Proficiency
Masterclass

Student's Book

Kathy Gude

Michael Duckworth

OXFORD UNIVERSITY PRESS

Exam Factfile

INTRODUCTION

There are five papers in the Cambridge Certificate of Proficiency in English (CPE) examination. Each paper is worth 40 marks, apart from Paper 4, Listening, which is worth 20. A total of 180 marks can be obtained and the pass mark is approximately 65% of the total marks awarded. There are five grades: pass grades are A, B and C; fail grades are D and E. For Papers 1, Reading, and 4, Listening, you will have to write your answers on a separate answer sheet (the OMR sheet).

PAPER 1   READING COMPREHENSION
(1 hour) 40 marks

SECTION A

Vocabulary multiple-choice

1   This consists of 25 sentences with blanks which you must fill in with one of a choice of four words or phrases. For example:

*She has been taken to hospital suffering from a
. . . . disc.*
   A *torn*   **B** *slipped*   **C** *broken*   **D** *sprained*

2   There is one mark for each correct answer.

SECTION B

Comprehension

1   This consists of three reading passages which vary in style. Passage 1 is longer and more general in subject matter; passage 2 is shorter and of a more specialized nature; passage 3 is more practical and may consist of one or more extracts.

2   There are 15 multiple-choice questions based on the passages. You have to read the passages then choose the most suitable answer, or finish a sentence, for example:

What did the writer think was out of place in the cafe?
  A *the modern decor*
  B *the respectable-looking students*
  C *the talk about the war*
  D *the presence of an army officer*

3   The questions test your understanding of the passages as a whole, rather than the meaning of specific vocabulary.

4   There are two marks for each correct answer.

5   You have to indicate your answer on a separate answer sheet (the OMR sheet), by shading in a lozenge.

Together Sections A and B carry 55 marks, which are scaled down to a mark out of 40.

PAPER 2   COMPOSITION
(2 hours) 40 marks

1   You have to write two compositions chosen from a total of five different types including discursive, descriptive and narrative compositions; a directed writing task; and a composition based on an optional set text.

2   The compositions should be about 350 words long, apart from the directed writing task, which should be 300 words long.

3   Marks are allocated for fluency, accuracy, naturalness and appropriateness of language. The relevance and organization of the material are also taken into account.

PAPER 3   USE OF ENGLISH
(2 hours) 40 marks

SECTION A

This consists of four different types of exercise testing structure and usage.

Cloze

1   This is a passage which has 20 gaps at irregular intervals. You have to fill in each gap using one word only, for example:

*... Devotees of soccer, rugby and rowing now regularly train to music; even those who take (**1**) . . . . in weight-lifting, which demands enormous physical strength, and (**2**) . . . . in athletics fields events, find that exercise to music is beneficial ...*

2   Various types of word are deleted but the majority of items test structure. The type of words which are omitted are verbs, determiners, connectors, adjectives, adverbs, prepositions and nouns.

Sentence transformations

1   These consist of eight sentences and eight incomplete sentences.

2   You have to finish each incomplete sentence to produce a sentence as similar as possible in meaning to the original. The initial word or words of the incomplete sentence are provided, for example:

*You should make an effort to get out and about more.
It's high time . . . .* .

Blank-filling

1   There are six sentences which you have to complete with a suitable word or phrase, for example:

*If this type of research . . . . ,
it must be carefully supervised.*

2   This section often tests knowledge of idiomatic or colloquial language.

Rewriting

1 This consists of eight sentences which you have to rewrite using one given word, for example:

You can avoid tooth decay by brushing your teeth regularly.
PREVENTED . . . .

2 The given word must not be changed in any way. You will have to add new words, and / or reorder the information in the original sentence.

SECTION B

1 This section tests your understanding and interpretation of a passage and your ability to summarize it coherently, including the relevant information. The passage will be 500 – 650 words long.

2 You have to read the passage of prose, and then answer 12 – 15 'short' questions.

3 Your short answers can consist of a phrase or a couple of sentences. The space provided on the examination paper gives an indication of the length required.

4 The emphasis is on producing relevant answers which do not repeat the exact words in the passage, and which show that you have understood what the question requires you to do.

5 You then have to write a summary of the text, or part of the text, in 50 – 100 words.

6 You are expected to follow the argument of the passage, presenting it through selecting the main points, and linking them correctly.

PAPER 4   LISTENING COMPREHENSION
(about 35 minutes) 20 marks

1 The listening test consists of three, four or five recordings in natural spoken English. Each recording is heard twice.

2 The written instructions on the paper are the same as those on the tape. You have to follow the instructions carefully and write your answers on the answer sheet.

3 There are various task types, such as box-ticking, note completion, multiple-choice, and true / false questions.

4 You can expect to hear recordings from a variety of contexts. The recordings could be announcements, radio programmes, news items, discussions, or conversations.

5 Included in the 35 minutes is time to check answers and transfer them from the question paper to the answer sheet (the OMR sheet). You may have to write one or two words in a box, or shade in a lozenge (for multiple-choice questions).

6 This paper carries 20 instead of 40 marks.

PAPER 5   INTERVIEW
(15 – 20 minutes) 40 marks

1 You will take part in a conversation with the examiner either individually, in pairs or in groups of three.

2 The conversation is based on a theme-related topic and consists of a) describing, comparing or contrasting one or more photographs then discussing the wider issues the photograph raises; b) commenting on the style, content, register and context of a passage related to the general theme of the interview; c) taking part in a broader activity, eg a discussion, rank-ordering or simulation, once again related to the general theme of the interview.

3 You will be assessed on the following areas: fluency; pronunciation (individual sounds); interactive communication; accuracy; pronunciation (sentences); and vocabulary.

4 In each area a mark of 0 – 5 is awarded for performance.

5 The interview carries 30 marks, which are scaled to a mark out of 40.

6 You can also choose to be examined on the set text you may have prepared for Paper 2 (Composition). All three parts of the interview will be based on the set text and the third activity will be a discussion about the text, writer, background, etc. The timing of the interview on the set text is the same as for the general theme-related interview.

1 IN SICKNESS AND IN HEALTH

One Man's Meat is another Man's Poison

talking points

A How do you rate the following suggestions as ways of ensuring physical fitness? Rank them starting with those you consider to be most effective. Be prepared to justify your choice by explaining how the suggestions may or may not help you.

- grow your own vegetables
- avoid 'junk' food
- sell your TV

- stop smoking
- buy an exercise bike
- take vitamin pills

- move to the countryside
- refuse to use lifts
- walk to work

Did you consider selling your TV to be an effective way of keeping fit?

B Look at the illustration of a couch potato. Describe the picture and decide what you think the term *couch potato* means.
Do you think the illustration is successful in showing what the expression means?
Give reasons for your answer.

reading

A Read this advice.

'It's high time you hung up your trainers and exercised your mind and not your body.'

Explain what this advice means. Who might it be given to? Is it sensible advice?

B Read the following magazine article about exercise. Decide whether the statements below it are true or false, according to what you read in the passage.

Muscle Binds

'**W**here's the virtue in sport, fitness and the body beautiful?' asks Dina La Vardera. 'It's high time you hung up your trainers and exercised your mind, not your body.'

5 Think about the things in life that give you most pleasure. Watching television, perhaps, while sipping chilled lager? How about eating *lasagne verde* by candlelight in
10 a favourite Italian restaurant? What do they all have in common? They all involve nothing more strenuous than sitting or lying down.

Why, then, this present mania for doing
15 things that necessitate remaining vertical or running around? I hate exercise and all forms of sport and I abhor the smugness and self-righteousness of those who think developing rippling muscles and flat
20 stomachs superior to the cultivation of personality, manners, good taste in art, music, literature and food. I hate the multi-million dollar propaganda that accompanies the body beautiful, with its
25 lure of glamour and eternal youth.

I was brought up to believe that physical exercise was bad for one, and experience seems to support my parents' philosophy that pain, suffering and ill-
30 health result from anything more strenuous than walking to the pillar box on the corner or digging the allotment. This has

been reinforced over the years by reports of footballers with torn ligaments, athletes
35 crippled by arthritis, or joggers dropping dead with heart attacks.

Most people's early experiences of exercise – after crawling into furniture and throwing building bricks under the settee
40 – come from school, and I suppose their future attitude to it is shaped then. The present decline in PE in schools only shows up the failings of a system that flourishes on the brutality of competition,
45 the fallacies of team spirit and character building, and the general humiliation of young and sensitive beings.

Don't let all the youngsters – and let's face it most of the oldsters, dressed up in
50 their snazzy purple shell suits with yellow flashes – fool you with their high-tech trainers and pump attachments to inflate their insoles and their egos. Apart from the odd football fanatic, muscle-man pumping
55 iron and aerobic freak, wouldn't they rather be eating a hamburger with their mates in town?

We are all followers of fashion in some way, and exercising is a fashion, an
60 ephemeral fad. It saves a lot of trouble if early on in life you put your cards on the table and announce to the world that exercise and sport are a bore, a real drag and you have better things to do.

65 It certainly saves you from requests to join in half marathons for charity and 'fun' five-a-sides with colleagues.

But people who take exercise don't see it like that. They are full of their own
70 importance and rightness. It's all so serious, like religion. And you are one of the pagans. It's difficult talking to sporty people: they get a far-off look in their eyes and their feet keep moving on the spot.

75 Exercising makes people think that they can live for ever. It puts off the moment of realisation that we are mortal. If you don't stay still long enough you don't have to think about such things. Coming to terms
80 with oneself, finding out who one is and where one is going, come from within, not from running round a park with 2,000 other people.

Exercise is repetitive and unending;
85 once you stop, the flab returns and the pulse slows down again. It is isolationist. All you get is an obsession with your body. And it's expensive: in terms of time, effort and material things like club fees,
90 equipment and special outfits.

But take heart, for the best club to join is free, has no age limit, requires no previous experience or special outfits. It's right there in your front room. Welcome,
95 Couch Potatoes, to your rightful place beside the fire. ■

Dina La Vardera, The Guardian

1	The things that give us the most pleasure in life involve us in very little physical activity.	T/F
2	The writer is a great believer in regular physical exercise.	T/F
3	Physical exercise is apparently a very dangerous thing to indulge in.	T/F
4	Competitive sports and a team spirit build up one's character.	T/F
5	Wearing sports clothes is no indication of a truly 'sporty' character.	T/F
6	By declaring yourself anti-sports you are spared participation in undesirable sporting activities.	T/F
7	Sports enthusiasts are sympathetic towards those who do not share their interests.	T/F
8	Exercise gives one a false sense of security.	T/F
9	Once you start exercising you have to continue with it.	T/F
10	The true path to contentment lies in becoming a couch potato.	T/F

C Style. The passage is written in a very chatty, informal style. Which of the following devices does the writer use to create this informality? What else does she use?

rhetorical questions   abbreviations   imperatives   repetition   slang   direct address

vocabulary

A **Words of disapproval.** The following words and expressions are all used in the article to convey the writer's disapproval of physical exercise and the attitudes of those devoted to it. Can you explain what they mean? Use a dictionary if necessary.

EXAMPLE *Mania* means a wild or violent mental disorder or an excessive, persistent enthusiasm.

1 abhor	4 failings	7 humiliation	10 a real drag
2 smugness	5 brutality	8 freak	11 pagans
3 self-righteousness	6 fallacies	9 an ephemeral fad	12 obsession

B **Expressions 1.** In the article we have the expression *come to terms with*. Look at the following diagram of this and other uses of the verb *come* and choose one in its correct form to complete the sentences below.

in for something
(be exposed to something unpleasant)

down (heavily) on somebody
(criticize or punish)

down with something
(catch an illness)

to terms with something
(accept a situation as it is)

come

out with something
(say something surprising)

up with something
(produce an idea)

to the point
(reach a conclusion)

round
(regain consciousness)

1 His wife died last year and he still cannot .... her death.

2 The new law .... those driving with no proper tax and insurance.

3 My little girl .... some strange expressions. Goodness knows where she hears them.

4 Although he's an entertaining speaker, it takes him ages to ....

5 After deliberating for several hours we finally .... a possible solution to the problem.

6 Soon after their arrival at the holiday resort they all .... gastric flu.

7 When he .... after the operation, he had absolutely no idea where he was.

8 I'm afraid we have .... a lot of criticism over our decision to close the hospital.

C **Expressions 2.** There are many colourful idioms like *couch potato* in English. Can you match the explanations on the right to the idiomatic expressions on the left? They are all connected with different kinds of people. *Couch potato* is done for you.

1	*a new broom*	a	someone who expresses opinions about things he/she knows very little about
2	*a wet blanket*	b	someone who has no fixed roots
3	*a stuffed shirt*	c	a pompous, self-opinionated person
4	*a couch potato*	d	a gossip who wants to know everything that happens to other people
5	*an armchair critic*	e	someone who stands by you only when things are going well
6	*a fair weather friend*	f	someone who likes to sit in comfort and do nothing
7	*a nosy parker*	g	a new person in charge who makes changes
8	*a rolling stone*	h	someone who does not want to join in and spoils the fun for everybody else

In pairs, choose ONE of the expressions above.
Either: write a short dialogue using the expression you have chosen, to act out in front of the class;
or: decide what kind of illustration would show what the idiom means in a humorous way.
Plan or sketch your illustration and be ready to tell the rest of the class about it.

The Sporting Life

A Can you identify these objects and suggest what sporting activities they might be used for?

B Which of the following places would you associate with the objects above?

rink   court   rapids   pitch   course   field   alley   gym

If you choose to take part in some sporting activity, you will probably undergo some form of training or practice. The following extract is taken from a newspaper article about a novel way to train. As you read it, try to decide what the missing words might be. The type of word is given, eg

- verbs
- determiners (eg *a*, *some*, *these*, *your*)
- connectors (eg *but*, *so*, *which*)

- adjectives
- prepositions
- nouns

Whether you are football crazy or keen on tennis, working out to music can improve the co-ordination of your mind and body. The suggestion that rock or pop music might ever

(1) . . . . (*verb*) a part in sports training would have

5 been **(2)** . . . . (*verb*) as a joke not so long ago. But today modern music is increasingly filling the gym as

(3) . . . . (*adverb*) as the front room.

The **(4)** . . . . (*noun*) of exercise to music is not new. For years, especially in eastern Europe, the benefits of

10 sportsmen and sportswomen **(5)** . . . . (*verb*) instruction in ballet and classical dance, with their stress

(6) . . . . (*preposition*) total body control and balance, have been **(7)** . . . . (*adverb*) recognized.

Figure-skating and ice-dance are **(8)** . . . . (*verb*)

15 to music and can be said to be specialized **(9)** . . . . (*noun*) of this type of exercise. But ballet and classical dance can be applied to other sports that are also **(10)** . . . . (*adjective*) to the eye, such as gymnastics and skiing, both of

(11) . . . . (*connector*) demand high standards of

20 balance, co-ordination and suppleness.

In western Europe and North America, much

(12) . . . . (*adjective*) interest has been shown in working out to classical music. Even sports which seem to

(13) . . . . (*verb*) muscular strength more than any

25 other physical requirement have taken **(14)** . . . . (*particle*) exercise to music as a valuable addition to

(15) . . . . (*determiner*) own specialized training schemes.

Devotees of soccer, rugby and rowing now regularly train to

30 music; even those who take **(16)** . . . . (*noun*) in weightlifting, which demands enormous physical strength, and

(17) . . . . (*noun*) in athletics field events, find that exercise to music is beneficial and **(18)** . . . . (*verb*) their movements more fluid.

35 Sport is benefiting from the keep-fit boom of recent years. Since the early 1980s, the advantages of aerobics,

(19) . . . . (*preposition*) particular, have been brought home to **(20)** . . . . (*determiner*) mass audience by television, tapes and books. ■

relative clauses

A **Defining and non-defining relative clauses.** Read through the cloze passage on page 4 and underline the relative clauses. How many can you find?

B **Answer the following questions.**

1 Look at these two sentences. Which is the defining and which the non-defining clause? What is the difference in meaning?
The footballers who attended the annual club dinner had won two previous championships.
The footballers, who attended the annual club dinner, had won two previous championships.

2 In which of these sentences could the relative pronoun be omitted? Why is this possible?
Ballet and classical dance techniques can be applied to other sports which are also pleasing to the eye.
Ballet and classical dance techniques can be applied to other sports which spectators find pleasing to the eye.

3 In which sentence could you not use *that*?

The money .... was collected at the turnstiles on Saturday was stolen.

The money, ... was collected at the turnstiles on Saturday, was stolen.

4 Why can we not use *that* in this relative clause?
Sports such as gymnastics and skiing, both of ...... demand high standards of co-ordination.

5 What does the relative pronoun refer to in this sentence and what does it mean?
That famous boxer, whose name I've forgotten, is supposed to have been involved in a financial scandal.

6 What does the relative pronoun refer to in this sentence?
He resigned as manager of the club, which shocked everybody.

C **Rewrite these sentences using a relative pronoun.**

1 An American journalist interviewed the tennis champion. The journalist reminded me of my brother.

The American journalist ....

2 The liver is about 30 centimetres long. It helps in the digestion of food.

The liver ....

3 We decided to engage the two young dancers. We had seen them perform on television.

We decided...

4 The new concert hall was opened yesterday. It holds two thousand people.

The new concert hall .... yesterday.

5 The manager of the pop group ICE has just resigned. The group is currently touring the USA.

The pop group ICE ....

6 I was amazed to learn that he had never had any formal education.

He had ....

D **Could you omit the relative pronoun in any of the sentences you have rewritten?**

rewriting

A **Study the example carefully.** You have to change the original sentence to accommodate the word given. The form of the word must not be changed in any way.

EXAMPLE There is no place whatsoever for sport in the school curriculum.

PART...
CLUE You need a verb to go with *part*.
Notice we must make two changes when rewriting this sentence: (a) the order of words;
(b) *There is no place for* becomes *plays no part in*.
ANSWER *Sport plays no part whatsoever in the school curriculum.*

B   Try rewriting the following sentences. Some clues are given to help you.

1   His new hobby is swimming.

TAKEN . . . .
CLUE Use a phrasal verb and *as a*. Begin *He*.

2   Exercise improves our health and enhances our appearance.

ONLY . . . .
CLUE Exercise does two things so use *not only*.

3   There were no volunteers for the school concert.

TAKE. . . . .
CLUE Use the verb *offered* and *take* as a phrasal verb.

4   The global interest in physical exercise has been a great boon to the leisure industry.

FROM . . . .
CLUE *Boon* means 'benefit'. Use the verb instead of the noun. Change *great* to an adverb.
Begin *The leisure industry*.

5   We can avoid serious injuries by wearing seat-belts in cars.

PREVENTED. . . . .
CLUE Begin *Serious injuries*.

6   When I saw Jim it suddenly dawned on me how much he must have suffered.

HOME . . . .
CLUE Use the verb *to bring it home to* meaning 'to make someone realize'. Begin *Seeing Jim*.

7   Great powers of concentration are needed to play tennis professionally.

DEMANDS . . . .
CLUE Change the word order.

8   An automatic gear box is a feature of the two different models of this car.

WHICH . . . .
CLUE Use *of which*.

Summary Skills

Carers and Curers

talking points

introduction to summary writing

The following list contains six physical complaints. However, the words have been arranged incorrectly. Can you rearrange them to discover what the complaints are?

- writer's elbow
- a sprained strain
- tennis ankle
- a torn disc
- eye cramp
- a slipped ligament

Have you ever suffered from any of these? Where / When / Why did they occur?

A   Some physical disorders necessitate a visit to hospital. Read the extract on the opposite page describing hospital conditions, and decide who wrote it. Choose one of the following options.

1   a nurse describing how patients and doctors feel
2   someone who has been both a doctor and a patient
3   a consultant explaining the frustrations of working in a hospital
4   someone who interviewed a doctor while he was a patient

COMMENT ON CARE

In his perceptive book *A Leg To Stand On*, Oliver Sacks describes how formal hospital ward rounds make patient–doctor communication virtually impossible. I have experienced this from both sides. As a junior surgeon you are constantly at the mercy of your bleeper – forever shuttling between clinics, the operating theatre, the wards and the administration. The essential work on the wards is the ordering of tests and the scheduling of operations, and you resent anything that distracts you from this task. You begin to think of the patients as the enemy and of the nurses as your first line of defence against them.

As a patient one gets quite a different perspective: the doctors are hiding from you all day, and when they do pop up everything has already been decided on.

'Just a couple of questions,' I stammered as the consultant's armada blithely sailed past.

'Lie back,' the nurse replied. 'We are just going to give you a little injection.' ■

B Answering comprehension questions.

1 Can you explain the implications of *constantly at the mercy of your bleeper* (line 7)?
If you don't know what the word *bleeper* means you might be able to guess from your knowledge of what the job entails, or by imagining the sound it might make. Then you could try and decide how the surgeon might feel about the constant intrusion.

2 What are the implications of the words *the patients as the enemy and the nurses your first line of defence* (line 15)?
Ask yourself these questions:
What is he comparing the hospital to?
Why is it a paradoxical comparison?

3 Explain these words: *I stammered as the consultant's armada blithely sailed past.* (line 23)
Ask yourself these questions:
What is the usual meaning of *armada*?
What is the meaning of *armada* in this context?
What effect does the metaphor have?
What does the word *blithely* convey about the attitude of the surgeons (from the patient's point of view)?
Why did the writer stammer?

4 Compare your answers with those of a partner. Were they similar? Which do you feel captured the meaning best?

C Summary. Choose the best answers to the two questions below. Then combine your answers to form a summary of how a junior surgeon and the patient really feel (about 40 words).

1 According to the writer, how does a junior surgeon really feel?
  A He is neglecting his patients and feels remorse.
  B It is the nurse's responsibility to order tests and schedule operations.
  C The patient is an intrusion into hospital efficiency.
  D Bleepers should only be used outside hospitals.

2 According to the writer, how does the patient really feel?
  A He feels frustrated by the lack of communication between the nurses and doctors.
  B He is unable to stand up and address the consultant face to face.
  C He is afraid of the medical preparations necessary for the forthcoming operation.
  D He feels convinced that he is quite simply a cog in a much larger wheel.

talking points

A Can you explain what these forms of alternative medicine are?

hypnotherapy   acupuncture
acupressure   herbalism

B Which might be suitable for curing the following?

an allergy   aches and pains
a smoking habit

listening

Listen to this radio programme. Eight people are being interviewed about their reactions to hypnotherapy treatment. Many of the questions focus on the feelings and reactions of the speakers. Before you listen to the programme, read through the items below. Look up any words you may not know, then, as you listen, choose the best answer.

1 How did the author feel before his first session of hypnotherapy?
  A curious
  B mistrustful
  C enthusiastic
  D fearful

2 Although the TV presenter was cured of insomnia, how does she feel about the effectiveness of hypnotherapy?
  A undecided
  B unconvinced
  C uneasy
  D disappointed

3 The boxer's first session of hypnotherapy left him feeling
  A relaxed and sleepy.
  B tired but resentful.
  C lucid and strong.
  D calm but sceptical.

4 The artist's experience left him feeling
  A sceptical.
  B contemptuous.
  C down hearted.
  D open-minded.

5 Two years' hypnotherapy helped the tennis champion
  A improve her tennis strokes.
  B react more positively to the crowd.
  C develop her understanding of the subject.
  D improve her application to the game.

6 Since he underwent hynotherapy, the psychic says he can now
  A put himself into an almost completely hypnotic state.
  B be certain that his psychic powers are genuine.
  C ensure he will never be afraid again.
  D have meaningful conversations with himself.

7 The columnist's attempt to give up smoking failed because of
  A the ineffectiveness of hypnotherapy.
  B his lack of freedom of choice under hypnotherapy.
  C his own lack of motivation.
  D his inability to take hypnotherapy seriously.

8 Since the actress took advice from a hypnotherapist, she has
  A undergone a personality change.
  B always been successful in overcoming her problem.
  C never been afraid during the night.
  D staged her own shows by herself.

speaking

A Describing actions. You may not fancy hypnotherapy but sometimes it is possible for you to treat yourself, if you are given the right kind of advice about what to do.

exam tip

In the interview you will be asked to give a brief description of one or more photographs. You may be asked to say what is happening or what you think the people are doing in the photograph(s).

1 Look at pictures 1–7 on page 9 showing massage techniques for dealing with neck pain.

2 Learn which verbs are not used in the progressive. Here are the most important verbs. You will need some to describe the pictures.

appear (to be)   can   know   look as if   look like   prefer   realize   recognize   seem (to be)   want

3 Now describe what the man in pictures 1–7 seems to be / looks as if he is doing. Use these words to help you:

arm   skull   wrist   head   fist   thumb   shoulder   neck   forehead   elbow   finger   hand

clasping   rotating   placing   massaging   pressing   clenching   drumming

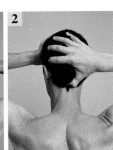
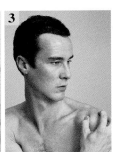
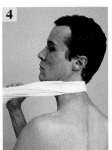
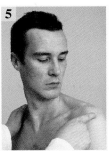
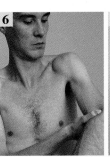

B Giving instructions. Here are the instructions for the actions in pictures 1–7. Match them to the appropriate picture.

a Press firmly on the shoulder muscle.

b Clasp the sides of the head with each hand and place thumbs at the edge of the skull at the base of the bone behind the ears.

c Clasp the shoulder, and with the index finger on the muscle massage firmly eight to ten times, in a downward stroke only.

d Using a loosely clenched fist, drum hard down on the back of the neck and down the side of the arm.

e Now press firmly on the tender point at the side of the arm at the elbow. Press hard. The sensation should be felt down into the hand. Hold for 30 seconds.

f Place one hand on the forehead, the other at the back of the head with the thumb pressed into the hollow at the base of the skull. Rotate the thumb for two minutes.

g Take a towel and, using a drying motion, massage the neck for two minutes.

C Now look at the pictures showing self-help techniques for dealing with insomnia.
Decide what the men seem to be / look as if they are doing then give your own instructions to illustrate what should be done. These words should help you:

press	*tightly*	*on*	*the knee*
place	*firmly*	*between*	*the eyebrows*
grip	*gently*	*below*	*the cheek-bone*
massage	*loosely*	*over*	*the second knuckle*
clench	*evenly*		*the arm*
	hard		*the fingers*

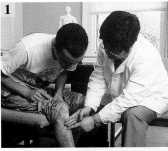

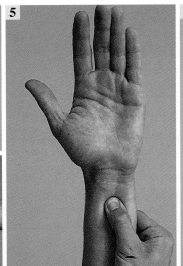

For and Against

Read the following example of a balanced discussion and answer the questions.

1 What was the title of the composition?
2 Which five sentences could be extracted from the composition unchanged to provide a reasonable summary of the arguments?

Recent advances in human embryology and genetic engineering have raised the issue of how this knowledge ought to be used, and it is now a matter of
5 *considerable public concern and debate.*

There are two main areas in which such research is widely regarded as being beneficial, and the first of these is in the field of conception. Doctors can help
10 *otherwise infertile couples to have children using the so-called 'test-tube baby' technique. Although there was considerable controversy when the first such experiments were introduced, there*
15 *is now a general acceptance that the process is both safe and useful.*

The second area is that of research into genetically transmitted diseases. Some of these only affect children of a
20 *particular sex, as is the case with haemophilia, which only affects males. In such circumstances, by determining the sex of the child in advance, doctors can ensure that the disease will not be passed*
25 *on. In addition to this, research into human genetics offers the potential of*

finding the causes for other diseases and their eventual cures.

On the other hand, there is deep-
30 *rooted hostility towards scientists who interfere with nature and human life. This suspicion has a long history, and is reflected in literary works such as Frankenstein and Brave New World. In*
35 *addition to this, however, there is widespread revulsion at the real-life 'experiments' that have been carried out in the past. As a result, there is a common fear that scientific developments*
40 *in genetics will inevitably be abused and that they will lead inexorably towards 'designer children' and other worse excesses.*

In conclusion, it can be said that
45 *research in these areas needs to be regulated rather than banned. There are many potential benefits as well as dangers, and therefore, if this research is to be continued, it must be carried out*
50 *under strict supervision and controlled by well-balanced legislation.*

A Question interpretation and outline planning. Always read the question very carefully and examine every part of it. This will usually enable you to come up with a very basic paragraph outline. Look at the example of the outline for the sample composition.

1 **Introduction** – brief comments on scientific developments
2 **Points in favour** – helping childless couples, curing disease
3 **Points against** – possible abuses – interfering with nature
4 **Conclusion**

B Write short paragraph outline plans for these questions.

1 *Do you agree that people should be allowed to keep potentially dangerous animals?*
2 *Discuss the view that there is no place for censorship in a modern society.*
3 *'Parents should be punished when their child breaks the law.' Do you agree?*

This stage of composition planning is where you work out the content of your composition. Think of as many ideas, points and examples as possible for each of the sections. At this stage they do not need to be in any particular order. One technique that may be helpful is to think of abstract ideas in terms of how different people you know might react to the idea and the kind of things they might say. The following activity is based on the title:

Conventional medicine has little to learn from alternative medicine.

Read through the following statements. Discuss:
a who they might have been made by (for example, a patient, doctor, alternative medical practitioner, someone who approves of alternative medicine, someone who doesn't, etc.);
b what issues each of the statements raise.

1 *'Ladies and gentlemen, I would like to welcome you to the 17th International Symposium on stress-related disorders ...'*
no all physical causes

5 *'It all sounds like a lot of mumbo jumbo to me.'*
people are sceptical

6 'I caught malaria in Africa and it comes back from time to time.' *not all diseases can be thoroughly cured*

2 'She did a three-week course in acupuncture in London ...' *confidence in training (short)*

7 'It is a serious condition and there is no known cure.' *same as 6*

3 *'Well, my next-door neighbour went to a hypnotist and hasn't smoked since.'*
alt. can be effective

8 'If your medicines and potions really worked, then proper doctors would use them.' *scientific proof → used by conv. doc.*

4 'As herbalists, we see illnesses as symptoms of an underlying imbalance involving the whole person.' *-ndsly in*
general approach causes
conventional - symptoms

9 *'After three days on penicillin, my leg cleared up completely.'*
conv. med. v. efficient in some cases

10 'It's natural, so it's good for you.' *artificial = bad. optimistic?*

stage 3 organization

Paragraph planning. When you have thought of the main points and examples that you need to include, work out a more detailed paragraph structure before you begin writing. For the purposes of the composition title in **stage 2**, your paragraphs might be as follows, but you could alter the suggested outline depending on your own views.

1 Introduction
2 Points in favour of the statement: Talk about the efficiency of conventional medicine – scientifically based, proven effectiveness; contrast with drawbacks of alternative – lack of scientific basis, results not always consistent.
3 Points against the statement: Limitations of conventional medicine – some illnesses incurable, some caused by psychological problems; contrast with alternative medicine, which can be effective in some circumstances, eg hypnotism.
4 Conclusion

stage 4 writing

Write a composition of about 350 words on the following topic.

Conventional medicine has little to learn from alternative medicine.

- Remember to go through the stages of outline planning, brainstorming and organization before you write.
- Remember to give both sides of the argument reasonable balance.
- Remember that the introductory sentence of each paragraph should provide a short summary of what the paragraph will be about.

stage 5 checking

Check your work carefully for grammatical mistakes.

exam tip

*Most compositions are required to be **about** 350 words. Do not waste your time counting them. Before the exam, work out approximately how many words you use per line, and how many lines your composition needs to be. Remember not to write too much, as you will be wasting time. However, you will be penalized heavily if you write substantially less than required.*

Overview 1

vocabulary

Choose the word which best completes each sentence.

1 The small boat drifted helplessly .... the mercy of the wind and waves.

   A in   **B** with   **C** to   **D** at

2 He'll never be able to come .... with his failure to win the tournament.

   A down   **B** round   **C** to terms   **D** up

3 She has been taken to hospital suffering from a .... disc.

   A torn   **B** slipped   **C** broken   **D** sprained

4 From time to time he .... himself to a weekend in a five-star hotel.

   A craves   **B** indulges   **C** benefits   **D** treats

5 Do you know that old saying 'a .... stone gathers no moss'?

   A wet   **B** new   **C** rolling   **D** rotating

6 We welcome the new regulations, which become .... on the first of next month.

   A effective   **B** efficient   **C** efficacious   **D** effete

7 In an act of defiance he raised a .... fist at the speaker.

   A clenched   **B** pressed   **C** gripped   **D** clasped

8 That pop star, ... name is on everyone's lips, is organizing an international charity concert.

   A which   **B** whom   **C** that   **D** whose

9 He's on his own now – he'll have to .... his own canoe!

   A row   **B** steer   **C** paddle   **D** ride

10 The performance was spoilt by the leading actor losing his train of thought and .... over his words in the final scene.

   A stammering   **B** stuttering   **C** spluttering   **D** stumbling

transformations

Finish each of the following sentences in such a way that it means exactly the same as the sentence before it.

1 You should make an effort to get out and about more.

   It's high time ....

2 It seems as if there is a slight deterioration in his physical condition.

   His physical condition ....

3 Happiness is elusive to rich and poor alike.

   Whether ....

4 I've forgotten that commentator's name but he's very well-known.

   That commentator, ...

5 We can say that the leisure industry will be the money spinner of the future.

   The leisure industry ....

6 Let's invite the Marshalls to a barbecue on Sunday.

   He suggested ....

7 It was overeating that caused his heart attack.

   If ....

8 Alternative medicine is a complete mystery to some people.

   Some people are ....

9 'Why don't you think about how you're going to play the character?' the hypnotherapist suggested to Annie.

   The hypnotherapist suggested ....

10 For gymnastics and skiing regular practice is needed.

Sports ....

blank-filling

Fill each of the blanks in the following sentences with a suitable word or phrase.

1 If this type of research ...., it must be carefully supervised.

2 Although .... many people now accept that infertile couples have the right to medical help.

3 Since .... acupressure, he has noticed a tremendous improvement in his condition.

4 He had tried several times .... up smoking.

5 For the first twenty-four hours the treatment worked because I didn't ....

.... like a cigarette.

6 By the time .... the train had just left.

7 I am really .... to seeing you and your family again.

8 How .... for a meal tonight?

9 It's time you .... some decision about your future.

10 Until recently the suggestion that pop music might be used to train athletes

.... as a joke.

rewriting

For each of the sentences below, write a new sentence as similar as possible in meaning to the original sentence, but using the words given in capital letters. These words must not be altered in any way.

1 You can avoid tooth decay by brushing your teeth regularly.

PREVENTED ....

2 I think cycling is preferable to walking.

RATHER ....

3 Most people regard him as being the best man for the job.

WIDELY ....

4 You aren't allowed to smoke on the tube.

BAN ....

5 They share a lot of hobbies and interests.

COMMON ....

6 Don't eat so many sweets and you won't have to visit the dentist so often.

SAVE ....

7 A sudden downpour resulted in the postponement of the football match.

PUT ....

8 The fact that he will never race again is something he cannot accept.

TERMS ....

9 From the educational point of view his childhood years had been well spent.

TERMS ....

10 I could tell by the tone of his voice how serious the situation was.

HOME ....

FIRST IMPRESSIONS

Master of the Universe

talking points

A Look at the photographs.

1 What is your first impression of these people's characters based on the pictures alone? Note down your reaction and the strength of it. Compare it with your partner's reaction.

2 List any factors which may interfere with a first impression, or make one difficult to get.

3 The following factors can contribute towards a first impression. Assuming that none of them is extreme, select three of the most important and three of the least important to you. Compare your answers with your partner's.

- what they say
- their clothes
- their eyes
- their hair

- their face
- their teeth
- their accent
- their posture

- the context in which you meet
- their reputation
- anything else

B Talk about your experiences.

1 How valid are first impressions? Can you give examples of when you have been right or wrong with your first impressions?

2 When do you try and create an impression that is slightly different from your true self? What do you do to achieve it?

3 It has been said that, at job interviews, a candidate's success or failure is usually determined within the first two minutes. What could you do to improve or reduce your chances of getting a job?

4 A relatively new word to come into the language from America is the term 'lookism', which refers to the prejudice of judging people by the way they look. Can you think of any other words ending in *-ism* that refer to prejudices?

reading

A The newspaper article on the opposite page is about one of the people in the photographs above. Read through the article and see how accurate your first impressions were.

B Comprehension. Read the article again and complete the matching exercise. The words on the left all appear in the passage. Deduce the meanings of any words you do not know from the context.

1	*chimera*	**a**	a person easily fooled
2	*quarry*	**b**	no longer existing
3	*whine*	**c**	once well developed but now of little use
4	*skeletal*	**d**	a non-expert
5	*joystick*	**e**	a high-pitched noise
6	*sucker*	**f**	an imaginary monster
7	*defunct*	**g**	extremely thin
8	*vestigial*	**h**	a device for controlling direction
9	*layman*	**i**	an object being hunted

A BRIEF HISTORY OF TIME

For 60 years, since Einstein revolutionised our understanding of the cosmos and Planck and Heisenberg undid the certainties of particle physics, scientists have been chasing a chimera – the Great Unified Theory that would describe and relate all the forces of the universe and, in the process, lay bare the secrets of nature. Now a profoundly disabled man has the quarry in sight; and it is no chimera, but a real beast, waiting to tear our philosophies apart.

A dull bumping noise and a mechanical whine from the corridor announce that Professor Stephen Hawking is ready to start his day's work. A nurse comes into the office, followed by an electric wheelchair with a large metal box on the back and a computer screen attached to the left arm. The seat is covered by a sheepskin mat on which rests what appears to be a bundle of clothes that have, by some extraordinary coincidence, formed themselves roughly into the shape of a man.

So the skeletal hands projecting from the crossed arms of the tweed jacket and the angled, alert head that emerges from the check shirt all come as a slight shock. The left hand is controlling the chair with a joystick on the right chair arm, while the right hand clicks away furiously at a computer control pad. Suddenly, a hard, inflectionless voice with a curious Scandinavian American accent issues from the chair. "Hello. How are you?" The voice is emitted from speakers on the metal box. Hawking calls up words on the screen, then sends them to the computer to be spoken. The process is slow – he manages about 10 words a minute – but can be speeded up if you read the words straight off the screen. I look over his shoulder to see what is coming up next.

"I want a dove..." it says. His secretary, Sue Masey, seems baffled. We wait nervously. Suddenly the voice bursts forth again. "I want a dove-grey van."

He had just wanted to specify the colour of a specially equipped van he is buying with the money he will receive for the Israeli Wolf

You can substitute the name "Hawking" for "Mankind"

Prize in Physics. In addition, his secretary reveals, he wants power steering, a stereo cassette and any other gimmicks that might be available. The Lucasian Professor of Mathematics at Cambridge University is a sucker for gadgets.

He is also the man most likely to produce an explanation for the entire history of the universe within the next few years. By his own estimate, there is a fifty-fifty chance mankind will come up with the answer by the end of the century; and, by everybody else's estimate, you can substitute the name "Hawking" for "mankind". If, of course, he lives.

For the terrible fact is that the intellect of one of the two or three greatest physicists of the century is sustained by an almost defunct body. Over the past 25 years motor neurone disease has caused a slow but savage deterioration in his condition. At 21 he was stumbling, by 30 he was in a wheelchair. He has some vestigial movement in his head and hands, and, disconcertingly, an immense, wide toothy grin.

Having dealt with his van problem, Hawking announces that he will have lunch at his College, Gonville and Caius. He then reverses out of the tiny office to have coffee in the shabby common room with the other members of the department.

Few people there pay any attention to the slumped, fragile figure with its whirring chair and the sudden loud interjections of its electronic voice. The talk is of equations and theories. One neighbour is announcing that Einstein's relativity was incomprehensible to him when explained in the usual layman's terms of clocks and spaceships, and it was only when he started doing the maths that it all became clear. Hawking has now reversed this process by producing the best-selling book *A Brief History of Time*, a non-technical guide to his thought, entirely free of mathematics.

Suddenly he announces he must prepare for his lecture and whirrs off. ■

Bryan Appleyard, *The Sunday Times*

C Multiple-choice questions. Choose the best answer.

1 The writer suggests that a Great Unified Theory
   A is only of interest to scientists.
   B is a mirage that will never be reached.
   C was formulated by Einstein.
   D may force people to re-evaluate their values and beliefs.

2 The writer was shocked because
   A he had thought there was no one in the wheelchair.
   B the Professor's hands were very thin.
   C the Professor had a very strange dress sense.
   D Hawking was very alert.

3 Hawking wants a van that
   A is practical and functional.
   B is fast and powerful.
   C is full of gadgets.
   D has two shades of colour.

4 The writer suggests that a full explanation of the universe
   A will be produced by scientists other than Hawking.
   B is most likely to be found, if at all, by Hawking.
   C will almost certainly not be found before the end of the century.
   D will be too complex for most people to understand.

5 According to the article, Hawking's disease
   A began as a result of a fall.
   B has left him unable to move his head.
   C has had a detrimental effect on his capacity to think.
   D has affected him physically but not mentally.

6 The people who are discussing equations
   A are arguing about Hawking's theories.
   B work in Hawking's office.
   C work in the same department as Hawking.
   D ignore Hawking completely.

vocabulary

Expressions. Discuss the meanings of the following idioms connected with time. Decide which idiom could replace the underlined words in each of the sentences below.

- *now's a fine time*
- *all in good time*
- *(be / come / leave) on time*
- *time and time again*
- *a bit pressed for time*

- *at the best of times*
- *to kill time*
- *to buy time*
- *just in the nick of time*
- *for the time being*

1 Please don't worry about painting the house – I promise I will do it <u>at some time when it is convenient</u>.
2 We were afraid we might miss our flight, but we got to the airport <u>with only seconds to spare</u>.
3 I'm afraid I can't talk to you at the moment. I'm <u>in a bit of a hurry</u>.
4 He's fairly rude and aggressive <u>in favourable circumstances</u>, but now that he's under so much stress, he's quite unbearable.
5 <u>This is a very inconvenient moment</u> to decide that you don't want to get married – your husband-to-be is waiting in the church.
6 The plane was not due to leave for another six hours, so she decided <u>to pass the time</u> by wandering around all the duty-free shops.
7 I often get to work late because the trains never seem to <u>arrive punctually</u>.
8 I doubt very much whether the cheque really is in the post; I should think they're just trying <u>to delay things</u>.
9 Your office won't be ready until next week, so could you use Room 11 <u>as a temporary measure</u>?
10 I really don't know what's the matter with him – I've told him <u>repeatedly</u> not to leave his car unlocked.

Structure

The Hawking Story

cloze development

A **The passage on the opposite page was taken from a newspaper.** Read it then decide whether the following statements are true or false.

1 Hawking's illness prevented him from working.   T/F
2 The Hawkings were initially unable to afford full-time professional nursing.   T/F
3 Jane Hawking gave up working when she had children.   T/F
4 Jane Hawking is dubious about her husband's work.   T/F
5 Jane Hawking and her husband share the same fundamental beliefs.   T/F
6 There are certain beliefs that Hawking does not discuss with his wife.   T/F

B Complete the missing words from the passage. The first letter of each word is given.

Jane Hawking met the man who was to become her husband in 1963, shortly before the beginning of his illness. They married two years later and, as Hawking got down to work, the disease progressed (1) i................... tandem with his fame.

5   A string of academic positions and awards came his way (2) a................... did an increasing dependence on his wife and those around him. For Mrs Hawking, (3) h..................., life became paradoxically easier. An American philanthropic organization provided the

10 (4) f................... for 24-hour nursing. For the first time in their marriage, she was no (5) l................... wholly (6) r................... for keeping him alive, and could devote more time (7) t................... concentrating on her own work and their three children.

15   Mrs Hawking has a neat, organized air, and a (8) v................... that is high-pitched and genteel. (9) N................... of which conceals the fact that she regards the world's belief that her husband is about to come up with an explanation for the universe (10) w...................

20 the deepest suspicion. It is ironic that his work threatens to undermine the foundations of her strongly

(11) h................... religious convictions, which have sustained her throughout the years of caring, and (12) w................... which he might not have been

25 able to continue his work.
    "There's one aspect of his thought that I (13) f................... increasingly upsetting and difficult to live (14) w...................," she explains. "It is the feeling that, because everything is reduced

30 (15) t................... a rational, mathematical formula, that must be the truth. He is now postulating a (16) t................... in which the universe is like the shape of the earth with no beginning and no end and no need for God at all.

35   (17) W................... I can't understand is whether his theory allows (18) f................... other interpretations or not. I can never get an answer and I find it very upsetting." What she does get, when the conversation (19) r................... a point beyond which he will not

40 go, is the Hawking grin, which can clearly be infuriating. For Mrs Hawking, a devout Anglican, it seems like an agnostic slamming a (20) d................... in her face. ∎

progressive aspect

A The progressive aspect can be used for a number of different reasons. What are the differences in meaning in the following sentences using the simple and progressive forms?

1 The calculations are done on the new university computer.
   The calculations are being done on the new university computer.

2 My brother is living with my parents.
   My brother lives with my parents.

3 I've read his book – it's fascinating.
   I've been reading his book – it's fascinating.

4 He's doing a lot of chat shows on TV.
   He does a lot of chat shows on TV.

B Read through the sentences below and indicate where the progressive aspect is being used:

   a to talk about an action that is, or was, in progress at a particular moment in time.
   b to talk about temporary states.
   c to talk about incomplete actions.
   d to talk about a repeated (but temporary) series of actions.
   e to emphasize that a repeated action is rather irritating.
   f to talk about a future arrangement.

   Which feature is the most prominent? The first one has been done for you.

1 He had to leave because he was seeing Jane at six.   ..f...

2 For 60 years, scientists have been chasing a chimera.   ......

3 She's always coming into the lessons ten minutes late. ......

4 This time next week he'll be flying to a conference in Geneva. ......

5 I've been reading an excellent book on the subject. ......

6 She will be giving lectures all over the States. ......

7 You're always forgetting your keys. ......

8 He told me he'd been trying to get through to you all day. ......

9 I'm having some people to stay this weekend. ......

10 I'm using my father's car until mine is repaired. ......

11 We'll be working here until they've completed the new building. ......

12 When I phoned, the Professor was giving a lecture. ......

*avoiding the
progressive aspect*

A Consider these three pairs of sentences. Which sentence in each pair sounds the most natural?

1 a The bridge has been being built for over two years now.
   b They have been building the bridge for over two years now.

2 a The government's immigration policy had been under review for several months.
   b The government's immigration policy had been being reviewed for several months.

3 a He has been being treated at the local hospital.
   b He has been having treatment at the local hospital.

B Complete the following sentences. Finish each sentence in such a way that it means exactly the same as the one printed before it. The clues help you to avoid the use of the passive in the perfect progressive tenses.

1 When they finished the meeting, they had been discussing the matter for hours.

   When they finished the meeting, the matter had been..
   CLUE Use the word *discussion*.

2 They've been selling Christmas cards since the beginning of September.

   Christmas...
   CLUE Use the phrase *on sale*.

3 She was unaware that the police had been watching her since her arrival.

   She was unaware that she ....
   CLUE Use the word *surveillance*.

4 He was tired when he left as they had been interviewing him all day.

   He was tired when he left because he..
   CLUE Use the phrase *to have interviews*.

5 The theory of relativity has been under attack recently by a number of scientists.

   A number ....
   CLUE Change the sentence from passive to active.

6 They have been teasing her at school because of her new glasses.

   She ....
   CLUE Use the phrase *to have a hard time*.

stative verbs

A Consider the following extracts from the text:

- … she *regards* the world's belief that …
- There's one aspect of his thought that I *find* increasingly upsetting …
- What I *can't understand* is …
- … it *seems* like an agnostic slamming a door in her face …

The verbs in italics are often referred to as 'stative' verbs. These are either not normally used in the progressive or change their meaning when used in the simple or progressive.

Look through the list of common stative verbs below and classify them into the groups suggested.

1   verbs related to the senses . . . .

2   verbs related to thinking . . . .

3   verbs related to possession . . . .

4   verbs related to emotional states . . . .

5   verbs related to appearance . . . .

6   others . . . .

appear   believe   belong to   contain   depend on   doubt   dislike   feel   find

guess   hate   have   hear   imagine   involve   know   like   love   mean

mind   own   prefer   realize   regard   remember   seem   smell   sound

suppose   taste   understand   want

B Meaning changes in stative verbs. In the following pairs of sentences, put the verb into the correct tense, and explain the differences in meaning between the simple and progressive forms of the verbs.

1   I'm surprised you aren't enjoying your music classes. I . . . . (think) they would be ideal for you.

2   I . . . . (think) about getting a new car soon, but I'll have to put it off until next year because I can't afford it.

3   The concept of infinity . . . . (be) very difficult for most people to grasp.

4   I told him he . . . . (be) unnecessarily difficult and that he ought to make a compromise.

5   There was no one downstairs; so she turned off the light again and decided that she must

. . . . (imagine) things.

6   You can tell your bank manager about your difficulties, but I . . . . (not / imagine) he will be all that sympathetic.

7   The last time I went to Stratford, Janet Suzman . . . . (appear) as Cleopatra.

8   They stated in their report that there . . . . (appear) to be a strong link between hooliganism and social deprivation.

9   I'm entirely in favour of the new law. I . . . . (always / feel) there was something morally questionable about blood sports.

10 If you . . . . (not / feel) very well recently, you ought to go and see the doctor.

talking points

How far do you agree or disagree with the following statement?

Men and women have different kinds of brain, so it follows naturally that men and women have different inherent skills and abilities.

What are your own views on the subject?

summary 1

Read the article and decide which of the four options best sums up the point the writer is making.

1 Women's brains work in a different way from men's.
2 Women failed to become scientists because of male prejudice.
3 Women feel resentful at the way they have been treated by men.
4 Men are afraid to accept the limitations of their own intellect.

A MEN'S CLUB

"A witch", wrote Thomas Vaughan in 1650, "is a rebel in physics, and a rebel is a witch in politics. The one acts against nature, the other against order, the rule of it. For both are in league with the devil."

Modern science was born in the 16th and 17th centuries, and its enemy was witchcraft. Witchcraft was a force of darkness that could not be understood by experiment, theory and observation. Science was a new way of knowing that seemed to be sweeping away such old darknesses. And it was a *masculine* way of knowing. Religious terror and male conviction resulted in the death of an estimated three million women in Europe during the 250 years of the systematic persecution of witches.

"The view was that the mind was masculine and nature feminine," says Dr Jan Harding, who works with the Fawcett Society to promote women in science. "It was not thought that women were equipped to do science, but they appeared to have access to some other form of knowledge. So it was

thought they must get that knowledge from the devil."

The Royal Society in London was where modern science was institutionalised and codified. Dominated for years by the titanic figure of Isaac Newton, it was the exclusive club in which the scientific dream was first dreamt. And it was utterly, rigorously and unarguably a men's club.

The view was that the mind was masculine and nature feminine

Margaret Cavendish, Duchess of Newcastle, was allowed entry in 1667 to see a demonstration of Boyle's celebrated air pump, but that was about it, and nobody had any doubts that neither she nor any other woman was capable of grasping the arcana of this new and staggeringly effective form of knowledge. It is worth knowing that Newton himself, having changed the universe, is thought to have died celibate.

Science has remained a men's club ever since, even though the fear of witchcraft may appear to have subsided. In the 19th century, Caroline Herschel was almost as great an astronomer as her kinsmen William and John. She discovered a phenomenal eight new comets. The name Herschel is now immortalised in the textbooks, but only as the surname of two men.

By then, however, the reasons for women's inadequacy in science were no longer seen as their associations with the devil. More kindly, yet equally disastrously, they were now believed to be constitutional. Augustus de Morgan wrote to the mother of his gifted pupil, Ada Lovelace. She was proving an alarmingly capable mathematician and de Morgan feared that mathematics demanded a "very great tension of mind" which would be "beyond the strength of a woman's physical power of application". Lovelace went on to work with Charles Babbage on the development of his difference engine, the precursor of the computer.

Bryan Appleyard, The Times Saturday Review

comprehension

A These adverbs all appear in the article. Match them with an equivalent meaning on the right, according to how they are used.

d 1 *utterly* 40   **a** evenly
e 2 *rigorously* 41   **b** astoundingly
h 3 *unarguably* 41   **c** catastrophically
b 4 *staggeringly* 51   **d** completely
g 5 *kindly* 70   **e** rigidly
a 6 *equally* 71   **f** disturbingly
c 7 *disastrously* 71   **g** generously
f 8 *alarmingly* 76   **h** indisputably

B Multiple-choice questions. These expressions are all in the article. Choose the meaning which best fits the expression.

1   in league with (line 6)
   A   a member of
   B   allied to
   C   dedicated to
   D   an offshoot of

2   systematic persecution (line 21)
   A   efficient collapse
   B   businesslike destruction
   C   precise indictment
   D   methodical victimization

3   titanic figure (line 37)
   A   tragic persona
   B   colossal number
   C   gigantic physique
   D   dominating persona

4   grasping the arcana (line 50)
   A   touching the levels
   B   understanding the mysteries
   C   holding the secrets
   D   embracing the subjects

5   precursor (line 85)
   A   forerunner
   B   inventor
   C   example
   D   embryo

C Reference devices. What do the underlined words refer to in the passage?

1   The one acts against nature, the other against order (line 4).
2   its enemy was witchcraft (line 8).
3   And it was a masculine way of knowing (line 15).
4   they must get that knowledge from the devil (line 32).
5   remained a men's club ever since (line 57).
6   By then, however, the reasons for women's inadequacy (line 67).
7   they were now believed to be constitutional (line 71).

summary 2

A Match one of the headings to each of the six paragraphs.

•   Exclusion of the 'opposite sex'   *4*
•   Fear of the unknown   *2*
•   The 'weaker sex'   *6*
•   The male / female divide   *3*
•   Defining terms of reference   *1*
•   A scientific family   *5*

B In support of his argument the writer mentions the following women:
   Margaret Cavendish   Caroline Herschel   Ada Lovelace

   Which of the above:
1   caused her tutor much concern?   *AL*
2   basked only in reflected glory?   *CH*
3   was the first female to gain access to one particular all-male domain?   *MC*
4   seemed unnaturally scientifically minded?   *AL*
5   was a woman of aristocratic birth?   *MC*
6   was a worthy member of a scientifically-minded family?   *CH*

C Linking sentences. Look at these two sentences.

1   Mary was never able to achieve the success she craved on account of the fact that she studied so hard.
2   Mary was able to achieve the success she craved despite the fact that she studied so hard.

   Do they sound logical? If not, how would you change them so that they do?

   Now combine the appropriate information to write one sentence about each of the women in the text using the information in **B**. Change the wording or add details as you think necessary and use either *despite the fact that* or *on account of the fact that* in each sentence.

listening 1

Listen to the following extract. A literary critic discusses the success of Hawking's book, *A Brief History of Time*.

1 According to the critic, the success of the book was
   A predictable.   B entirely unforeseen.   ʼC surprising.   D undeserved.

2 The critic suggests that the sum of money Hawking received before writing the book was
   A very low.   B standard.   C slightly above average. ⟍D unusually high.

3 According to the critic, most people
   ⟍A feel reassured because Hawking seems to have solved some important questions.
   B want to understand complex mathematical concepts.
   C are no longer interested in old religious questions.
   D want to fully understand what Hawking says in his book.

4 The anecdote about the physicist and the businessman implies that the book
   A explains complex concepts clearly.
   ʼB oversimplifies certain concepts.
   C is baffling for the average reader.
   D is of little interest to experts in the field of astronomy.

5 The critic views Hawking's aim in writing the book as
   A intellectually suspect.   ⟍B laudable.   C indefensible.   D misguided.

speaking

A Ranking. Discuss in groups what would make you buy a new book, either fiction or non-fiction, that was not connected with your studies or work. List these factors in order of persuasiveness.

- publicity on TV and in magazines
- prize winner
- by an author whose other books you like
- recommended by a friend

- attractive cover
- serialization on TV
- favourable reviews

B Picture discussion.

1 Work with a partner to discuss what each of the three books might be about. Compare your answers with other students in the class.
2 What kind of readers are each of the covers trying to appeal to and how do they try and achieve this?
3 What are the main differences in style between the three covers?

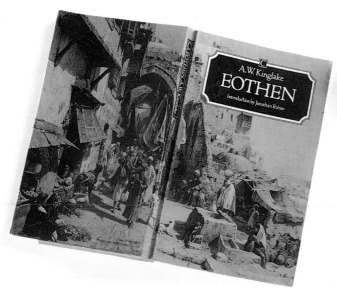

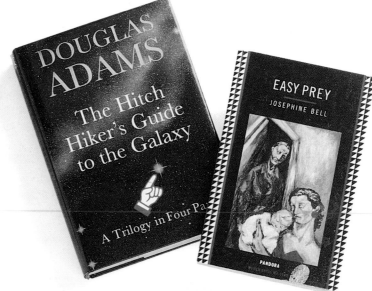

A I ascended one day to the citadel, which commands a superb view of the town. The fanciful, and elaborate gilt-work of the many minarets gives a light, and florid grace to the city as seen from this height, but before you can look for many seconds at such things, your eyes are drawn westward – drawn westward, and over the Nile until they rest upon the massive enormities of the Ghizeh pyramids.

B He struck most of the friends he had made on earth as an eccentric, but a harmless one – an unruly boozer with some oddish habits. For instance he would often gatecrash university parties, get badly drunk and start making fun of any astrophysicists he could find till he got thrown out.

 C We didn't find any place near enough for a person to stoop down and wash anything – such as a cosh. Nor their clothes and shoes, which would be splashed with blood, almost certainly. We tried particularly hard for traces of blood on the ground, and footprints near the site of the body, but there weren't any.

4   Look at the above extracts from the books and match the extracts with the covers.
5   What are the main differences in style between the extracts?
6   Write a short summary of one of the books for the back cover. Read your piece to a partner and see if he / she can guess which book it is for.
7   Is there an equivalent in your language of the proverb *Don't judge a book by its cover*?

vocabulary

A **Expressions.** Discuss the meaning of the following expressions connected with books. Then use the correct expression to replace the underlined words, making any necessary changes.

- *to throw the book at someone*
- *to turn over a new leaf*
- *to do something by the book*
- *to be in someone's good books*
- *to speak volumes about someone*
- *to take a leaf out of someone's book*

1   If the police catch you driving without a licence and with no insurance, they will punish you severely.
2   I think you ought to behave in the same way as her and let a lawyer deal with the problem.
3   He decided that it was time to change, and that in future he would try and be much kinder and more sympathetic to people less fortunate than himself.
4   I think the fact that she hasn't had the good grace to apologize is very indicative of her character.
5   Mrs Lawson is very pleased with me at the moment because I helped her clear the garden.
6   Our accountant is a little slow, but he is absolutely reliable and he follows all the correct procedures in everything he does.

B **Story-telling.** Prepare a short story lasting for about 30 seconds that will use and illustrate one of the idioms above. When you are ready, tell the anecdote to your partner.

listening 2

Listen to the following extract. It is from a humorous science fiction book by Douglas Adams called *The Hitch Hiker's Guide to the Galaxy*. In this episode, a powerful computer called Deep Thought is about to make an important announcement. Indicate whether the following statements are true or false.

1   There was a new computer on the desk in the room.   T/F
2   Phouchg and Loonquawl were accustomed to speaking to the computer.   T/F
3   The two men had been extensively prepared for the moment of the Answer.   T/F
4   The computer was worried the men might not like the Answer.   T/F
5   The computer was proud of having worked out the Answer.   T/F
6   The two men were worried about having to speak to the crowd.   T/F
7   The two men realized the full significance of the Answer.   T/F
8   The computer said it would work out the Ultimate Question.   T/F

The Descriptive Composition

A **A good piece of descriptive writing conveys feelings and reactions as well as simple facts.**

1 Look at the two pictures. What are the similarities and differences?
2 Read these two extracts. Which of them contains the most information and what kind of information is it?

Passage A *She is 71 years old. She has an oval face, a straight nose, blue eyes and a wrinkled face. She has wavy grey hair which she keeps in a bun.*

Passage B *When she laughs, her sparkling blue eyes flash with youthful delight and shine brightly from behind the mask of her wrinkled face.*

B **Practice.** Write two similar sentences about someone you know, the first with purely factual information and the second with some indications of the person's character.

A **Character adjectives, when used in moderation, can help to bring a description of a person into focus.** Work with a partner, using a dictionary if necessary, and match the words on the left with words of similar meaning on the right. Do any of the words describe you?

1	*callous*	**8**	*self-effacing*	**a** lacking energy		**h** arrogant
2	*placid*	**9**	*retiring*	**b** irritating		**i** honest
3	*sullen*	**10**	*frivolous*	**c** loutish		**j** sociable
4	*vivacious*	**11**	*condescending*	**d** unfeeling		**k** bad-tempered
5	*listless*	**12**	*gregarious*	**e** moody		**l** modest
6	*irksome*	**13**	*petulant*	**f** calm		**m** superficial
7	*boorish*	**14**	*frank*	**g** lively		**n** shy

exam tip

One of the criteria for marking a composition is vocabulary. Try and avoid simplistic adjectives like nice, lovely, *etc. Choose more interesting adjectives where appropriate to show that you have an extensive vocabulary.*

B **Word building.** These words can also be changed to form nouns and adverbs, as in the following example.

Jamie is going through a stage of almost unremitting sullenness. He rarely smiles, and when he does not get his own way, he behaves very petulantly, which can be irksome to his parents.

Look back at the list. How would you change the words on the left to form nouns?

A **In addition to character adjectives, almost any item or object can be used to help to delineate a character.** Look at the following example.

- jacket
- hair
- voice

*One of the students in the class is painfully shy. She always wears an extra-large waxed cotton **jacket** that envelops her almost completely, and which comes up to her chin; with a shake of the head, most of the rest of her face can be hidden behind her long black **hair**. All this, together with a **voice** that is never raised above a whisper, makes you wonder sometimes whether she is there at all.*

B **Practice.** Write short sketches of people (real or imaginary) incorporating the following items.

1 boots	**2** a posture	**3** eyes
a dog	a tone of voice	a pencil
hands	a fire	a room

significance

A **Think of a friend or member of your family.** If you were writing a creative description of them, which of the following items might you find useful?

- their hair
- their facial features
- their problems
- things they have done
- things they like to do
- things they have said
- their hands

- their attitudes and beliefs
- their relationships
- their shoes
- their gestures and reactions
- their furniture
- the walls in their room
- their clothes

- their skin
- their possessions
- their age
- their habits
- their hobbies
- their build
- their occupation

B **Practice.** Read the following extract from a description of an orphan. Indicate which of the items from the list above have been used and compare your answers with a partner.

He was brought to the asylum at the age of three, when the staff at the orphanage could no longer cope with his unruly behaviour, and he has been here for the last eight years. He is surrounded by the despairing cries of the other fifteen or so children who share the room, which is illuminated by a single electric bulb hanging from the ceiling, just out of reach.

There is no warmth surrounding him, so for much of the day he sits on the stone floor in his ragged, threadbare clothes, clasping his knees tightly to his thin body and burying his head; there are moments of fury as well, when he batters his pale, scarred face with his fists or beats his head against one of the walls. At other times he simply sits there, rocking relentlessly backwards and forwards, his wide open, jet-black eyes staring feverishly at the grey concrete walls and at a terrifying, endless future as bleak as despair itself.

writing task

Answer the following sample question.

Write a description of the person whom you would most like to see again.

Stage 1 General approach. Take care in the planning stage to pay full attention to the implications of the title and the possible ways of interpreting it.

Stage 2 Brainstorming. Think of the most significant features about the person. Consider whether you will use 'character adjectives' or external items to help you.

Stage 3 Organization. Arrange your thoughts into several clearly defined paragraphs. You could begin with some general information about the person, where you met, and explain why you have not seen them recently; then you could take one or two paragraphs to describe their personality in some detail and give examples; then you could finish by talking about the likelihood of seeing them again.

Stage 4 Write a composition of about 350 words. Time how long it takes you just to write – do not include the time for planning.

Stage 5 Check your work carefully.

Overview 2

Choose the word which best completes each sentence.

1 Their eventual choice of house was .... by the time Peter would take to get to the office.
   A related **B** consequent **C** determined **D** dependent

2 Her business must be going rather well, ... by the car she drives.
   A deducing **B** deciding **C** inferring **D** judging

3 My cousin obviously didn't .... much of an impression on you if you can't remember meeting her.
   A create **B** do **C** make **D** build

4 I was kept awake for most of the night by the .... of a mosquito in my ear.
   A whine **B** moan **C** groan **D** screech

5 If you would like to wait a moment, sir, I will just .... your file on the computer screen.
   A call up **B** pull down **C** bring in **D** pick up

6 He looks very aggressive and threatening, and so his soft, gentle voice is rather ....
   A disembodied **B** disconcerting **C** dismissive **D** discordant

7 If I were you, I would regard their offer with considerable ...., because it seems too good to be true.
   A suspicion **B** doubt **C** reservation **D** disbelief

8 My sister's confidence in her ability to play the piano was badly .... by her last music teacher.
   A subsided **B** weakened **C** undermined **D** loosened

9 He got an excellent grade in his examination .... the fact that he had not worked particularly hard.
   A on account of **B** because of **C** in spite of **D** although

10 I was astonished that he turned down the job – I .... it would have been ideal for him.
   A have thought **B** would have thought **C** am thinking **D** had been thinking

11 Next month TV and cinema star Paul Nicholas will be .... as Aladdin at the Apollo Theatre.
   A casting **B** playing **C** acting **D** appearing

12 On leaving prison, Vic decided to turn over a new .... and to give up his old life of crime.
   A book **B** page **C** chapter **D** leaf

13 Most people buy their houses with a loan which they then pay back .... 25 years.
   A over **B** during **C** with **D** throughout

14 It was only .... he told me his surname that I realized that we had been to the same school.
   A then **B** until **C** as soon as **D** when

15 Now's a .... time to tell me you're going out this evening – I've spent the whole day preparing supper for you.
   A suitable **B** reasonable **C** right **D** fine

Fill each of the blanks in the following sentences with a suitable word or phrase.

1 He managed to get to the airport on time .... that the traffic had been unusually heavy.

2 He uses a voice synthesizer .... it would be virtually impossible for him to communicate.

3 In addition .... a full-time job, she also manages to look after her family.

4 We can't move to our new offices until January, so .... being we are working from home.

5 I'd co-operate with the police if I were you, because if you don't they'll ....

.... at you.

6 The club was founded in 1822 as a men's club and it has remained one ....

....

7 The barman was sacked on account .... he had been stealing from the till.

8 She entered politics in 1989, and went .... become a minister two years later.

9 She must be out – I .... through to her all day without success.

10 It's your own fault the car was stolen – I've told you time .... to lock it up.

transformations   *Finish each of the following sentences in such a way that it means exactly the same as the sentence printed before it.*

1 The government have been reviewing their immigration policy for some time.

The government's ....

2 A new flu vaccine has been on trial since the beginning of the year.

They ....

3 If anyone succeeds in solving the problem, it will probably be him.

He is the most ....

4 He met Jane, whom he later married, when he was at Cambridge.

He met Jane, who was ....

5 His behaviour is beginning to annoy me more and more.

I am beginning to ....

6 I only heard her husband's side of the story when I met him in France.

It was only ....

7 'I'm in a bit of a hurry, but I'll ring you tomorrow,' he said.

He said he was a ....

8 I find it surprising that she didn't like her present.

I would ....

9 Most of the students ignored what the teacher was saying.

Few ....

10 She discovered eight new comets in the course of her work.

Her work resulted ....

SAFETY AND DANGER

War and Peace

Look at the pictures and, in small groups, discuss the following:

- Who are the people in the pictures and what are they doing?
- Should military service be abolished / compulsory?
- Should women have to do military service? If so, should they be taught to do different things from men?
- How long should people be made to do military service?
- Can you think of any short- or long-term benefits in doing service of this kind?

Be prepared to report back to the rest of the class on your group decisions.

The war saved my life. I really do not know what I would have done without it. On 7 August, the day war was declared on Russia, I enlisted as a volunteer gunner in the artillery for the duration and was instructed to report to a
5 garrison artillery regiment in Cracow. In my elation I was reluctant to go straight home to pack my bags (my family had by now all returned to Vienna), so I took a taxi to the Café Museum.

I should say that I joined the army because it was my
10 civic duty, yet I was even more glad to enlist because I knew at that time I had to *do* something, I had to subject myself to the rigours of a harsh routine that would divert me from my intellectual work. I had reached an impasse, and the impossibility of ever proceeding further filled me
15 with morbid despair.

By the time I reached the Café Museum, it was about six o'clock in the evening (I liked this café because its interior was modern; its square rooms were lined with square honey-coloured oak panelling, hung with prints of
20 the drawings of Charles Dana Gibson). Inside it was busy, the air noisy with speculation about the war. It was humid and hot, the atmosphere suffused with the reek of beer and cigar smoke. The patrons were mostly young men, students from the nearby art schools, clean-shaven,
25 casually and unaffectedly dressed. So I was a little surprised to catch a glimpse in one corner of a uniform. I pushed through the crowd to see who it was.

Georg, it was obvious, was already fairly drunk. He sat strangely hunched over, staring intently at the table-top.
30 His posture and the ferocious concentration of his gaze clearly put people off as the three other seats around his table remained unoccupied. I told a waiter to bring a half litre of *Heuniger Wein* to the table and then sat down opposite him.

35 Georg was wearing the uniform of an officer, a lieutenant, in the Medical Corps. He looked at me candidly and without resentment and, of course, without recognition. He seemed much the same as the last time I had seen him, at once ill-looking and possessed of a
40 sinewy energy. I introduced myself and told him I was pleased to see a fellow soldier as I myself had just enlisted.

'It's your civic duty,' he said, his voice strong and unslurred. 'Have a cigar.'

45 He offered me a Trabuco, those ones that have a straw mouthpiece because they are so strong. I declined – at that time I did not smoke. When the wine arrived he insisted on paying for it.

'I'm a rich man,' he said as he filled our glasses.
50 'Where're you posted?'

'Galicia.'

'Ah, the Russians are coming.' He paused. 'I want to go somewhere cold and dark. I detest this sun and this city. Why aren't we fighting the Eskimos? I hate daylight.
55 Maybe I could declare war on the Lapps. One-man army.'

'Bit lonely, no?'

'I want to be lonely. All I do is pollute my mind talking to people... I want a dark, cold, lonely war. Please.'

'You'd better keep that to yourself.'

60 He raised his glass. 'God preserve me from sanity.'

I thought of something Nietzsche had said: 'Our life, our happiness, is beyond the north, beyond ice, beyond death.' I looked into Georg's ugly face, his thin eyes and glossy lips, and felt a kind of love for him and his
65 honesty. I clinked my glass against his and asked God to preserve me from sanity as well.

---

reading

A **Read the passage above, and try to imagine which period of history it is set in.**

B **Multiple-choice questions.** Now look at the following questions and choose the best answer. Distractors could be:

- correct statements which do not answer the problem posed in the stem.
- carefully worded incorrect statements which seem correct at first glance.
- statements which may have an element of truth in them but are too narrow in their scope to be correct.

1 The writer found himself in the army because
  A he had been instructed to report to a regiment in Cracow.
  B it was the perfect excuse to get away from home.
  C he was getting nowhere with his work at the time.
  D he had wanted to save the lives of his fellow-countrymen.

2 What did the writer think was out of place in the café?
  A The modern decor.
  B The respectable-looking students.
  C The talk about the war.
  D The presence of an army officer.

3 Why was Georg sitting alone?
  A He had had too much to drink.
  B He was not an art student.
  C He made the other customers feel uneasy.
  D He had argued with some other customers.

4 Georg confessed to the writer that he
  A was not suffering from a mental illness.
  B preferred to be on his own.
  C wanted God to make him sane again.
  D did not want to fight the Eskimos.

vocabulary

A **Words which create atmosphere.** The passage has a gloomy feel to it which is reflected in the rather pessimistic vocabulary. However, some words and expressions convey the opposite feeling. Find the words and expressions which conjure up feelings of (**a**) optimism and (**b**) pessimism. Look up in the dictionary any words you do not know.

B **Similar but different.** In each of the sentences below, choose the word which best completes the sentence. Some of the words appeared in the passage.

1 Two dead bodies were .... from the wreckage after the bomb went off.
  A recovered　　B saved　　　　　　C salvaged　　　　　D liberated

2 He .... to be an expert in bomb disposal.
  A pronounced　　B certified　　　　　C professed　　　　　D declared

3 He was not .... to taking on all the extra responsibilities the promotion entailed.
  A hesitant　　B unenthusiastic　　C reluctant　　　　D averse

4 As fog had closed the airport, they had to .... the relief flight elsewhere.
  A distract　　B divert　　　　　　C deflect　　　　　D detract

5 There was a(n) .... of freshly baked bread coming from the field kitchens.
  A reek　　B scent　　　　　　C odour　　　　　D aroma

6 During the rioting several houses in the area had their windows ....
  A clinked　　B banged　　　　　C crashed　　　　　D smashed

Now choose **one** word from each set of three incorrect options above and use it in a sentence of your own. Use a dictionary if necessary.

C **Use your eyes! Related word groups.** In the passage we had the words *glimpse* and *gaze*. The words on the left are all connected with using the eyes. Match them to their appropriate explanation on the right.

1	glimpse	**a**	close the eyelids rapidly
2	gaze	**b**	to have a quick look (through)
3	stare	**c**	look closely at (as if trying to see more clearly)
4	glance	**d**	see briefly (often before it disappears)
5	peep	**e**	look at steadily in surprise or astonishment
6	peer	**f**	look at intently / longingly
7	blink	**g**	close one eyelid only
8	make out	**h**	see with difficulty
9	weep	**i**	take a quick look when you shouldn't (eg through a keyhole!)
10	wink	**j**	cry

D **Expressions.** We came across the expression *done without it*, meaning 'managed without it' in line 2 of the text on page 29. Look at these uses of *do*, then use the correct expression to replace the underlined words, making any necessary changes. In some cases it is necessary to change the word order or add an extra word.

wonders for　　　　　　　　　　　　　*time*
something up　　　　　　　　　　　　*someone a good turn / favour*
the donkey work　　　　*do*　　　　*a lot of harm / good or no harm / good*
something with your eyes closed

1 I'm fed up with being responsible for all the hard work in the barracks.
2 The café was in a mess. We had to redecorate it.
3 Running a smooth operation is not difficult. It's second nature to me now.
4 I think too much army-type discipline is counter-productive.
5 Could you help me? I need someone to pick up an urgent consignment of supplies.
6 Some people say that military service is very good for character building.
7 He spent several years in prison for being a conscientious objector.
8 You'll gain no benefit from a life of hardship.

Minimizing the Risks

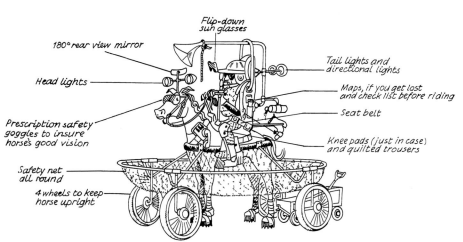

Flip-down sun glasses

180° rear view mirror

Head lights

Tail lights and directional lights

Maps, if you get lost and check list before riding

Seat belt

Prescription safety goggles to insure horse's good vision

Knee pads (just in case) and quilted trousers

Safety net all round

4 wheels to keep horse upright

talking points

Occupational Safety & Health Admin

Cowboy after O.S.H.A. During an address before some risk managers in Calgary, Alberta – home of the famous Calgary Stampede – the figure on the left was projected on the screen. The audience reacted with uncontrolled shrieks and howls. Can you think why?

- What precautions do we take in everyday life to ensure our personal safety?
- What can we insure ourselves against?

cloze development

Apparently you can even insure yourself against rain on holiday! Quickly read through the following article about someone who is not too disappointed when the weather turns out to be inclement, then fill in the missing words. Choose one of the four possible answers in **1–20** following the passage. Indicate which you think is the most suitable by underlining it.

It appears that a rainy day is defined as one that includes four hours of rain between 9 in the morning and 5 in the evening. Being nine-tenths water, I am not bothered when a drop (**1**) ....*more*.... falls
5 on me from the skies. That is if it's pure sky-distilled water, of (**2**) ....*course*...., and not one of the acid brews, (**3**) ....*though*.... even from a stiff acid downpour near the Danube in Hungary, I've never yet (**4**) ....*had*.... my clothes
10 dissolve. The occasional shower is
(**5**) ....*more*.... than welcome and when it comes down cats and (**6**) ....*dogs*...., it stirs one's Viking blood.
    Those who feel this way are fortunate
15 (**7**) ....*as*.... travellers. When rain falls, then so (**8**) ....*do*.... prices. Cultivate the rainy seasons for cheap, independent travelling. Heavy relentless rain is a perfect (**9**) ....*excuse*.... not to climb a mountain or cross a rope bridge above
20 a swollen river. (**10**) ....*Besides*...., after the rain the world is brilliant.
    It seems (**11**) ....*likely*.... from the anecdotal evidence that all over the world rain is

falling at (**12**) ....*times*.... when it shouldn't,
25 and I often find local citizens
(**13**) ....*apologising*.... to me for these solecisms of the climate. No offence (**14**) ....*taken*...., I reply, it reminds me of home.
    Not (**15**) ....*everybody*.... shares this view of
30 rain, and with a row of sodden offspring trailing in my
(**16**) ....*wake*...., grumbling about the low grade of entertainment, I too might class the episode as a marred holiday. People in this sort of
(**17**) ....*predicament*...., persecuted by mischievous
35 rain gods, prompted the revelation this week of a wheeze called Holiday Rain Insurance,
(**18**) ....*claimed*.... to be the first of its kind.
    Now there's nothing new about insurance against the havoc caused by robust weather to public events.
40 I remember (**19**) ....*raising*.... a legal umbrella against the showers that might drive away my audience for an open-air theatre production. The document was called a Pluvius Policy: no
(**20**) ....*doubt*.... Plautus and Terence had
45 the same worry – though not Seneca, because his plays were meant for reading indoors! ■

1	again	other	more	also
2	fact	course	sorts	note
3	though	despite	if	whereas

4 been	gone	suffered	had
5 other	more	better	sooner
6 kittens	rabbits	dogs	mice
7 as	for	being	such
8 did	do	have	are
9 excuse	grounds	evasion	disguise
10 Otherwise	Whereas	Notwithstanding	Besides
11 likely	bound	probably	liable
12 occasions	times	opportunities	terms
13 bemoaning	apologizing	blaming	complaining
14 believed	suffered	understood	taken
15 anybody	everybody	one	all
16 queue	waves	wake	row
17 predominance	preconception	predicament	prediction
18 challenged	claimed	demanded	insisted
19 rising	arousing	raising	arising
20 doubt	apprehension	confusion	ambiguity

vocabulary

Synonyms and paraphrases. In the article on page 31 you will find synonyms or paraphrases of the nine words below. Match the explanations to the appropriate words. **NB** None of the words appeared in the gaps. The nouns are all given in the singular and the verbs in the infinitive form, and they are all in the order in which they appear in the passage.

1 disintegrate   *dissolve*
2 arouse   *stir*
3 seek out   *cultivate*
4 soaked   *sodden*
5 complain   *grumble*
6 spoil   ....
7 victimize   ....
8 disclosure   ....
9 chaos   ....

Now use one of the answers you found in its correct form to complete each of the sentences below.

1 Torrential rain caused ..*havoc*.... late last night in the north-west.

2 The holiday was a resounding success, ..*marred*.... only by the fact that our flight was delayed.

3 Take two tablets ..*dissolved*.... in water every four hours.

4 The jury was shocked by the ..*revelation*.... that the man they had just decided was not guilty had had five previous convictions.

5 Stop ..*grumbling*.... about the weather! You'll just have to put up with it while you're in this country.

6 Having walked for two hours across the moors in the pouring rain, we were absolutely ..*sodden*... .

7 The film showing the effects of the present famine ..*stirred*.... strong emotions in the audience.

8 In the past many people have been .... for their political or religious beliefs.

9 She's such a snob. She considers that her neighbours are just not worth ..*cultivating*... .

uses of have

A Look at the following examples and answer the questions.

1 What is the difference between these two sentences?

   a *We've put central heating in.*
   b *We've had central heating put in.*

   Who performed the action in **b** and why?

2 What is the difference between the use of *have* in **1b** and in this sentence?

I had my car stolen last night. _not arrange – victim of event_

3 What word could replace *had* in *We had the house painted by Gilbert and Son*, if we changed the sentence as follows?

We ...got..... *Gilbert and Son to paint the house.*

4 In the passage the writer said *I've never yet had my clothes dissolve.* _st to happen without_

What does the writer mean by this? What is the difference in construction between this example and the ones in **1**, **2** and **3**?

5 What is the difference in construction between these examples of *have* and the ones in **1**, **2** and **3**?

I won't have you staying / stay out late. _I won't allow you_

I'll have you know that I did all the work myself.

6 What is the meaning of *have your grandmother complaining* in the following sentence?

If you don't stop making that noise, you'll have your grandmother complaining. _predict what might happen_

Which of the sentences above is closest in form to this one?

7 This sentence has the same construction as **5** and **6**:

After several hours I had them singing in unison. _instrumental_

What is the meaning of *have* here?

B **Look at the following sentences.** Finish each sentence in such a way that it means exactly the same as the one printed before it. Use each of the forms above.

1 **a** The police have never arrived on our doorstep in the middle of the night before.

We've ....

b My hair has never fallen out in handfuls before!

I've never ....

2 **a** The gas explosion blew out all the shop windows.

All the shops ....

b A thief picked my pocket on the tube.

I ....

3 **a** They laid a new carpet yesterday.

We ....

b They're fitting the windows tomorrow.

We're ....

4 We had double glazing put in by the builders.

We got ....

5 They are not allowed to smoke in my classroom.

I won't have ....

6 They'll all want to stay the night if we don't ask them to leave now.

We'll have ....

7 She managed to walk around the room with a little encouragement from me.

With a little encouragement I had ....

rewriting

Write these sentences in *two* different ways.

EXAMPLE Someone came to clean the office carpets today.
HAD *We had the office carpets cleaned today.*
WERE *The office carpets were cleaned today.*

1 I never thought of going to Iceland for my holidays.

OCCURRED . . . .
CLUE Begin with *It*.

HEAD . . . .
CLUE Begin with *It* and use an idiomatic expression with *head* meaning 'to have an idea', or change the order and begin with *Going to*.

2 His holiday insurance scheme failed through lack of support.

BACK . . . .
CLUE Use *because no one was prepared*.

BACKING . . . .
CLUE Use *because he was unable*.

3 The last day of the holiday was disastrous.

IN . . . .
CLUE Use *ended*.

CATASTROPHICALLY . . . .
CLUE Refer to the previous clue.

4 It poured down all day.

DOGS . . . .
CLUE Use *raining*.

TORRENTS . . . .
CLUE Use *came down*.

5 It seems likely that the company will fold.

PROBABILITY . . . .
CLUE Use *in all*.

ODDS . . . .
CLUE You need *the odds*.

6 Nobody plays football in front of my house!

HAVE . . . .
CLUE Begin *I*.

FORBIDDEN . . . .
CLUE Begin *Playing*.

7 No one agrees with me.

VIEW . . . .
CLUE Use *shares*.

OPINION . . . .
CLUE Use *of the*.

8 Physical exercise is not a modern pastime.

NEW . . . .
CLUE Use *nothing*.

HILLS . . . .
CLUE You need an idiomatic expression meaning 'very old'.

9 I hope my remarks haven't upset you.

OFFENCE . . . .
CLUE Use *You … taken.*

AMISS . . . .
CLUE Refer to the previous clue.

10 There are some people who didn't agree with the decision.

EVERYBODY . . . .
CLUE Use *not.*

UNANIMOUS . . . .
CLUE Begin *The decision.*

Summary Skills

Taking a Chance

talking points

Which of the following do you consider diminish our life expectancy most, or pose the greatest risk to us? When you have decided, check your answers with the key on page 215.

- exposure to radiation
- riding in cars (10,000 miles per year)
- being male rather than female
- being bitten by an animal or insect

- remaining unmarried
- choking on food
- working as a coal miner
- being struck by lightning

summary 1

Read through the following passage and summarize in one sentence what it is about.

In a classic and oft-quoted treatise published in *Science*, 'Social Benefit versus Technological Risk', Chauncey Starr pointed out several interesting premises about risk in our society that can be empirically validated.

Starr first divided risks into two categories: voluntary and involuntary. For the voluntary risks, you subject yourself, as an individual and by your own decision, to a risk. Examples might be hunting, flying your own airplane, or skiing. Involuntary risks, on the other hand, are imposed on you by society without your consent. These could include military service, nuclear power generation, or highway bridge design. Starr's analysis revealed that the *average person will accept roughly 1,000 times as much risk voluntarily as he or she will involuntarily.* As Starr so aptly puts it, 'We are loath to let others do unto us what we happily do to ourselves.'

He validated this 1,000:1 ratio in a variety of ways. In one such experiment certain activities were measured in terms of their probability of fatalities per hour of exposure versus the average annual benefit a person would receive by that exposure. Typical activities included traveling by automobile, game hunting, or using electrical power. In all cases, the risk of voluntary activities exceeded that of involuntary ones by 1,000 times.

Starr further showed that for most of us acceptability of risk is inversely related to the number of people who participate with us in that risk. Automobiles, for example, were originally considered to be sporting vehicles — driven by daredevils. But as more and more people began to drive, the amount of risk considered to be acceptable (in terms of fatalities per person-hour of exposure) was reduced. Moreover, tolerable risks for both general and commercial aviation demonstrate this same idea by continuing to drop as more of us utilize those modes for transportation.

A corollary to this relationship between acceptable risk and numbers of people involved is that advertising has a positive influence on the acceptance of greater risk by the general public.

Whether or not misery loves company, there seems to be within us a subconscious willingness to take risks that we can see others also accepting. Without question, the superabundance — and cleverness — of alcoholic beverage advertising can be credited with the rising per capita consumption of alcohol, despite the alarming dangers of drunken driving, physical diseases, and sociopsychological ills it produces.

As a final glimpse of modern society's response to risk, Starr demonstrates that the probability of dying from disease seems to be, psychologically, a benchmark or yardstick in setting the limit of voluntarily accepted risk. In most sporting activities (whether skiing, race driving, hunting, or athletic contests), the risk of death is surprisingly close to the risk of death from disease. It is as though we all have a subconscious computer that sets our courage at a level equal to, but not exceeding, the statistical mortality due to involuntary exposure to disease. Could this unique probabilistic barrier be that fine line that separates boldness from foolhardiness? ■

Managing Risk by Vernon L. Grose

comprehension

The following expressions were used in the passage. Choose the explanation you think best fits the original meaning and justify your answers.

1   loath to let others do unto us (line 18)
   A   forced to comply with what others impose on us
   B   reluctant to be subjected to what others impose on us
   C   willing to allow others to subject us to their will
   D   hesitant about imposing our will on others

2   in terms of fatalities per person-hour of exposure (line 37)
   A   defined as the number of hours one is exposed to a risk without injury
   B   with reference to the numbers of people involved in taking the risk
   C   as an example of the time necessary to expose a person to a fatal risk
   D   in relation to the number of deaths occurring each hour of the risk-taking

exam tip

Read the passage through and try and pinpoint what each paragraph is about before looking at the comprehension and summary questions.

3   a corollary to this relationship (line 43)
   A   a conclusion we can draw from this relationship
   B   a contradiction inherent in this relationship
   C   a coincidence we can perceive between this relationship and…
   D   a counterbalance noticeable between this relationship and…

4   the rising per capita consumption (line 52)
   A   the increase in the number of related illnesses
   B   the fluctuation in the number of excessive consumers
   C   the increase in the average amount consumed
   D   the growing cost of consuming large amounts

5   a benchmark or yardstick (line 59)
   A   a means of solving a problem
   B   a compromise reached by both sides
   C   a point of no return
   D   a standard used in judging

6   this unique probabilistic barrier (line 68)
   A   the only logical obstacle
   B   this incomparable prospective limit
   C   this apparently feasible obstruction
   D   the original obstacle envisaged

summary 2

A   Summarize the main point of each paragraph. The first one has been done for you.

1   Chauncey Starr claimed that some theories about societal risk can be proved by experiments.

2   ....

3   ....

4   ....

5   ....

6   ....

B   Connecting ideas. Define the two types of risk mentioned in the passage in your own words as far as possible.

1   ....

2   ....

Now join the two definitions above using these connectors:

whereas   however   while

Which connector could appear in two different positions?
Can you define *boldness* and *foolhardiness* and link them in the same way?

Just my Luck!

exam tip

You may not know what the pictures are trying to convey so use your imagination and 'think on your feet', reason aloud – you will be assessed on the language you produce, not on your opinions!

A Can you describe these pictures? What are they trying to show?

B Expressions. What do you think these expressions mean? Match them with the explanations on the right.

1	*the luck of the draw*	**a**	to be fortunate enough to find what you are looking for
2	*beginner's luck*	**b**	unexpected success at your first attempt
3	*to push one's luck*	**c**	good or bad luck depending on fate
4	*to strike lucky*	**d**	to expect (wrongly) your luck to be good all the time
5	*to take pot luck*	**e**	to take a risk/chance without knowing what the outcome will be

listening

A Have you ever been in the wrong place at the wrong time? Cindy Talbot certainly was! Listen to the introduction to Cindy's strange story. She is being interviewed on the radio programme *Young hero or heroine of the week*. Read through the sentences before listening and identify the type of information you will need to fill in, eg numbers, categories, places.

1 Cindy is in her . . . . year at . . . .

2 She was on the . . . . day of her . . . . day trip in Colorado.

3 Lightning kills . . . . Americans each year.

4 To survive a direct hit is . . . .

B Which option should I choose? Read through numbers **1** to **5** before listening to the rest of the interview, then, as you listen to the people talking, put a small pencil dot beside the answer you think is correct.

1 On her trip Cindy was
  A alone.
  B with two boys.
  C with university friends.
  D with another girl.

2 Cindy was struck by lightning
  A on Middle Bald Mountain.
  B under the trees.
  C after the storm.
  D while she was resting.

3 Cindy reached the track
  A on foot.
  B on her hands and knees.
  C with some help.
  D as the rain started.

4 When Rod and Mark saw Cindy they were
  A walking in the woods.
  B working in their timber business.
  C driving along the path.
  D looking for a particular type of wood.

5 Which of the following statements is true according to Cindy?
  A She will never go hiking during an electric storm again.
  B She is now very frightened of hiking long distances.
  C She has no intention of giving up her hobby.
  D She is not as strong-willed as she thought she was.

C **Sound discrimination.** Look at the following pairs of words. Read them aloud and decide which appeared in the interview. They are all in the order in which they occurred. If you cannot remember, listen to the interview again.

	A	**B**		**A**	**B**
1	object	subject	9	a life	alive
2	so so	solo	10	crawl	cruel
3	peak	beak	11	track	truck
4	grumbling	rumbling	12	searching	surgeon
5	backpack	knapsack	13	scares	scars
6	frame	fame	14	hips	hits
7	surging	scorching	15	scared	scarred
8	belt	bolt	16	equitable	a quitter

vocabulary

Expressions. The British love talking about the weather. It's a neutral topic and there's always something to say on the subject! Consequently there are many idioms in the language based on the weather. Read the following expressions and decide which ones could replace the underlined sections of the sentences below.

- *a storm in a teacup*
- *under a cloud*
- *make heavy weather of*
- *the calm before the storm*
- *under the weather*
- *get wind of*
- *bright and breezy*
- *it's an ill wind that blows nobody any good*

1 You're <u>very cheerful</u> for a dismal Monday morning.
2 Things are quiet at the moment but it's <u>an uneasy truce.</u>
3 It seems like a tragedy now, but <u>someone will derive some benefit from it.</u>
4 He <u>finds doing his</u> homework <u>very difficult indeed.</u>
5 She's <u>not very well</u> at the moment.
6 We tried to keep the party a secret but they've managed to <u>find out about it somehow.</u>
7 He's <u>in disgrace</u> because of the way he behaved at the party last night.
8 The whole affair is <u>a lot of fuss about nothing.</u>

speaking

Coping in a crisis. In Part Three of the interview you may be asked to take part in a simulation.

In small groups decide what you would do in the following situations. When you have decided, tell the rest of the class what decisions you reached.

1 As you are driving home one evening, you notice a car which seems to have broken down on a lonely road in the countryside. There appear to be two people inside it and you notice the word HELP scrawled across the condensation on the back window.
2 Your plane has made a forced landing in a clearing in the middle of a forest. Although no one was injured, one of the passengers is suffering from shock. There seems to be no sign of life anywhere and it is very cold.
3 There is a fire in your hotel. You are in the restaurant when the fire alarm goes off. You suddenly remember you have left your most treasured possessions in a safe in your bedroom.
4 You see a teenage boy fall into a river. He seems to be in difficulties but you cannot swim.
5 You are on holiday in a foreign country. When you get back to your hotel you discover that your money, travellers' cheques and passport have all been stolen.

exam tip

Try to be as imaginative and resourceful as possible when asked to perform a speaking task. Remember, the examiner can only assess you on the language you produce.

introduction

In the task-based composition, you may be asked to write a report, letter or article in a particular style. You will be given some key information that may be presented in a variety of formats such as telexes, graphs, notes, comments, etc. In tackling this kind of composition, you need to pay particular attention to the following:

- Fulfil the task set – read the instructions carefully to see exactly what is required and make certain you answer the question fully.
- Extract the information – make use of the information that is presented to help plan your paragraphs, but remember that the order of what you write does not need to follow the order of the information that is presented, and you may have to add new information.
- Write in an appropriate style. Newspaper articles, official reports, formal and informal letters all vary in language and organization.

sample composition

A Read the following composition title and the sample answer.

Write a report for a local evening newspaper about a hurricane that devastated your home town. (About 300 words)

1 *Severe hurricane force winds buffeted their way across Kent and much of the south-east of England last night, leaving a trail of devastation in their wake. Vast tracts of the county have been flattened, and damage to property is estimated at hundreds of millions of pounds.*

2 *Yesterday evening there was little warning of what was about to come. The wind began to pick up just after 11 p.m. and by 2 a.m. storm force winds had hit towns on the south coast. Later, the winds increased in violence until they eventually reached hurricane force in the early hours of the morning, lashing the country with gusts of over 130 miles an hour. Hospitals were warned to expect casualties.*

3 *Kent has been very badly hit. In Sevenoaks, an entire forest was flattened by the blast and uprooted trees were littered over the countryside like matchsticks. Elsewhere there has been considerable damage to crops and buildings. David Hart, from Lamberhurst, awoke to find that his roof had been blown off: 'I was woken up by an incredible noise – it was just like a bomb going off. I could see the roof flapping about in the wind. Then it just flew off, and slates and bricks came crashing down through the ceiling.'*

4 *Concern has been raised at the failure of the authorities to provide adequate warning. A spokesperson from the Meteorological Office explained that storm force winds had been forecast, but that the hurricane itself had been caused by a combination of freak weather conditions.*

5 *The first priority for Kent County Council is the restoration of communications, and the government is considering giving emergency aid. Meanwhile, insurance companies are bracing themselves for a deluge of claims that could well run to nearly a billion pounds.*

B Language focus. Read the text again and answer the following questions.

1 What headings could be provided for each of the five paragraphs?
2 In paragraph **2**, what link words and other devices are used to indicate the progression of the storm?
3 How many examples of the passive are there in paragraphs **3** and **4**?
4 Find at least five different verbs or phrases which describe the wind and its effects.
5 To what extent is the personal viewpoint of the writer made clear?

writing task   **Read the following sample question.**
Write an article for a local evening newspaper about a severe flood, using the information provided. (About 300 words)

Extract from Local Government report: 'Danger of flooding'.

```
The Committee has been advised that
this particular combination of
weather conditions is unlikely to
arise, and is therefore of the view
that expensive measures to prevent
flooding cannot be justified.
```

Here are some comments from residents whose homes were flooded:

'I've lost everything – carpets, curtains, furniture, books, you name it. And what I want to know is why weren't we warned about it because we could have done something. I think it's an absolute disgrace.'

Penny Winter, resident

'The land will recover given time, I suppose. But a lot of my farm machinery is still submerged and I should think it'll be very expensive to repair if it can be repaired at all, but I've had all my crops wiped out completely.'

Charlie Tomkins, farmer

Extracts from a newsroom printer:

11.43   WEATHER STATIONS REPORT SEVERE EASTERLY WINDS INCREASING IN FORCE

12.18   MET OFFICE ISSUE WARNINGS OF HEAVY THUNDERSTORMS

14.20   TORRENTIAL DOWNPOUR IN CITY – FOUR INCHES OF RAIN IN PAST HOUR

16.35   WATER LEVEL IN RIVER INCREASING ALARMINGLY. RESIDENTS IN LOW-LYING PROPERTIES ADVISED TO LEAVE BY POLICE

17.12   RIVER BREAKS ITS BANKS – SEVERE FLOODING REPORTED AND A NUMBER OF TOWNS ALREADY SEVERAL FEET UNDER WATER

18.23   GOVERNMENT ORDERS ARMED FORCES TO HELP EMERGENCY SERVICES IN EVACUATING FLOODED AREAS

18.24   LOCAL OFFICIAL DESCRIBES FLOOD AS ECONOMIC CATASTROPHE OF MAJOR PROPORTIONS

Stage 1   Outline planning. For the purposes of this composition, follow the five paragraph model in the sample composition to give:
- a news summary
- details of the progression of the storm
- personal viewpoints and eye witness reports
- reactions to the disaster / criticism of the authorities
- comments about the future.

Stage 2   Brainstorming. Read through the information carefully and extract what you consider to be the most relevant points.

Stage 3   Organization. Make a detailed paragraph plan showing where the information given will be used and make up any extra details that are necessary.

Stage 4   Writing. Keep to the style of a newspaper article, remembering the points discussed in the **Language focus** section.

Stage 5   Checking. Try not to repeat key words too often. You may find the following items helpful.

a flood   flooding   rain, storm   to flood   to submerge to pour down   to break its banks   to swamp   to gush to come pouring in   torrential, heavy   violent

Overview 3

vocabulary

Choose the word which best completes each sentence.

1 Many countries have .... compulsory military service.
   A aborted   B absconded   C abolished   D abstracted

2 Media reports on the outcome of military intervention often .... the true facts.
   A divert   B detract   C depose   D distort

3 He gave her a mischievous .... as she handed him his order.
   A peer   B peep   C wink   D blink

4 Despite their initial objections, we soon .... them all playing football together.
   A made   B had   C organized   D persuaded

5 We may win, we may lose – it's just the .... of the draw!
   A strike   B odds   C chance   D luck

6 You are under no obligation to help as assistance is purely ....
   A free   B voluntary   C charitable   D donated

7 Trespassers will be ....
   A perpetrated   B persecuted   C proscribed   D prosecuted

8 War is .... as open-armed conflict between countries or factions within countries.
   A delineated   B declared   C defaulted   D defined

9 I hope you won't take it .... if I suggest an alternative remedy.
   A offence   B amiss   C upset   D heart

10 Claims for compensation could .... run into billions of pounds.
   A far   B much   C well   D most

transformations

Finish each of the following sentences in such a way that it means exactly the same as the sentence printed before it.

1 The decorators have finished the whole of the first floor.

   We have. . . .had. . . . .

2 It is difficult to know what one's reaction would have been in such a situation.

   If I . had. . . . .

3 Tell me, Cindy, what were you actually doing when the lightning struck?

   I asked . had. . . . .

4 The children are in disgrace for being so badly behaved.

   The children are under . . . .

5 My car has never broken down on a motorway before.

   I've never had my car. . . . .

6 Her hobby is one thing that she does not intend to give up.

   She has. . . . .

7 Freak weather conditions resulted in the hurricane which devastated the area.

   The hurricane which devastated the area was. . . . .

8 The authorities failed to provide adequate warning, which has caused considerable concern.

   Considerable concern. . . . .

9 The restoration of communications and essential services is of prime importance for the council.

   The first . . . .

10 The storm completely wiped out all my crops.

I've... had ....

blank-filling

Fill each of the blanks in the following sentences with a suitable word or phrase.

1 The car can't have broken down, I .... only had it .... serviced last week!

2 If I ...... had been in that .... situation, I certainly wouldn't have had the courage to do what you did.

3 Although he had a difficult time during the war, it ..... did him no .... harm.

4 It's no ..... good .... the cold and wet, you'll just have to put up with it!

5 I won't have .... their cars in the street outside the entrance to my house!

6 In times of hardship we have to learn to do .... without .... some basic necessities.

7 I'm .... death of spiders!

8 I heard the thunder ..... rumbling .... in the distance.

9 He's been .... weather for ages and still isn't back at work.

10 We made the uniforms ourselves as we couldn't ..... afford to have them .... made.

rewriting

For each of the sentences below, write a new sentence as similar as possible in meaning to the original sentence, but using the words given in capital letters. These words must not be altered in any way.

1 The regiment's reputation was greatly damaged by his outrageous conduct.

HARM ....

2 The ships were hardly visible through the thick fog.

MAKE ....

3 The rain was coming down in torrents.

CATS ....

4 A treaty will very probably be signed soon.

ALL ... In all probability ....

5 There's nothing new about defence alliances.

HILLS ....

6 We are unanimous regarding the formation of a new alliance.

SHARES... E.O. Shares ....

7 The disagreement is a lot of fuss about nothing.

TEACUP ....

8 A government official leaked the story to the world press.

WIND ....

9 It was with great reluctance that they came to our aid.

LOATH ....

10 Organic vegetables are said to be very healthy.

WONDERS ....

STRANGER THAN FICTION

Reading

Suspension of Belief

talking points

Discuss how strongly you agree or disagree with the following statements.

1 I am not superstitious, but would not make any important decisions on Friday 13th.
2 Ghosts exist only as figments of the imagination or as optical illusions.
3 The experience of *déjà vu* suggests that reincarnation is possible.
4 Clairvoyants are charlatans.
5 Mediums with psychic powers can communicate with the dead during séances.
6 Reading horoscopes in the paper or magazines is a waste of time.
7 We live in a pre-determined and entirely mechanistic world.
8 I would never believe the predictions of a palmist or other fortune-teller.
9 I am highly sceptical of claims that some people have telepathic powers.
10 It is unwise to dabble in the occult.

reading

A Read the first part of the article and answer the questions that follow it.

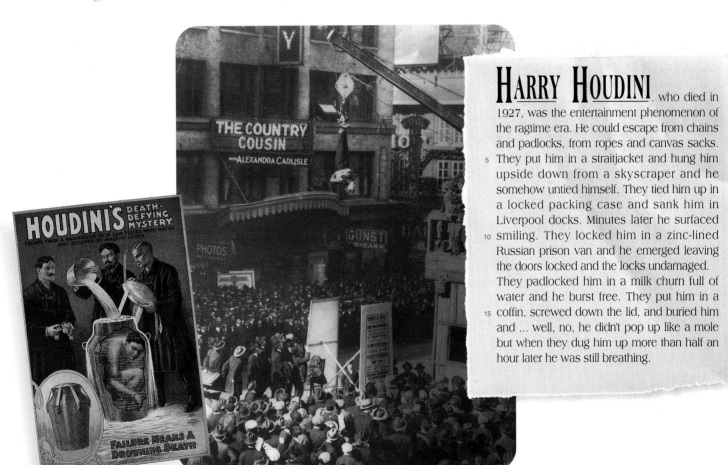

HARRY HOUDINI, who died in 1927, was the entertainment phenomenon of the ragtime era. He could escape from chains and padlocks, from ropes and canvas sacks.
5 They put him in a straitjacket and hung him upside down from a skyscraper and he somehow untied himself. They tied him up in a locked packing case and sank him in Liverpool docks. Minutes later he surfaced
10 smiling. They locked him in a zinc-lined Russian prison van and he emerged leaving the doors locked and the locks undamaged. They padlocked him in a milk churn full of water and he burst free. They put him in a
15 coffin, screwed down the lid, and buried him and ... well, no, he didn't pop up like a mole but when they dug him up more than half an hour later he was still breathing.

1 Which of these feats seem the most impressive to you?
2 Which of these activities would you least like to try and do yourself?
3 Discuss briefly how you think Houdini might have managed to do these things.
   Then read the rest of the text to see whether you were right.

Houdini would usually allow his equipment to be examined by the audience. The chains, locks and packing cases all seemed perfectly kosher, so it was tempting to conclude that he possessed super-human powers. Sir Arthur Conan Doyle's Sherlock Holmes was the very paragon of analytical thinking but Conan Doyle believed that Houdini achieved his tricks through spiritualism. Indeed, he wrote to the escapologist imploring him to use his psychic powers more profitably for the common good instead of just prostituting his talent every night at the Alhambra. However, Houdini repeatedly denounced spiritualism and disclaimed any psychic element to his act.

The alternative explanation for his feats of escapism was that Houdini could do unnatural things with his body. It is widely held that he could dislocate his shoulders to escape from straitjackets, and that he could somehow contract his wrists in order to escape from handcuffs. His ability to spend long periods in confined spaces is cited as evidence that he could put his body into suspended animation, as Indian fakirs are supposed to do.

This is all nonsense. If you ever find yourself in a straitjacket, it's difficult to imagine anything less helpful than a dislocated shoulder. Contracting your wrists is not only unhelpful but, frankly, impossible because the bones of your wrist are very tightly packed together and the whole structure is virtually incompressible.

As for suspended animation, the trick of surviving burial and drowning relies on the fact that you can live for short periods on the air in a confined space. The air shifted by an average person in a day would occupy a cube just eight feet square. The build-up of carbon monoxide tends to pollute this supply, but, if you can relax, the air in a coffin should keep you going for half an hour or so.

The chains, locks and packing cases all seemed perfectly kosher

In other words, there was nothing physically remarkable about Houdini except for his bravery, dexterity and fitness. His nerve was so cool that he could relax in a coffin six feet underground until they came to dig him up. His fingers were so strong that he could undo a buckle or manipulate keys through the canvas of a straitjacket or a mail bag. He made a comprehensive study of locks and was able to conceal lock-picks about his person in a way which fooled even the doctors who examined him. When they locked him in the prison van he still had a hacksaw blade with which to saw through the joins in the metal lining and get access to the planks of the floor.

As an entertainer he combined all this strength and ingenuity with a lot of trickery. His stage escapes took place behind a curtain with an orchestra playing to disguise the banging and sawing. The milk churn in which he was locked had a double lining so that, while the lid was locked onto the rim, the rim was not actually attached to the churn. Houdini merely had to stand up to get out. The mail sack he cut open at the seam and sewed up with similar thread. The bank safe from which he emerged had been secretly worked on by his mechanics for 24 hours before the performance.

All Houdini's feats are eminently explicable, although to explain them, even now, is a kind of heresy. Houdini belongs to that band of mythical supermen who, we like to believe, were capable of miracles and would still be alive today were it not for some piece of low trickery. It's said of Houdini that a punch in his belly when he wasn't prepared for it caused his burst appendix. Anatomically, it's virtually impossible that a punch could puncture your gut, but the story endures. Somehow the myth of the superman has an even greater appeal than the edifice of twentieth century logic.

B Multiple-choice questions. Choose the best answer.

1 Houdini's burial alive is mentioned to show that
  A his tricks sometimes went disastrously wrong.
  B he was not always able to do what he claimed he could.
  C he was capable of extraordinary feats of survival.
  D he had overcome his fear of confined spaces.

2 The writer of the text suggests that Conan Doyle
  A was less rational and analytical than one might have expected.
  B asked Houdini if he could include him in a Sherlock Holmes story.
  C felt that Houdini could make more money in other ways.
  D thought there were scientific explanations for all of Houdini's feats.

3 The writer suggests that Houdini
  A had an unusual bone structure.
  B needed less air than most people.
  C was able to put himself in a trance.
  D was not physically abnormal.

4 Houdini was able to escape from straitjackets by
  A using hidden lock-picks.
  B undoing buckles through the material.
  C cutting the canvas with a hacksaw.
  D turning keys he had concealed.

5 When Houdini escaped from the milk churn
  A the role of the orchestra was important.
  B he made use of the hacksaw to escape.
  C the container had been worked on beforehand.
  D he was in full sight of the audience.

6 According to the text, many people
  A want to hear the scientific explanations for Houdini's feats.
  B prefer to believe that Houdini had mystical powers.
  C think that Houdini is still alive today.
  D do not believe that Houdini ever really existed.

language focus

Could, was able to, managed to. The article discusses at length what Houdini could and couldn't do. In the following sentences, discuss whether it is possible to use the forms of *be able to*, *could* or both of these.

1 Houdini .... escape from chains and padlocks, from ropes and canvas sacks.

2 They once hung him upside down in a straitjacket and he .... break free in minutes.

3 When he was in the coffin, he .... hear the sound of footsteps above him.

4 Until now, no one has .... explain how he did these things.

5 Perhaps in the future someone might .... repeat some of his feats.

In the following sentences, discuss whether it is possible to use forms of *manage to* or *could*.

6 Some people thought that Houdini .... put himself into suspended animation.

7 Once he .... stay underground in a coffin for half an hour, without using up the air.

8 When he was in the coffin, he .... hear muffled voices above him.

9 One day someone might .... repeat some of his more daring feats.

10 So far nobody .... copy all of Houdini's dramatic escapes.

vocabulary

A **Expressions.** The article used the word *tie* in its literal sense: *… he somehow untied himself. They tied him up in a locked packing case.…* In sentences 1–5 below, which of the phrasal verbs with *tie* mean the following?

  a to organize
  b to correlate
  c to be busy
  d to be invested on a long-term basis
  e to restrict

1 I'm afraid I can't make our lunch date today – I'm tied up at the office.

2 It'll take a few weeks for me to get the cash – most of my money is tied up in stocks and shares.

3 The police held the two suspects for further questioning because their stories did not tie in with each other.

4 He's a freelance journalist – he says he'd feel tied down if he worked for just one paper.

5 The expedition is all arranged except for one or two small details that need to be tied up.

B **Fill in the blanks with a suitable phrasal verb with *tie*.**

1 The contract is nearly ready to be signed – there are just one or two loose ends that need ....

2 He's reluctant to get married because of his fear of ....

3 I'm sorry I'm so late – I .... because of those visitors and I couldn't get away.

4 That newsflash from Reuters seemed .... the rumours they had heard that morning about the Prime Minister.

5 She only has a small income as most of her money .... in property.

The Camera Never Lies

cloze development

Read the following extract taken from a book about the *Titanic*, then fill in the blanks.

exam tip

Read the whole passage through first, ignoring the spaces, then go back and consider the missing words.

Of all the accounts of premonitions, one of the most dramatic and most easily verifiable concerns the sinking of the *Titanic* in 1912. In 1898, author Morgan Robertson wrote a novel called *Futility* which bore many striking

5 **(1)** similarities to the loss of the *Titanic* 14 years
(2) later . Robertson's ship, the *Titan*, was the largest ship afloat, and **(3)** had the most modern equipment and the most highly qualified
(4) crew members. The only thing that she
10 **(5)** lacked was a sufficient
(6) numbers of lifeboats to accommodate everyone **(7)** on board. However, this did not seem to **(8)** matter as the *Titan*
(9) was believed to be unsinkable.
15   It was April when the voyage in question took
(10) place , and *Titan* was steaming at
(11) greatfulltop speed. On each of her two masts

the crew had hoisted great triangular
(12) sails to help the ship make a record
20 crossing. So intent on breaking this record
(13) were the crew that when they rammed a windjammer they did not stop to pick up anyone who might have **(14)** survived . A curse was shouted by one of the sailors in the water, calling **(15)** down
25 the wrath of God on the doomed vessel.
     Later, on a foggy **(16)** but moonlit night, *Titan* encountered an iceberg. She did not strike it squarely, but slid up a gradual slope of ice **(17)** until she was almost completely out of the water; the severely
30 **(18)** damaged ship then slid backwards into the water, after also **(19)** having her starboard lifeboats smashed in the process. **(20)** Out of 3,000 people on board, only 13 survived when *Titan* sank. ∎

discussion

A Look at the photograph of the *Titanic*. At the top of the first funnel is the figure of a man. Answer the questions below.

1 Why would it not be possible for a human to survive in the funnel when the ship was moving?

2 If you had seen the man, would you have interpreted it as a bad omen?

3 What explanation can you suggest for the photograph?

April 1912

B Infinitives. Read these comments about the photograph of the *Titanic* and fill in the blanks in the transformations with the correct infinitive form.

1 Perhaps it *is* a genuine photograph.

   It might ...... be ...... a genuine photograph.

2 Perhaps the man in the photo *is standing* in front of the funnel.

The man in the photograph might ..... *be standing* in front of the funnel.

3 Maybe someone *tampered* with the photo.

Someone might ... *have* .... with the photo.

4 Perhaps the man in the picture *was repairing* something in the funnel.

The man in the picture might ... *have been* ..... something in the funnel.

5 Perhaps the mystery *will be solved* in the future.

The mystery might ... *be solved* ...... in the future.

6 Maybe one photograph *was superimposed* on to another one.

One photograph might ... *have been* .... on to another one.

must, mustn't and variations

A Join up the two parts of the following sentences before answering the questions below.

c	**1**	He must be in the garden …	**a**	because I can't open it.
f	**2**	The application form must be returned …	**b**	but his car broke down.
d	**3**	The back door must be locked so …	**c**	because I can hear the lawn mower.
a	**4**	The back door must be locked …	**d**	that burglars don't get in.
h	**5**	He should have been wearing a tie …	**e**	because it never arrived.
g	**6**	I had to study Latin …	**f**	by the end of next week at the latest.
b	**7**	He was supposed to pick Jane up from the airport …	**g**	when I was eleven.
e	**8**	You must have sent the letter to the wrong address …	**h**	but he wasn't, so they didn't let him into the restaurant.

1 Which sentences express a definite positive deduction? *1, 4, 8*
2 Which sentences express a present or future obligation? *2, 3*
3 Which sentences express a past obligation that was not fulfilled? *5, 7*
4 Which sentence expresses a past obligation that was fulfilled? *6*
5 Which forms of the infinitive can follow *must* to express obligation? *plain inf -active*
6 Which forms of the infinitive can be used with *must* to express deduction? *all 6 forms* *→ passive*

B Transformations. Rewrite the following sentences.

1 It is essential that you get to the airport on time.

You .. *must* ....

2 I am convinced that there is some mistake with this bill – it's astronomical.

There ...... *must be* ....

3 You should have got here over an hour ago – what kept you?

You ..... *were supposed to* ....

4 If you hadn't been speeding, the police wouldn't have stopped you.

You must ... *have been* ....

5 They made us go to church every Sunday when we were at school.

We had .. *to go* ....

6 It's a pity you didn't come to the party, because you'd have loved it.

You should ... *have come* ....

7 It is essential that no one is told about our plans.

You ... *mustn't tell* ....

8 It was wrong of you not to call the doctor at once.

You should ... *have* ....

*necessity and
lack of necessity*

A *Need* **and** *should.* The forms *needed to*, *didn't need to*, *needn't have* and *should (n't) have* are each used in specific limited circumstances, the correct choice depending on the necessity of the actions and whether or not the action took place. Read through the sample sentences.

1 They said we needed to have a vaccination { so we did.
{ but we never got round to it.

2 They said we didn't need to have any vaccinations { but we did anyway, just to be on the safe side.
{ so we didn't.

3 They said we needn't have had any vaccinations   but by then it was too late because we'd already had them.

4 They said we should have had vaccinations   and that was why they were refusing us entry.

5 They said we shouldn't have had vaccinations   because they were now thought to be unsafe.

B **Say which of the following forms show the features below.**

needed to   should have   shouldn't have   didn't need to   needn't have

1 action was not necessary, but has already been taken anyway
2 action was necessary or obligatory, and it was wrong not to have taken it
3 action was not necessary, or was prohibited, and it was wrong to have taken it
4 action was not necessary, and may or may not have been taken subsequently
5 action was necessary and may or may not have been taken subsequently

C **Fill in the blanks below.** Use either *needed to*, *didn't need to*, *should have*, *needn't have* or *shouldn't have* and a suitable verb. The first one has been done as an example.

1 I *didn't need to take* the parcel to the Post Office because Sonia very kindly took it for me.

2 We discovered when we arrived on the island that we .... in advance because there were lots of villas for rent.

3 We only realized when we got to the island that we .... in advance as there was nowhere to stay.

4 Although we .... comprehensive insurance, we got it anyway just to be on the safe side.

5 I think you deserve to be punished – you .... the car without asking your father first.

6 He told the taxi driver he .... to the airport as quickly as possible, as the plane was due to leave soon.

7 I .... so much time worrying about the test, because in the end it was really easy and I passed first time.

8 The policeman was furious with me and said that I .... so fast in a residential area.

*can, could,
may and might*

A **Look at sentences 1–10 on page 49.** In which of the sentences do the modal verbs express the following?

  a ability
  b permission
  c deduction / supposition
  d future possibility
  e irritation
  f an unfulfilled possibility

1 It's very late in the day to cancel – I do think you might have let me know a little earlier.
2 He could have been a great politician, but he chose instead to become a priest.
3 Judging from the architecture, this photo might have been taken in Spain.
4 I was wondering whether I could come and see you next week.
5 You can't have phoned on Tuesday, because I was in all day.
6 It was such a bad line, I couldn't hear what she was saying.
7 You could have phoned to tell us you were all right. Why on earth didn't you ring?
8 There could be severe unrest if the economy doesn't improve before the winter.
9 Excuse me, sir. Might I ask whether you intend to stay at the hotel for another night?
10 If I pass all my exams, I may take a year off and travel round the world.

B Sentences 1–5 below can be completed in two ways. Match each sentence with two possible endings, then discuss how the meaning of the modal verb changes in each pair.

EXAMPLE **1 d, h**

1d *They could have sold their house if they had been more flexible about the price.*
The first part of this sentence could be rephrased as: 'They would have been able to sell their house …'. *Could* expresses ability.

1h *They could have sold their house so they might not be able to put you up.*
The first part of this sentence could be rephrased as: 'Maybe they have sold their house …'. *Could* expresses speculation.

1 They could have sold their house …

2 You may see Peter tonight …

3 My car can't be stolen …

4 You might have written to us …

5 He could have caught an early train …

a because it's impossible to open the door without the right key.
b because we went to a lot of trouble preparing for your visit.
c as long as you do all your homework first.
d if they had been more flexible about the price.
e but our filing system is in a mess, so I have no record of it.
f so he might be here in half an hour or so.
g because I bought it from a reputable dealer.
h so they might not be able to put you up.
i because he said he'd try and come to the party.
j but he decided to spend the night in London instead.

C Discussion. Look at the photographs below. How do you think they can be explained?

Good and Evil

Hieronymus Bosch 1450–1516

talking points

A Look at the picture. How has the artist tried to symbolize concepts of good and evil?

B What kind of things do you consider to be good/evil?
In small groups make two lists of items under *good* and *evil*, then compare your lists with those of another group.

summary 1

Read the passage on page 51 about our perceptions of the devil and summarize each paragraph briefly in note form.

comprehension

A Find words and phrases in the passage which mean the same as the following explanations. They are all in the order in which they appeared in the passage.

1 very religious, pious *devout*
2 intense fear *horror*
3 twist and move violently *jerks*
4 ascribed to *attributed to*
5 inflicted by oneself *self-injurious*
6 out of the ordinary *paranormal*
7 descriptions relating to one (national) group of people *racial & ethnic*
8 a scholarly piece of writing *monograph*
9 notorious *infamous*
10 flagrant misinterpretations *gross misdiagnosis*
11 to give another example of an extreme case *at other end*
12 imminent fear and loathing *impending terror & revulsion* *spectrum*

B Now explain these words and phrases according to how they are used in the passage.
The questions will help you to give a more precise explanation.

1 is actually present (line 16). Does *actually* mean *momentarily*, *nowadays* or *really*?
2 some malign and external force (line 26). Does *malign* mean *hostile*, *rejected* or *unknown*?
3 divine inspiration (line 36). Does *divine* mean *intuitive*, *sacred* or *imagined*?
4 the witch hunters of the Inquisition (line 67). Why does *Inquisition* have a capital letter?
5 unresponsive to external stimuli (line 96). Why does *stimuli* end in *i*?
6 preceded by an aura (line 102). Does *aura* mean *halo*, *something golden* or *atmosphere*?

C Reference devices. The writer links the information in this article in various ways.
For example, in the first paragraph he uses *Another individual ...*, *A third individual*.
Go through the passage again and underline the devices used to link the information given to the reader. You should look for devices such as pronouns to replace nouns, the use of *do/did* to replace verbs, another noun used to replace one already mentioned, eg *scale*, *spectrum*; *case*, *disease*.

Handwritten margin notes:
① Descriptions of 3 cases abnormal behaviour
② Tempt to attribute these to good or evil forces
③
④ More logical explanation of 2nd – epilepsy

5 min

The PARANORMAL

15 – 18 c

more logical explos

Suddenly, a normally well-mannered, quiet and devout individual begins to jerk and twitch and, to his own and everyone else's horror, starts to curse and swear uncontrollably, using foul language he would ordinarily never even consider using in public. Another individual, following a sensation of profound dread and terror, appears to be thrown violently to the ground where he begins to writhe and thrash about, sometimes severely enough to break bones or even to cause death. A third individual is overcome by a shimmering, brilliant vision of a bright light, when no light is actually present. The vision may contain various shapes and structures.

In all these cases, the individual is not in control of the behaviors he or she is exhibiting and believes, correctly, that he or she has absolutely no ability to control them. This being the case, it is easy to understand how control of the behaviors would be attributed to some malign and external force, such as the devil or demons. This would be especially likely to be the explanation of the behaviors in the first two cases, where the foul language, self-injurious behaviors, and lack of control all would be easy to interpret as the work of demons. In the final case, the experience could equally well be attributed to some type of divine inspiration or message.

In fact, the three cases described above are examples, not of demonic possession or inspired visions, but of three different neurological diseases that have for centuries been taken as evidence for paranormal experiences.

Beyerstein (1987–88) has traced the relationship between these three diseases and belief in demonic possession and inspired visions in an excellent paper. The first case is one of Gilles de la Tourette's syndrome, a rare disease that has become the focus of considerable interest in neurology recently because of its strange symptoms, including uncontrollable twitches and, in severe cases, uncontrolled swearing and use of racial and ethnic epithets. An entire monograph (Friedhoff and Chase, 1982) has been devoted to the symptoms, possible neurochemical causes, and treatments of this disease.

It is clear from the work reported in that volume that Tourette's syndrome is a neurological disease, not a psychological disorder. Shapiro and Shapiro (1982) have noted that the infamous *Malleus Maleficarum*, published in 1489 as a "manual" for the witch hunters of the Inquisition, contains descriptions of behaviors said to be demonstrative of having consorted with the devil; these are similar to those seen in Tourette's syndrome.

The behavior of the little girl in *The Exorcist* (Blatty, 1971) is very similar to what is seen in severe cases of Tourette's syndrome. Such gross misdiagnoses of the syndrome are not, then, limited to the Middle Ages, but can still occur. Shapiro and Shapiro (1982) note that twenty-four of their Tourette's syndrome patients had undergone exorcism for their disorder, but none had been helped by the process. Drug treatment may provide some benefit, but the pharmacology of the disorder is not yet well understood (Friedhoff and Chase, 1982).

The second case described above is one of epilepsy, a neurological disorder much more common and well-known than Tourette's syndrome. The symptoms of epilepsy vary greatly from individual to individual. At one end of the scale are the "absence spells" where the individual is simply unresponsive to external stimuli for a minute or so and appears to be staring off into space. At the other end of the spectrum is the much more dramatic and dangerous grand mal seizure, as in the case described.

Seizures are often preceded by an aura that is sometimes a feeling of impending terror and revulsion. When, immediately following this, some mysterious outside force seemingly takes over one's body and causes it to behave in self-injurious ways, the inference that demons or the devil are responsible is an easy one to make.

Pseudoscience and the Paranormal by Terence Hines

summary 2

A **Look at the following questions and the 60-word summary which relate to the first case mentioned in the passage.**

1 What type of behaviour is exhibited?
2 What interpretation could we give of this behaviour?
3 What scientific explanation can we give for this behaviour?

The first case illustrates a usually docile, well-behaved person, who unexpectedly exhibits jerky body movements and uses bad language in a reckless manner. This lack of control could be put down to some evil influence. A more likely explanation, however, is that the person is suffering from the rare Tourette's syndrome, which is a disease of the brain.

B **Now answer the same questions about the other two cases and write a summary of your own.** Each summary should be 60 to 70 words long.

talking points

A Describe what you can see in the picture.

B Describe briefly some of the main mythical or legendary creatures from your own ancient culture or from another culture with which you are familiar.

1 In what ways are these creatures similar to humans and how do they differ?
2 In what ways do ancient myths and legends seek to explain concepts such as fortune, the afterlife, or psychological conditions such as love?
3 What place do you think ancient myths, folk-tales and fairy stories should have in the education of a modern child?

listening 1

A Listen to the tape. A writer and researcher are discussing a book the writer has recently completed on fairies. Choose the best answer to the questions below.

1 Peter Wilson wrote a book about fairies because he
  A wanted to clarify the mass of information about them.
  B had seen fairies on a number of occasions.
  C greatly enjoyed traditional fairy stories.
  D wanted to persuade people of the existence of fairies.

2 The writer says that many people
  A are unaware that fairies depend on humans.
  B are afraid of the power that the fairies have.
  C overestimate the similarities between humans and fairies.
  D are jealous of the lives that fairies lead.

3 During the talk, the interviewer is accused of being
  A sceptical.
  B sentimental.
  C illogical.
  D simplistic.

4 According to the writer, Knockers
  A are unusual Goblins.
  B are a considerable nuisance to miners.
  C can be relied on to be helpful.
  D are very fond of fruit.

5 Peter Wilson says that a changeling is
  A a human baby that has been stolen.
  B a fairy with a short life expectancy.
  C an unusually sick child.
  D a replacement for a baby.

6 The writer says that looking for fairies
  A is always a dangerous pastime.
  B will not greatly increase one's chances of seeing them.
  C is most profitably done in woods and gardens.
  D can be a very frustrating experience.

B **Listening and note-taking.** Listen to the tape again and complete the following notes using these words and phrases.

alien   capricious   churlish   favourably disposed   inimical
magical   malicious   mischievous   spiteful   troublesome

harmful
hostile

The fairy kingdom represents (**1**) .. magical .... power, and it is

(**2**) .. inimical .... to humans because it is incomprehensible to us. Although the

fairy kingdom is largely dependent on humans, fairies are very different from us; they are

(**3**) ... alien .... creatures whose ethics and values have very little in common

with ours. In general, Goblins look extremely ugly and are intensely

(**4**) ... malicious .... creatures. However, the Goblins in Devon and Cornwall, known

as Knockers, are generally more (**5**) . favourably disposed . to miners, yet even they are

capable of being extremely (**6**) ... capricious ....

Most fairies are capable of being (**7**) . mischievous .... and (**8**) .. spiteful ....

Brownies are generally thought of as being helpful, but if they are teased or angered, they

can turn into Boggarts, who are (**9**) .. churlish ...... and (**10**) .. troublesome ....

bad manners
not well bred

listening 2

A **Visions of the future.** Say if the following statements are true or false according to the passage.

1   Nostradamus worked as a doctor after leaving university.   T/F
2   Nostradamus' first wife was killed by the Black Death.   T/F
3   Nostradamus began writing his prophecies before his second marriage.   T/F
4   The prophecies predicted what would happen over the next ten centuries.   T/F
5   Nostradamus' divining technique was based on ancient methods.   T/F
6   Few people were convinced by Nostradamus during his lifetime.   T/F
7   Nostradamus is believed by some people to have predicted the rise of Hitler.   T/F
8   One of the quatrains pinpoints Napoleon's birthplace.   T/F
9   One quatrain is believed to warn of a nuclear war around the year 2000.   T/F
10 Much of Nostradamus' work is open to considerable interpretation.   T/F

B **Discussion.**

1   On the evidence of the listening passage, do you believe that Nostradamus made accurate predictions?
2   How seriously do you think you might take some of his other predictions?
3   Look at two other extracts from Nostradamus' works. They are said to predict modern technological developments. Can you guess what they are said to refer to?

    They will think they have seen the sun at night
    When they will see the pig half-man

    Noise, song, battle in the sky perceived
    And one will hear brute beasts talking

4   Have you ever had an experience of a premonition or a dream that has come true?
5   Have you ever had your fortune told? If so, how, and what predictions were made? If not, would you like to?

speaking

Possibility and probability. Look at the table showing different ways of expressing probability and the example sentences below. Notice the different sentence structures.

Pattern A   It's **probable** that Manchester United will win the cup.
Pattern B   Manchester United are **likely** to win the cup.
Pattern C   **In all probability** Manchester United will win the cup.
Pattern D   **I imagine that** Manchester United will win the cup.
Pattern E   Manchester United **will probably** win the cup.

Pattern A	Pattern B	Pattern C	Pattern D	Pattern E
a foregone conclusion	bound	There's no doubt that	I'm quite convinced that	will certainly
inevitable	certain	The chances are that	I'm certain that	will definitely
probable	likely	There's little chance that	I imagine that	will probably
quite possible	sure	There's little likelihood that	I wouldn't have thought that	probably won't
possible	unlikely	There's no chance that	I shouldn't think that	certainly won't
just possible		In all probability	I doubt very much whether	definitely won't
unlikely		Maybe		
doubtful		Perhaps		
inconceivable				

Work in pairs or small groups. Select a sentence from the following list and get another student to re-phrase it, using a pattern of your choice.

1   It's a foregone conclusion that you're going to pass your exam.
2   The economic situation is unlikely to improve.
3   The chances are that we'll have to do another composition this week.
4   I wouldn't have thought that she'd invite you to the party.

Writing

Telling a Story

introduction

One of the standard types of composition is a narrative. The question often asks you to write a story that begins or ends with a particular sentence. Below is an example of how you can tackle the narrative composition following a number of clearly defined steps. The question on which the example is based is:

Write a fairy story that ends '… it was only then that it dawned on him how lucky he was to be alive.'

*planning
and writing*

Stage 1   General approach. Work out a basic plot that answers the question. A basic plot might look as follows:

The central character, walking through the mountains at night, finds a cave. In the cave is a malicious fairy, a Duergar. During the night they sit by the fire. The fairy asks him to get some wood from the other side of the cave, but the man is suspicious and stays where he is. In the morning he wakes to find that the cave has vanished and that he is on the very edge of a high cliff, and would have died if he had gone to fetch the logs for the fire. Then comes the final sentence.

exam tip

A Duergar is the correct technical name for this kind of fairy; in your own compositions you should not invent nouns, though you are free to invent surnames.

Stage 2   Brainstorming.

1   Work out more details and think of a few choice expressions. To help with this step, ask yourself lots of questions about the basic plot that you have thought of. For example:

Where did this all take place and when? Who was this traveller? Where was he going and why? What time of day was it when the story began? What was the weather like? Who are the Duergars? How did he find the cave? What did he see when he went into the cave? How big was the cave? What did the Duergar look like? How did he feel when he saw the Duergar?

2   Think of another five questions that you might ask about the story. Compare your questions with those of someone else in the class.

3   Words and images. As you are asking and answering these questions, note down important points of the story in any order. In addition, as words and images come to you, jot down the most powerful and most descriptive ones so that they can be incorporated later in the finished story. The kind of words and images that might come to mind are:

evil   towering pine trees   a rocky stream   menacing face   a vast, empty cavern gnarled hand   flickering shadows   black thunderclouds heavy with rain slanting green eyes.

Stage 3   Organization. Arrange the ideas into a clear paragraph structure. For example:

1   Introduction – time, place – information about Duergars.
2   The night and weather – need for shelter – discovery of the cave – goes towards it.
3   Description of the cave – size – the fire.
4   The sight of the Duergar – description of the creature.
5   The Duergar's trick – across the cave – the traveller does not fall for trick.
6   The morning – wakes at cliff top – explanation of the Duergar's trick.

Look carefully at the words and images in **stage 2** above. Which paragraphs would they most probably appear in?

Stage 4   Writing. Here is an example of what the finished composition might look like.

1   *Many years ago, a young man was travelling one night through a forest inhabited by Duergars, an evil race of fairies, who liked nothing better than to lure unsuspecting humans to their death.*

2   *As he was making his way down the narrow path, he looked up at the towering pine trees. Black thunderclouds heavy with rain were racing across the sky, and he knew that he would soon have to find shelter. Presently he saw the glow of a fire on the hillside and left the path to clamber up the steep slope that led to the entrance of the cave.*

3   *He stood at the entrance and looked in. It was a vast, empty cavern whose sides rose up to a vaulted ceiling. On the ground in the centre a space had been cleared and a warm fire was throwing flickering shadows across the floor. He went cautiously towards the fire and sat down.*

4   *As his eyes slowly grew used to the dim light, the menacing face of a Duergar began to emerge. The creature was sitting motionless on the opposite side of the fire; it stared at him through its slanting green eyes but said nothing.*

5   *An hour passed, then two. The fire was dying down, so the Duergar picked up a log from the other side of the cave and threw it onto the flames. When the fire began to die down again, the Duergar waved its gnarled hand frantically at the traveller to indicate that it was his turn to collect more wood. Suspecting some devious trick, he stayed where he was, ignoring the glowering looks of the furious Duergar.*

6   *The next morning, woken by the sound of mountain songbirds, the traveller was suddenly filled with terror and shock. Both the cave and the Duergar had vanished, and he found himself perched at the very edge of a massive cliff – he could just make out a rocky stream in the valley thousands of feet below. He realized that if he had walked across the cave to get more wood for the fire, as the Duergar had wanted, he would have plunged to his death. It was only then that it dawned on him how lucky he was to be alive.*

Stage 5 Checking. This final stage is extremely important. Read through this paragraph and see if you can find ten mistakes. When you are ready, compare your corrected version with the correct version in paragraphs **3** and **4**.

He stood at the entry and looked in. It was a vast, empty cavern who's sides were rising up to a vaulted ceiling. On the ground in the centre a space was cleared and a warm fire was throwing flickering shadows across the floor. Cautiously did he go towards the fire, and sat down.

As his eyes slowly were used to the dim light, the face menacing of a Duergar began to emerge. The creature was sat motionless on the opposite side from the fire; it stared at him by its slanting green eyes but said nothing.

focus on
narrative tenses

At certain points in a story, it is often necessary to describe scenes in some detail. Look carefully at the tenses used in the following examples.

1 Which tense is used to carry the plot forward and to describe actions that happen in sequence? One example is *he **looked up** at the towering pine trees* …. Find five examples of this in paragraphs **2** and **3**.
2 Which tense is used to describe permanent features? One example is *the steep slope that **led** to … the cave.* Find another example from paragraph **3**.
3 Which tense is used mainly for describing scenes? One example is *A young man **was travelling** one night.* Find three more examples from paragraphs **2** and **3**.
4 Which tense refers to actions that took place before the events in the narrative? One example is *Both the cave and the Duergar **had vanished.*** Find another example in paragraph **3**.

writing task

Look at the following sample question.

Write a fairy story that ends with the words '… and at these words, he crumbled to dust on the doorstep.'

You may choose your own story or use the composition notes to help you if you wish.

Stage 1 General approach. Basic plot outline: a young man goes out one summer's day, and sits down beneath a tree on a hill; he hears a beautiful fairy melody and drifts off to sleep. In his dreams, he visits a beautiful castle where strange and wonderful creatures are having a celebration. He watches for a while. He then wakes up to find that the tree is old and withered. He walks home, but the house seems much older and covered in ivy. When he speaks to the people in the house, he realizes that he has been away for a hundred years, and crumbles to dust.

Stage 2 Brainstorming. Ask yourself a series of questions about the story and work out some of the details. Think of some phrases that can be used when you come to write the final version.

Stage 3 Organization. Plan paragraphs carefully, and assign the images and phrases to the paragraphs.

Stage 4 Writing. While writing, pay particular attention to the tenses; towards the end, when you describe the changes to the house, you may need to use the past perfect fairly extensively.

Stage 5 Checking. Check your composition carefully.

Overview 4

vocabulary

Choose the word which best completes each sentence.

1 My sister showed great .... in selling her house when she did because soon afterwards the market fell dramatically.
   A premonition   B forecasting   C prediction   **D** foresight

2 The jury began to believe the accused man might be guilty because his story did not tie .... with those of the witnesses.
   A in   B on   C up   D down to

3 It turned out that we .... rushed to the airport as the plane was delayed by several hours.
   A hadn't   B should have   **C** needn't have   D mustn't

4 Judging by the latest results, the team look .... to return without a single medal.
   A doomed   B forecast   C convicted   D sentenced

5 My brother's son is a very .... child, but he has a very sweet nature so it is difficult to be angry with him.
   A malevolent   B malicious   **C** mischievous   D malignant

6 In the Middle Ages, women who were found guilty of .... were sometimes burned at the stake.
   A wizardry   B magic   C conjuring   **D** witchcraft

7 When his accomplices failed to turn up at the meeting point, it .... on him that he had been tricked.
   A dawned   B broke   C awoke   D became clear

8 He claimed that he was not a particularly remarkable businessman, but that he had simply had the good .... to be in the right place at the right time.
   A fortune   B fate   C destiny   D opportunity

9 In the last century, it was widely .... that Indian fakirs were capable of superhuman feats.
   A held   B grasped   C kept   D shaken

10 Do you know what the main characteristics of your .... sign are?
   A zodiac   B astrology   C horoscope   **D** star

blank-filling

Fill each of the blanks in the following sentences with a suitable word or phrase.

1 I imagine it ....*must have*.......... come as a terrible shock when you found out that you were adopted.

2 With the new spell-check program on my computer, it's virtually ....*impossible*.......... .... make a spelling mistake.

3 I've been ringing her all morning but so far I ....*haven't managed / been able*.......... through.

4 The robbers ....*managed to / able to*.......... get into the bank by climbing through a skylight in the roof.

5 You're terribly late – you were ....*supposed to*.......... be here over an hour ago.

6 As it turned out, we ....*didn't need/ needn't have*.... called the fire brigade because the fire went out by itself before they arrived.

7 Although they ....*didn't have to* / *need to*.......... get rear seat belts fitted, they did anyway because they felt it would be safer.

8 I really do think that you might ....*have let me know*.......... know a little earlier that you weren't coming for the weekend.

9 Mary isn't here – but she ....*can't have*.......... taken the car because there's no petrol in it.

10 The ....*chances are*.......... that you'll get through the exam – after all, practically everybody does.

rewriting

*For each of the sentences below, rewrite **two** new sentences as similar as possible in meaning to the original sentence, but using the words given in capital letters. These words must not be altered in any way.*

1 He stood no chance of passing his exams.

BOUND...

INEVITABLE ...... *that he would fail* ....

2 I'm sure that he missed the eleven o'clock train.

MUST ....

CAN'T. *possibly have caught* ....

3 I'm annoyed with you for not phoning me to say you'd be late.

MIGHT ...... *You* ....

EARTH ...... *Why on earth* ....

4 I hardly think she will agree to giving you a pay rise.

DOUBT .... *whether she will agree* ....

LIKELIHOOD ...... *little* ....

5 It seems to be a foregone conclusion that Davis will win the gold medal.

CERTAIN ...... *is/seems certain* ....

DOUBT .... *little* *no doubt* ....

6 The house has got everything except a large garden.

LACKS .... *only thing it* ....

FROM ...... *got et apart from* ....

7 I'm afraid to say that we haven't got any oil left.

UP .... *we've used up* ....

RUN...

8 The film is similar to Shakespeare's *Hamlet* in a number of ways.

BEARS ...... *bears some resemblance* ....

COMMON ....

9 In all probability we will finish the project on Thursday.

CHANCES..

SHOULDN'T...... *Project shouldn't take* ....

10 The Embassy said it would not be necessary for me to get a visa.

NEED....... *no need* ....

REQUIRED ...... *a visa is not required* ....

IT BROADENS THE MIND

Mindless in Gaza

Reading   **Traveller or Tourist?**

Genoa
Better Way?

LONDON
PARIS
MADRID   TURIN
ROME

AND TRAVEL
Express

talking points   **Travel companies often use eye-catching adverts to attract potential customers' attention.** Look at the following captions. They are all playing with language.

Vnice

EXAMPLE TURIN Europe
TURIN means 'Touring (Europe)'.

Can you work out what these captions mean?

PISA cake

CANNES do

T a k e
votre Dame

ROME around Europe

PARIS Happy, so is Ma

reading   **A**   **What do you consider to be the difference between a traveller and a tourist?** Read the following newspaper article about travellers and tourists and decide on a suitable title for it, then compare your answer with its original title on page 215.

Here is a speck of comfort for anyone not planning to canoe up the Amazon or trek across Siberia – contrary to what anyone will tell you, travel does not broaden the mind.

It was the Victorians who were really obsessed with travel. They lived at a time when travel really did harden the body and improve the spirit. It took a
5 rare breed of man to trudge through some malaria-infested swamp in a pith helmet after the native bearers had drunk all the whisky, stolen the rations and run off with the compass.
10 Since then, travellers have thought of themselves as faintly noble and they look down on mere tourists who stay in comfortable hotels and ride in air-conditioned buses. To travellers it is a
15 mark of pride to suffer as much as possible. They get a perverse joy from spending all day squatting over a sordid cesspit.
Paul Theroux, a best-selling travel
20 writer, is one of the people caught up in the myth: "The nearest thing to writing a novel is travelling in a strange country." Travel, he declares, is a creative act. It isn't. It may be fun.
25 It may be interesting, but travellers get

no insight into eternal truths.
Travellers learn a lot about shopping (good in Singapore, bad in China). They learn how to avoid the
30 young boys that follow you everywhere begging (look at them with a condescending smile). They discover how to find a *pensión* in Spain or what sort of Mexican food to sample. In
35 doing so they find out very little about Orientals, Spaniards or Mexicans. A knowledge of Indian railway timetables and hotel prices is not the same as understanding Indian culture.
40 Travellers acquire useless skills, such as how to make trivial conversation with new acquaintances – discussing cameras or makes of car is a sure-fire way of provoking long and
45 boring discussions.
Many people use travel as an idiotic form of escapism. Oxford graduates, who would not be remotely interested in getting to know British working-
50 class people on council estates, find it

uplifting to go sightseeing among the poor of the Third World.
The worst travellers are the long-term ones – often people with personal
55 problems who are keen, not so much to see the world, as to avoid returning home. As a rule, the only people who travel for more than a year are simpletons, social inadequates, or New
60 Zealanders.
Travel can sometimes close the mind altogether. I once hitched a lift with a van-load of Aborigines. They had already picked up one hitch-hiker who
65 had been travelling round the world for four years. He had no fixed home and no fixed job and didn't care what his next destination was.
In desperation for something to talk
70 about, I told my fellow traveller that I was going to a famous beauty spot in Queensland. Did he know it? "Oh yeah," he said, "I think there's a good Salvation Army hostel somewhere near
75 there." **G**

Jack Shamash, Weekend Guardian

B **Which adjective best sums up the mood of the passage?**

a hilarious   **b** disparaging   c superficial   d argumentative

C **Multiple-choice questions.** These often focus on the moods or attitudes expressed in the passage. Choose the best answer to the questions below and be prepared to justify your choice by quoting the relevant sections from the article.

1 Those of us who are less adventurous in our attitude towards travelling should feel
  A guilty.
  B reassured.
  C self-satisfied.
  D resentful.

2 To the Victorians travel was something
  A addictive.
  B commonplace.
  C to be avoided.
  D compulsory.

3 Modern travellers have a tendency to regard themselves as
  A scapegoats.
  B casualties.
  C tormentors.
  D martyrs.

4 The knowledge travellers have of the world is
  A imperative.
  B inaccurate.
  C insufficient.
  D invaluable.

5 The writer dismisses the motives of many travellers as being
  A paradoxical.
  B unadventurous.
  C inexplicable.
  D uninteresting.

6 The hitch-hiker's main interest was
  A the beauty spots of the world.
  B somewhere to sleep.
  C the length of time he had been travelling.
  D the desire to put down roots somewhere.

vocabulary

A **Unfavourable adjectives.** These words appeared in the article. They are all used in a negative sense. Can you use them to complete the sentences below?

a idiotic   e sordid
b obsessed   f condescending
c infested   g trivial
d perverse

1 The government spokesman addressed the press in a very superior, *condesc.* tone.

2 Robbing the rich to help the poor always seemed *perverse* logic to me.

3 Politicians are invariably *obsessed* with their own self-importance.

4 The orphaned children were squatting on the floor of one of the most *sordid* -looking buildings I have ever seen.

5 Pulling the alarm for a joke was a particularly *perv.* thing to do.

6 I once shared a flat which had a cockroach- *infested* kitchen.

7 Please don't bother me with *trivial* matters when I am about to make one of the most important decisions of my life!

B **Negative prefixes.** The prefixes *mis-*, *dis-*, *ig-*, and *un-* can all be used to give a word a rather negative meaning. The prefix may help you to guess the meaning of the word.

mis- = 'wrongly, badly' or 'not done' (*mismanage*)
dis- = 'away from, the opposite of, lack of' (*distaste*)
ig- = 'not, lacking in' (*ignorant*)
un- = 'not, lack of, the opposite, reversal or removal of' (*undo*)

Here is some advice to help you choose the correct prefix.

- *dis-* can be used to form verbs, eg *dissatisfy*; adjectives, eg *dishonest*; and nouns, eg *disability*.
- The prefix *ig-* appears only before the letter *n*.

Make opposites for these words (all of which are from the passage) using one of the prefixes on page 60. You can check your answers in a dictionary.

comfort   comfortable   noble   interesting   understanding   provoking

C   Suffixes. The title of the article was *Mindless in Gaza*. The suffix *-less* can denote 'not being', 'a lack of' or 'being without'. The opposite concept can be implied by using the suffix *-ful*. Which of the following words have a *-less* and / or *-ful* form? Some have both, some have only one.

use   care   worth   point   hope   youth   motion   stress   resent   meaning

D   Expressions. In the article we had the verbs *run off with*, *look down on* and *caught up in*. Can you explain their meaning?
Look at the phrases below. In pairs, match *run*, *look* and *catch / be caught* with phrases **a–j**.

a   *a business*
b   *red-handed*
c   *on the bright side*
d   *out of*
e   *short of*

run
look
catch / be caught

f   *down your nose at*
g   *for it*
h   *like a drowned rat*
i   *someone's eye*
j   *a gift horse in the mouth*

Now match one of these expressions to the explanations below.

1   attract someone's attention
2   flee from
3   be cheerful / optimistic
4   be ungrateful for what you are given
5   have no more left

6   apprehend in the act of doing or trying to do something
7   feel superior to
8   have an insufficient supply of
9   manage a company
10 be completely soaked

Structure	# The Intrepid Explorer

talking points

Look at these pictures of more unusual forms of moving around. In small groups, identify them and discuss where and for what purpose they are suitable.

exam tip

In the interview you may be handed a picture and asked to describe an object whose exact name you do not know. Do not worry – describe what the object is for or what it does.

cloze development

Read the following article about an explorer who needed a dog sleigh and huskies to reach his final destination, the Greenland ice cap. Twenty words are missing but there are no gaps to indicate where – only numbers in the right-hand margin. Mark a / to show where the missing words should come before trying, in small groups, to decide what the words might be. The first has been done for you and the missing word is *was*.

1 *was*   2 the
3 covered   4 out
5 last
6 got
7 followed
8 over
9 saw   10 after
11 had
12 member
13 estab
14 see/estab
15 more   16 an
17 of   18 `
19 air/opp
20 use

On 5 May 1931, my uncle, August Courtauld / spending his 150th day alone on the ice cap. Since last week of March his tented igloo had been by snow; his food was now running, there was no light and he was smoking tea-leaves in his pipe. On that day his paraffin primus stove gave its gasp; August had just decided that he would have to walk back on 1 June if he could out, when suddenly there was an appalling noise like a bus going by, by a confused yelling. The voice of his expedition leader came down the ventilator pipe, and his five-month incarceration through an Arctic winter was.

But August never it as an ordeal, never said he wished he hadn't gone. He had, all, volunteered to stay alone at the ice cap station, and take recordings of the weather there, which never been done before.

Uncle August was a of an expedition which had gone to Greenland in the summer of 1930, to map the coast and mountain ranges. It was also important in considering the of a regular air route over Greenland to North America, to what the weather was like on the ice cap, particularly in winter.

There was, however, to the expedition than that. Its members had average age of 25, many of them had not long ago been at university and there was a clubbable spirit youthful adventure among them. But the of gentlemanly amateurishness could be deceptive: most significantly, and contrast to Scott's expedition to the South Pole, they learnt how to dogs for sledging. ■

vocabulary

A Shades of meaning. The following words were all in the original passage. Decide whether you think their meanings are negative, neutral or positive. Some words may have more than one meaning. Use a dictionary if necessary and be prepared to explain why you think they should be graded as such.

EXAMPLE *incarceration (negative)*

running out	clubbable	volunteered	deceptive	ordeal
youthful	appearance	significantly	incarceration	alone
appalling	confused	adventure	contrast	feasibility

B Describing attitude. Look at the following list of adjectives. Which would you choose to describe Uncle August and his attitude as portrayed by his nephew? Justify your answers with reference to the passage.

brief consise

dejected   resigned   disillusioned   afraid   laconic   amateurish insensitive   courageous   practical

rewriting

Rewrite the following sentences in *three* different ways, using the words given.

EXAMPLE Uncle August did not suffer from his experience.

WORSE *He was none the worse for his experience.*
HARM *His experience did him no harm.*
UNSCATHED *He came through his experience unscathed.*

1 Initially they had far more supplies than they needed.

SPARE / OVER / SURPLUS
CLUE All three words above mean 'in excess of requirements'.

2 After such an experience nowadays, Uncle August would have been subjected to counselling.

UNDERGO / SUBMIT / THROUGH
CLUE *Submit* takes *to*, and *through* is part of a phrasal verb. (**NB** *submit* has a rather negative meaning as the person involved might not have wanted to do this!)

3 He was eager to see his fiancée again.

FORWARD / EXCITED / WAIT
CLUE Watch the constructions that follow *forward* and *excited. Wait* is part of an idiom meaning 'too excited to wait'. You will need to use *not* with *wait*.   *couldn.t wait*

4 They were married a year later.

PLACE / CELEBRATED / BECAME
CLUE Each sentence will require the addition of, or a change of vocabulary.

5 The reporter asked him about his experience.

EXPRESS / AFFECTED / REACTION
CLUE *Express* needs *his feelings, affected* needs *how* and *reaction* needs *to*.

6 He returned from the treacherous Antarctic expedition in good health and completely unharmed.

HALE / SOUND / KICKING
CLUE All these are idiomatic expressions consisting of pairs of adjectives joined by *and*. The adjectives are *safe, alive* and *hearty*.

wishes and regrets

A **In the passage it says: (*Uncle August*) *never said he wished he hadn't gone.*** What exactly does this mean? Can you answer the following questions about these sentences expressing wishes and regrets?

1 **a** Look at the sentences below.

    I regret not going on the expedition.
    I regret not having gone on the expedition.
    Is there any difference in meaning between these two sentences?   *no*

   b In the following sentence we need a different form of the verb in brackets. What is it?

    I regret (inform) you that we no longer have those supplies in stock.
    How is this sentence different from the ones in **a**?   *about to say*

2 **a** What form of the verb in brackets is needed in the following three examples?

    I can play the guitar quite well but I wish I (can) sing better.
    Using public transport is so inconvenient. I wish I (have) a car.
    We hate city life. We wish (be living) in the countryside.   *none are true*
    What do these three sentences imply?

   b When *wish* introduces a request, what form of the verb follows it?

    I wish (know) exactly what happened.

   c What tone is the speaker conveying in the following sentence?   *concern/irritation*

    I wish you didn't take so long in the bathroom every morning.

3 When there is a chance that things might happen or other people (not yourself!) might change their (irritating) habits, what form of the verb is used?

   I wish he (not smoke) cigars in the house.
   I wish they (tell) me what's worrying them.

4 Fill in the form we need when we express regret for what happened or existed in the past.

   I wish we (not tell) him the news. He was very upset.

5 *If only* follows the same patterns as *wish*. Which do you think is more emphatic? Complete the sentences below.

   If only I (not have to do) so much homework.
   If only I (apply) for that job! I'm sure I would have got it.
   If only he (not interrupt) when I'm speaking. It really gets on my nerves!

B Complete the following sentences so that they mean exactly the same as the ones printed before them.

1 **a** He knows he shouldn't have said those terrible things.

  He regrets ....

  b We are sorry that your job application has not been successful.

  We regret to ....

2 **a** I have to admit I'm a chain smoker.

  I wish ....

  b It's a pity you aren't teaching next year.

  We wish..

3 **a** I hope it rains soon, everything's so dry.

  I wish ....

  b She's always phoning me at work when I'm busy.

  I wish ....

4 They should have let us know they were moving house.

  I wish ....

5 They are sorry they did not buy the land.

  They wished..

6 I can't stand the way he falls asleep in the middle of dinner.

  If only..

7 Why didn't I take up his offer of a job!

  If only..

Summary Skills

A Necessary Evil?

talking points

Look at the following newspaper headlines. What arguments do they present for and against tourism?

DRUNKEN TOURISTS ARRESTED IN NIGHT CLUB BRAWL

NO ROOM AT THE INN Tourists come first say Hotel Managers

Report by Julian Sands

CITY A GHOST TOWN AS TOURISTS STAY AWAY

RECORD-BREAKING GAINS FOR TOURIST INDUSTRY PREDICTED THIS SUMMER

WHERE TO GO TO AVOID THE DREADED TOURIST

A special report by Bernard Manting

AIRPORT SAFETY CHECKS COULD RUIN TOURIST INDUSTRY

UNDER COVER THEME PARK SET TO ATTRACT TOURISTS

comprehension **Read these seven paragraphs from a leaflet setting out the arguments for and against tourism in the Lake District.** Then answer the questions, following the advice given.

Tourism: A Mixed Blessing

1 Tourism creates employment. It is estimated that in the Lake District 30 per cent of jobs can be directly attributed to tourism. But the fact that visitors spend their money in a variety of different ways affects other things too. Many village shops would
⁵ have to close if they were not supported by income from tourists and the money spent on local souvenirs can prevent local industries from going out of business.

2 Many of the roads in the Lake District are extremely narrow and tourist cars cause congestion. Some farmers and local traders
¹⁰ complain that the traffic makes it difficult for them to do their work. Because car parks fill up during busy periods, many visitors cause obstructions by parking across gateways, etc.

3 The popularity of the countryside has led to the growth of many organisations dedicated to protecting it. Many areas also operate
¹⁵ conservation schemes or trusts, supported by voluntary contributions. In some parts of the country, tourist operators have set up their own trusts and give money to local conservation projects.

4 The Lakes are a popular attraction for people who enjoy
²⁰ watersports. Most lakes have a speed limit for boats of 16 km per hour. One of the few lakes where fast boats are permitted is Windermere, which has recently become polluted. This is partly due to boats pumping sewage directly into the water. There are also problems with litter.

5 In the summer, thousands of people use the network of footpaths across the fells. Often, the grassy surface is worn away, leaving rough stone or mud. This makes the path look unsightly and it can be dangerous to walk on. Repairing the paths can be very expensive, particularly higher up in the fells where access is
³⁰ difficult.

6 The income from visitors can help support local services and industries. In a sparsely populated rural area it can be expensive to keep bus services running. Because large numbers of visitors use the buses during the holidays, it is possible to keep them
³⁵ running at quieter times too.

7 Because of the number of people using the lake shores for picnics and to land their boats, some of the vegetation around the lakes is being destroyed. This can be harmful to wild animals which build their nests along the shores. The creation of wildlife
⁴⁰ refuges around some of the lakes has helped protect these natural habitats. ■

exam tip

Examiners only expect one or two sentences paraphrasing the extracts from the passage, or answering the shorter questions. Do not write too much!

a Explain *jobs can be directly attributed to tourism* (line 2).
Begin *Tourism …*
Use *instrumental in*.

b Explain in your own words *cause congestion* (line 9).
Explain the meaning of *congestion* in this sense and what form it would take.

traffic jams, blocked roads

c What does the writer mean by *dedicated to protecting it* (line 14)?
You need to focus on the usual associations of *dedicated* and what it is directed towards here.

pros of countryside

d Explain *pumping sewage directly into the water* (line 23).
Not a pretty description! Describe exactly what happens to the sewage.

boats discharge

e Explain why the path could *be dangerous to walk on* (line 28).
Here you need to show that you understand the meaning of *thousands of people (walking) across the fells* and the effect that has on the paths, together with what might happen as a result of that.

pressure – slippy

f Why would it be expensive to keep a bus service running in an area of this kind?
Show that you understand *sparsely populated rural area* and how this would affect the financial feasibility of a bus service.

few fares

g How can the wildlife refuges help protect the natural habitat?
Explain what effect tourism has had on the vegetation then describe what *refuge* means and how it would prevent this from occurring.

destroy

summary

A Give each paragraph a short heading according to its subject matter. Compare your headings with those of a partner then arrange your paragraph headings under the arguments for and against tourism in the table below.

Advantages	Disadvantages
1. Econ. benefits	Traffic cong.
2. Envir. help	Pollution
3. amenities provide	Erosion walkways
	threat habitats

Write one sentence summarizing the main point in each paragraph.

B Linking additional and contrasting information. Now link your sentences to write two paragraphs only, one expressing the arguments for and one against tourism. Choose two or three of these words and phrases to link similar ideas in both paragraphs.

in addition (to this fact)   moreover   besides   furthermore

Now link the two contrasting paragraphs, using one of the following words or phrases.

nevertheless   in contrast   on the other hand   conversely

Listening and Speaking

Time Traveller

talking points

Can you describe the various stages in mankind's development depicted above?
In his film *Back to the Future*, Steven Spielberg's characters were able to travel into the past and the future in a 'time machine'. If you could travel back in time, which of these periods in time would you most / least like to visit? Explain why.

- The Bronze Age
- Classical times
- The Middle Ages
- The eighteenth century
- The nineteenth century
- A period in your own lifetime

listening 1

Listen to a description of a journey back through time. Fill in the missing information.

The exhibition spans (**1**) .... *800 y* .... of the history of
(**2**) .... *Oxford u* .... Visitors experience the (**3**) .... *sights sounds smells*
of the past. During the visit there is a roll call of (**4**) .... *famous former ss* .... The
visitor travels round the exhibition in (**5**) .... *scholar's desk* .... .The visit is
recommended as (**6**) .... *major tourist attrat* .. the city. The exhibition opens at 9.30
except for (**7**) .... *Nov to mar* .... , when it opens at 10.00.

listening 2

A **Note-taking.** Although life in the past often seems romantic and glamorous, the reality of day-to-day living was very different. Listen to two commentaries in the exhibition *The Oxford Story*. The first is about life in the halls and lodgings. The second is about the relationships between the scholars themselves and between the scholars and the townsfolk.

As you listen, make notes. Use symbols, abbreviated forms (ie = that is; eg = for example; •.• = because of; .•. = therefore; ➔ = resulted in) and other devices to help you remember as much as possible. Do not attempt to write everything as you will not have time.

<u>Suggested headings for your notes</u>

1 Halls and hostels run by .... *grad who were principals* ....

2 Food and heating paid for by .... *ss* ....

3 Students ate .... *at 10 a.m.* ....

4 At mealtimes students spoke .... *Latin > Eng* ....

5 Students usually lived .... *squalor halls/host* ....

6 Relationships between masters and scholars and town traders .... *poor strained* ....

7 Disturbances in town often caused by .... *drinking Ale* ....

8 Worst riot .... *1355 St Scolastica* ....

B **Group discussion.** After listening to the tape and making notes individually, divide into groups of three or four and compare notes so that you can form an accurate picture of what happened in those days. When you have finished either compare your notes with those of another group or listen to the tape again to check your information.

C **Homophones.** The words on the left have exactly the same pronunciation as those on the right but their meaning is different. Listen to some sentences on the tape and circle the word you think is being used. One word in each pair appeared in **A**.

1	**a** right	**b** rite		**8**	**a** main	**b** mane
2	**a** hall	**b** haul		**9**	**a** ale	**b** ail
3	**a** principal	**b** principle		**10**	**a** brewed	**b** brood
4	**a** bread	**b** bred		**11**	**a** sold	**b** soled
5	**a** beer	**b** bier *movable frame coffin*		**12**	**a** great	**b** grate
6	**a** tales	**b** tails		**13**	**a** days	**b** daze
7	**a** place	**b** plaice				

Can you explain the differences in meaning?

speaking

A time video. You are preparing a video to send with a video cassette player and TV in an unmanned spaceship on a trip to a faraway planet. On the video you want to show a selection of items which might give another civilization an idea of what life is like on earth. In small groups decide what you would include on the video.

The Narrative / Descriptive Composition

introduction

A fairly common kind of question in the examination is the narrative / descriptive composition. In questions like this you are asked for a description which may be of a person, place or journey. In addition there may be a requirement to blend this together with, for example, the story of how you met someone or why you visited a particular place. Great care is needed in the planning stage to ensure that the various parts of the question are given sufficient weight.

sample composition

A **Read the following composition and complete the exercises that follow.** The title of the composition is:

Write an account of an unusual journey that was spoiled by a travelling companion.

There had been rumours that the Ethiopian military authorities had opened the railway from Addis Ababa to Dire Dawa, and so one weekend some friends and I decided to get out of the
5 capital and see some of the countryside.
We arrived at the station early in the morning, and pushed our way through the crowds to the ticket office. Two Revolutionary Guards with machine guns seemed unconcerned at our
10 presence, so we made our way along the busy platform to the comparative calm of the carriage. I found an empty window seat and settled in.

The train started on the long twelve-hour haul to Dire Dawa, hundreds of miles east across the
15 plains. City buildings drifted past the window and the train soon reached the green hills of the open countryside, dotted with round thatched farmers' huts.

It was nearly midday when the train began to
20 move slowly uphill into a region of volcanoes. At first, the trees became more and more scarce, and small pebbles were scattered on the ground.

The train clanked on up to a desolate plateau, which stretched out as far as the eye could see,
25 like some vast lunar landscape covered with pitted and pock-marked rocks.
The final stretch, from mid-afternoon onwards, was the journey across the lowlands. There were thorny green acacia trees on the plain, and
30 vultures on their branches stood out against the pale light of the late afternoon sun.

It was early evening when the train finally came to a halt in Dire Dawa, an oasis in the wilderness. I hired one of the horse-drawn carriages at the
35 station, and breathed in the sweet smell of fresh rain. I leaned back in the carriage as it swept through the empty, tree-lined avenues of the town towards the only hotel, and savoured the silence.

It was a delight not to have Emma's voice
40 ringing in my ears. She had got onto the train at the beginning of the trip and had not stopped talking the whole time, which had ruined what would have been a wonderful journey.

B **Grading.** Read the composition title again. Bearing that in mind, what would you say is very good about the composition? What is very bad about it? What grade do you think it would get? *lang is good; not tosk*

C **Paragraph planning.** The main – and very serious – flaw with the sample composition is the failure to deal adequately with both parts of the question; however good a piece of writing might otherwise be, irrelevance will always be penalized very harshly. Spend five minutes on each of the following titles, and work out a paragraph structure for each of them. When you have finished, compare your paragraph plans with a partner.

1 *Describe a country that would best suit your ideal lifestyle.*
2 *Write a descriptive account of a stay in a place where your surroundings were at variance with your feelings.*

style improvement

A Read the following passage. What is wrong with it?

We went down the rough track towards the jungle until we reached the river that went across the road. We parked the Land Rover in the shade of some rubber trees and got out. We went across the river, which fortunately was not too deep, and then, as we were in no hurry, went through the rice fields on the other side towards the forest. The path that went through the trees was entirely overgrown, so we went along it with considerable difficulty. It was nearly mid-afternoon when we finally went out of the thick undergrowth and went to the bottom of the mountain. Although we were all by now feeling exhausted, we went up the steep slope and went to the rendezvous point just as the sun was going down.

B Rewrite the passage, trying to include the following verbs. You may also need to make a number of other small changes, for example, to prepositions. The verbs below are not in the right order.

arrive   clamber   cut   drive   emerge   hack one's way   lead   reach   wade   walk

writing task

Answer the following question.

Write a description of a nostalgic journey.

Stage 1 General approach. Plan the basic outline. There needs to be two elements to the composition – firstly, the journey and, secondly, an account of why it was nostalgic.

With this title, you could talk about either the journey itself or you could concentrate on the destination but, if you do this, you must say at least a little about the journey there. You also need to give considerable weight to the word 'nostalgic'. You will need to talk about a place that was important to you in the past and that has many memories for you. It is better to integrate these memories with each of the paragraphs in the composition rather than write two completely separate halves.

Stage 2 Brainstorming. Try and think of details that will be included – the exact places and memories that you will talk about. Note down any good expressions and images that may be useful.

Stage 3 Organization. Work out the final paragraph structure and, if possible, try and include a basic underlying structure for the whole composition. In the sample composition, there was a basic underlying structure of the journey from morning to night – this helped to give the passage a certain cohesion so it was more than just a collection of images. For this title you could concentrate on the journey itself, or the destination. If you choose the former, you can give your composition a simple underlying structure of:

A going to the place   **B** a description of the place   **C** the journey back.

If you decide to concentrate on the destination itself, try and find some other underlying structure to give your composition cohesion.

Stage 4 Write your composition.

Stage 5 Check your work carefully for grammatical mistakes.

exam tip

*When checking your work, look for any words (not only verbs) that have been repeated. Where possible, see if you can improve the style by choosing a different word that is more appropriate and that adds some extra information, as you did in the **style improvement** section. You will be given credit if you demonstrate extensive vocabulary.*

Overview 5

vocabulary

Choose the word which best completes each sentence.

1 It is advisable to .... any contact with potentially rabid animals.
A escape **B** avoid **C** prevent **D** evade

2 The bedroom was .... with bugs and beetles.
A infected **B** inflated **C** infested **D** infused

3 I'm afraid this vase is anything but antique – in fact, it's ....
A pointless **B** worthless **C** meaningless **D** hopeless

4 Never .... a gift horse in the mouth.
A feel **B** look **C** catch **D** hold

5 The crowds .... riot through the streets.
A incited **B** caused **C** went **D** ran

6 He gave a .... of surprise when he saw the damage the crash had caused.
A pant **B** puff **C** gasp **D** gulp

7 A traveller looks down on anyone who seems to be a(n) .... tourist.
A only **B** sole **C** mere **D** lone

8 They live in a very .... populated area of Italy.
A sparsely **B** scarcely **C** hardly **D** barely

9 There wasn't a .... of dust anywhere in the hotel.
A drop **B** fleck **C** speck **D** pinch

10 Tourism provides people with jobs – albeit often rather .... ones!
A superficial **B** menial **C** trivial **D** remedial

transformations

Finish each of the sentences in such a way that it means exactly the same as the sentence printed before it.

1 I should have bought that car.

If only ....

2 Oh dear! I didn't realize it was so cheap.

I wish ....

3 They were seasoned travellers, which we had not expected them to be!

Contrary...

4 It would be nice to be able to understand the language when I go to France.

I wish ....

5 Trudging through malaria-infested swamps demanded tremendous strength of character.

It took ....

6 What I would give to be able to pass my driving test first time!

If only...

7 He was looking forward to going home again.

He couldn't...

8 I'm sorry you're leaving so soon.

I wish ....

9 Unfortunately, he hasn't phoned me for days.

I wish ....

10   You don't understand Spaniards just because you can find a *pensión* in Spain!

Being.. *able* ....

blank-filling   Fill each of the blanks in the following sentences with a suitable word or phrase.

1   Don't get too down-hearted – try and ... *look on the* .... bright side.

2   Their untimely arrival .... *caught* .... us on the hop.

3   I wish you ... *wouldn't leave* .... the top off the toothpaste!

4   If only I ..... *hadn't* .... spent so much money yesterday!

5   The dispute ... *arose* .... from a disagreement between a landlord and some students in a tavern.

6   In addition ...... *to our own* ....luggage, we had to carry the old lady's as well!

7   They telephoned us to see ...... *if we wanted to* .... go on a day-trip to the city.

8   Although we .... *were exhausted* .... we decided to carry on up to the summit of the mountain.

9   We regret .... *to inform you* .... you that flight AZ 107 has been unavoidably delayed.

10   Many local shops would have to close if ... *they were not supported* ... by income from tourism.

rewriting   For each of the sentences below, write a new sentence as similar as possible in meaning to the original sentence, but using the word given in capital letters. These words must not be altered in any way.

1   The police arrived as the thieves were committing the crime.

RED-HANDED ....

2   We don't seem to have much sugar left!

RUNNING ....

3   He celebrated his birthday last Saturday.

PLACE ....

4   They lost not only their money but their passports as well.

ADDITION ....

5   Bad weather delayed the flight.

DUE ....

6   They arrived at their destination alive and kicking.

SOUND ....

7   Travellers consider themselves superior to those who lead a more sedentary life.

DOWN ....

8   Why does life have to be so difficult!

ONLY .... *weren't* ....

9   My jewellery has been stolen!

OFF ..... *run off* ....

10   What you do with the money is of no interest to me.

CARE ....

ART FOR ART'S SAKE?

Under the Hammer

talking points

A **An elderly and distant relative has left you a small legacy.** In his will, he has stated that you (Student A) and your cousin (Student B) can each choose two objects, but may not have them valued professionally first. You visit the house and find the following objects. Take it in turns to select the items you want, trying to pick the most valuable ones.

When you have finished, compare your choices with the actual values given on page 215.

B **What makes items valuable?** Think of three factors and compare your ideas with the rest of the class. What modern everyday items might be valuable to collectors in 50 years' time?

reading

A **Read the following article.**

IN PRAISE OF IMAGINATION

A woman in this country had in her possession – acquired when or where I do not know, though lawfully – a preserved human head. It was the tattooed head of a Maori warrior, and experts assigned it to the early 19th century. Anyway, the woman in our story apparently saw no difference between a human head and an inlaid escritoire, and sent the object to Bonham's, the auctioneers, to sell for her. Bonham's, for their part, made no demur, and prepared to offer one human head, in good condition, with tattoo, to the highest bidder at a forthcoming sale. Now read on.

Autres temps, autres mœurs; many a ritual once thought perfectly normal has come to seem abhorrent, from cannibalism to burning witches. And yet there is in England a woman and a firm of auctioneers who between them are unable to see that they might be doing anything odd by trading in human heads. Maori leaders have called the impending sale 'a degrading and deeply offensive desecration', and that strikes me as scoring very high marks for both succinctness and accuracy.

Let us examine the nature of this more closely. If a human head is to you a toy, an ornament or another acquisition for your *cabinet de voyeur*, it does not mean that you are wicked, but it does mean that there is something missing in your make-up. I think I know what the missing element is, and there is a curiously recondite yet useful test for defining it.

The touchstone will be found in the twenty-second book of *The Iliad*. Achilles, having refused to take any further part in the war, is roused to fury and to battle by the death of his friend Patroclus at the hands of Hector. Achilles goes forth to face the victorious Trojan, and kills him. Up to that point there is nothing special for a reader to feel; this is a war, after all, and people get killed in wars. But mark the sequel. Achilles ties the body of Hector, by the heels, to his chariot, and drags the noble corpse round the walls of Troy.

There is your test. If you can read the passage without feeling a profound pity and revulsion, you could buy a tattooed Maori warrior's head; if not, you couldn't. Go on to the sequel, in which Priam begs for the mangled body of his son, so that he can bury it with dignity and the proper rites; if, the boon granted and the obsequies held, you feel a deep sense of fitness and resolution in the story (though Hector, after all, is still dead, and his father still heartbroken), then you have in you that precious element that those who feel nothing as Hector is laid to earth do not have.

Imagination is the missing ingredient. That Maori head once spoke; in a strange tongue, no doubt, but spoke. It kissed its wife; it cursed its enemies; it got wet in the rain; it died and was severed from its shoulders. The body below the head was just as real; take its hand and feel the warmth of a living being. Imagination stirs, does it not?

You think these questions are pointless and childish? Then you are probably an auctioneer at Bonham's or the owner of the controversial lot. Homer knew better.

It is imagination that is dying out in the world. If imagination dies, it will make the world a desert. For imagination informs every culture; it is the blood of art, the mark of maturity, the guide-dog of ethics, the cornerstone of religion. But if it comes riding back in arms to claim its rightful kingdom, we shall hear no more of the selling and buying of human heads.

B   Comprehension questions. Answer the following questions using your own words as far as possible.

no details but not illegal

1   Explain what the writer knows about how the woman came to own the head.
2   What effect is the writer trying to achieve in the sentence in paragraph **1** beginning *Bonham's, for their part …?*   *ironical – lang. of auctioneers*
3   What opinion does the writer have of the Maori leaders' attitude towards the sale?   *well founded*
4   What does the *test* the writer mentions define?   *whether person can judge   · expressed*
5   In what way can one feel a *deep sense of fitness* at the burial of Hector?   *regains dignity*
6   What is missing in people who feel nothing at the burial of Hector?   *lack imagination*
7   What is meant by the phrase that imagination is *the guide-dog of ethics*?   *that we are blind in sense of morality, but imag. will lead us in right direction*

vocabulary

A   Read the text carefully to find a word or phrase that means:

1   objection *– demur*
2   outrage *desecration*
3   conciseness *succinctness*
4   standard by which something is judged *touchstone*

5   enraged *roused to fury*
6   request *boon*
7   cut off *severed*
8   morality *ethics*

B   Adjectives. Read through the following list of some of the adjectives which appeared in the passage. Classify them as negative or neutral / positive.

impending *N*	wicked *N*	recondite *–*
forthcoming *–*	pointless *N*	victorious *–*
abhorrent *N*	childish *N*	noble *–*
degrading *N*	normal *–*	rightful *–*

Negative . . . .

Neutral / Positive . . . .

C   Complete the following sentences using six of the adjectives from the list above.

1   As the election approached, the unpopular President felt a sense of . . . *impending* . . . doom.

2   As dolphins are such intelligent creatures, it must be . . . *degrading* . . . . for them to spend their lives performing tricks in dolphinariums.

3   After the Russian revolution, a woman called Anastasia claimed to be related to the Tsar and

said she was the . . . *rightful* . . . . . . heir to the throne.

4   It is . . . *pointless* . . . . . trying to get him to change his mind; he will not listen to you.

5   After the battle, the . . . . *victorious* . . . . army ransacked the town and looted all the houses.

6   Sentencing the accused to life imprisonment, the judge said she was horrified by the

. . . *abhorrent* . . . . crimes he had committed.

role-play

STUDENT A   You are a Maori leader visiting England for the first time. Your aim is to persuade the woman not to sell the head of the warrior, who may be distantly related to you. You feel that the head belongs to New Zealand and that she should return it. Try and persuade Student B to see things your way.

STUDENT B   You are the owner of the controversial head, which you inherited from your great-grandfather, who bought it when he was in New Zealand. You cannot see what all the fuss is about, and you see no reason why you should give it back or why you should not sell it for as much as you can get. Try and persuade Student A to see your point of view.

Absolutely Abstract

Cossacks by Kandinsky

talking points

A Look at these comments about Kandinsky's painting. Do you agree or disagree with them?

It looks very abstract and modern.
I can't see anything that looks remotely like a Cossack.
It looks as if it was painted by a five-year-old.

B Discuss the following questions using the structures above.

1 Are there any parts of the painting which look calm / dramatic / violent?
2 Can you see anything that looks like a flock of birds / a castle / a lance / a sword?
3 Can you identify two horses rearing up / a battle going on / the sun shining?

cloze development

The following extract is about the Russian painter Kandinsky. Some lines are missing a word, which is printed in bold in the margin. Decide where each of the missing words should go, and show where you would insert them by using a /.

	The doctrine of Expressionism provided a great impetus for experimentation
of	in the field of art. One of the central tenets this doctrine was that
what	mattered in art was not the imitation of nature but the expression
to	of feelings through the choice of colours and lines; this naturally led the
away	idea that art might be made more pure by doing with all subject matter 5
on	and by relying exclusively the effects of tones and shapes. And it
without	was the example of music, which gets on so well the crutch of words,
that	had suggested to artists and critics the dream of a pure visual music.
one	However, it was thing to talk about such possibilities in general terms
another	and quite to actually exhibit a painting without any immediately 10
that	recognizable object. It appears the first artist to do this was the Russian
whose	painter Wassily Kandinsky (1866–1944). He was essentially a mystic
made	dislike of the values of progress and science him long
of	for a regeneration the world through a new art of pure 'inwardness'.
somewhat	In his confused and passionate book *Concerning the Spiritual in* 15
way	*Art*, he stressed the psychological effects of pure colour, the in
like	which a bright red can affect us the call of a trumpet. His conviction
it	that was possible and necessary to bring about in this way a
gave	communion from mind to mind him the courage to exhibit these first
at	attempts colour music in paintings such as *Cossacks*, which really 20
came	inaugurated what to be known as abstract art.

intensifiers

A ***Very*** **and** ***absolutely.*** Discuss which of the following adjectives could be intensified with the word *very*, and which could be intensified with the word *absolutely*. What is the reason for this?

EXAMPLE   *good* can go with *very*   *I thought the exhibition was very good.*
               brilliant can go with *absolutely*   *I think Rodin's sculpture is absolutely brilliant.*

....*very*.... good   ....*absolutely*.... awful   ....*very*.... expensive

.... attractive   ....*very*.... gloomy   .... cheap

....*absolutely*.... amazing   ....*absol*.... incredible   ....*very*.... complicated

....*very*.... pleasant   ....*very*.... bad   ....*absol*.... perfect

....*abs*.... brilliant   ....*abs*.... astonishing   ....*absol*.... fine (meaning 'well' or 'OK')

exam tip

The use of ungradable adjectives with intensifiers is very much a part of conversational English. Use this kind of language in your interview, but not in a formal composition.

B **The adjectives which can be intensified with the word** ***very*** **are called gradable adjectives.**
For example, the word *good* is gradable, because a thing might be *quite good*, *reasonably good*, *very good* or *exceptionally good*.
The adjectives which can be intensified only with words like *absolutely* are called ungradable adjectives, because they are already extreme or complete in themselves. For example, it is not possible to be only *a little bit diabolical*, *brilliant*, *stupendous*, etc.

Look through the following lists. In each set, choose the odd one out. Here are two examples.

difficult   hard   complex   *incomprehensible*
(*incomprehensible* is ungradable or extreme, the other three are gradable)

diabolical   awful   *bad*   unspeakable
(*bad* is gradable, the other three are ungradable)

good	reasonable	marvellous	fair
dreadful	ghastly	terrible	poor
gorgeous	magnificent	stunning	pretty
upset	sad	devastated	disappointed
hot	warm	boiling	mild
terrified	worried	frightened	scared
weary	shattered	tired	weak
ridiculous	absurd	ludicrous	foolish
large	vast	huge	enormous
content	thrilled	ecstatic	delighted

listening

A **Helena is phoning a friend to tell her about an exhibition she has just been to.** During the conversation they use the adjectives below. Listen carefully to the tape and write down which intensifiers are used with each of the adjectives. The first two have been done as an example.

Ungradable adjectives   **Gradable adjectives**

1 ...*absolutely*... fantastic   2 ...*pretty*... reasonable

3 ...*absolutely*... wonderful   4 ...*incredibly*... good

5 ...*totally*... unbearable   6 ...*amazingly*... easy

7 ...*just*... brilliant   8 ...*terribly*... lucky

9 ...*utterly*... devastated   10 ...*very*... crowded

11 ...*really*... amazing   12 ...*really*... interesting

13 ...*quite*... magnificent   14 ...*quite*... expensive

1 Which intensifiers are used only with ungradable adjectives? *abs/ totally, just utterly — proper*
2 Which intensifiers are used only with gradable adjectives? *pretty, incredibly, amazingly, terribly*
really – **3** Which intensifier is used with both kinds of adjective and has the same meaning? *very*
4 Which intensifier is used with both kinds of adjective but changes its meaning?
quite – churral

B *Quite* **with gradable and ungradable adjectives.** Listen to the following sentences. For each sentence say whether the meaning of *quite* is:

a surprisingly	**c** fairly
b not very	**d** absolutely

1 Auctions of paintings are held quite regularly. ...*c*...

2 The prices for lesser-known works are quite reasonable. ...*a*...

3 The cost of Impressionist paintings is quite ridiculous. ...*d*...

4 Nowadays forgeries are becoming quite common. ...*c*...

5 The Modern Art exhibition was quite good. ...*b*...

6 The range of paintings in the National Gallery is quite magnificent. ...*d*...

C **Differences in meaning.** There are a small number of adjectives which can go with both kinds of intensifier. In the following pairs of sentences, which show a difference of register only, and which show a difference in meaning?

Your hair is very fine.   *I thought she was very beautiful.*

Your hair is absolutely fine.   more informal   *I thought she was absolutely beautiful.*

Can you think of any other adjectives that could be used with both sets of intensifiers?

D **Personal reactions.**

How would you feel if you passed Proficiency with a grade A?
How would you feel if someone in the class proposed to you?
How would you react if you discovered you had a twin brother or sister?
Tell your partner about your favourite film of all time.
How surprised would you be to find out you were going to have a baby?

collocations

A **Match the adverbs in the middle with the sets of adjectives on the outside.** The adverbs must collocate with all of the adjectives in any set. One has been done as an example.

disappointed resentful cold	**DEEPLY**	hurt (emotionally) offended moved
changed different mistaken	**BITTERLY** **GREATLY**	amused trained qualified
	HIGHLY	
ill injured wounded	**SERIOUSLY** **FULLY**	kind generous helpful
simple fair reasonable	**PERFECTLY** **MOST**	aware insured conscious

B **Complete these sentences using each of the adverbs and a suitable adjective.**

1 The sergeant was *seriously wounded* in the battle and had to be flown home to hospital.

2 I can't understand why you're having such trouble with the video – it's really *perfectly simple* to operate.

3 I am just warning you that you would be *greatly mistaken* to think I'm going to give in without a fight.

4 It is *bitterly cold* in North Canada in the winter – the temperature is never above zero.

5 It was *most kind* of you to lend me the car, and I'm just writing to say how much I appreciated it.

6 She only needed a local anaesthetic, so she remained *fully conscious* throughout the operation.

7 Many people in the audience were *deeply moved* by his tragic story and began to cry.

8 People who leave university are often *highly qualified* but lack any practical work experience.

Summary Skills

talking points

p 77

Traditional Values

A **Put the words in the following descriptions in the right order and match them to the appropriate item in the picture.**

1 with brass studs   in a pineapple pattern   decorated   from Zanzibar   carved   a chest
2 with a plaited raffia collar   one of a pair   from southern Sudan   of wood dancers
3 beaten iron   an Indian   made from   oil jar
4 from   carved figures   West Africa
5 vase   porcelain   tall   Japanese   a
6 skull   a dolphin   fish   a   skull   and
7 on the   turtle   wall   hanging   shells
8 three-legged   Ethiopia   a   tribal   from   stool

B **If money was no object, which items would you choose to decorate a room of your own?**

summary 1

Verbal summary. Read the magazine article about Mara Amats then, in small groups, discuss the following points:

1 the two fields Mara has specialized in
2 places where she has spent a lot of time working
3 what she has been trying to encourage people to do

A ROOM OF MY OWN

MARA AMATS

**used to restore frescoes until
she decided restoring people was somewhat more valuable.**

By this she meant giving people whose lives were as distinctive as the icons she worked on the chance to maintain their own ways. Her change of tack began when she discovered that
5 the beggars hanging around the church where she was working in Addis Ababa had been embroiderers in Haile Selassie's palace and that their only sources of work now were infrequent church commissions. She looked at their designs,
10 advised how they could sell them more effectively and in years to come found herself working among the people in other parts of Africa as well as India and the Caribbean.

That is why her room in a small flat just off
15 London's Baker Street is filled with exotica – of which she herself could claim to be an example. She was born in Latvia, half-Russian on her mother's side, and spent her childhood years in displaced persons' camps before settling in
20 France, where she was apprenticed to an icon master who trained her as a restorer. Her artistic sensitivity is balanced by a strong practical streak and her adventurous spirit sustains her in her travels to isolated and often
25 dangerous parts of the world.

Her flat is in what began as a block of artisans' dwellings, purpose-built at the turn of the century, and mostly occupied then by glove-makers and other craftsmen: she believes three
30 families lived in the fairly cramped space that is now her base whenever she is in London – 'the navel of the world, the crossroads for all these other places'. She has worked on development projects in poor countries in the belief that
35 many of the textiles, pottery and sculpture such countries produce can sell in the West in their own right and not just on the guilt principle. 'I start from the other end, designing products that can sell because they are the best in their price
40 range.' Financial aid from the West often went down the plughole of grandiose bureaucratic enterprises. 'One walks across that field or into that hut and there is very seldom any of that aid visible, though billions are spent. Now I think
45 we are beginning to have ideas and look at our methods.'

She went on contract from the Common-wealth Secretariat to the Caribbean where the mechanization of banana-loading meant that the
50 women who used to hump the bananas to the ships needed new jobs. She experimented with banana fibre and found it made rather fine paper. Then she went to Nepal, where people had been making paper since the eleventh
55 century, using the bark from trees of the daphne family. The trees were never replanted, contributing to the 40 per cent loss of ground cover in the Himalayas. 'I found a water hyacinth that makes splendid paper and now the
60 people are producing it for several top British firms.' She has also helped them market a species of black mushroom that needs to be harvested, dried and sold within two months. She brought a sample back with her and now it
65 is sold in the West End of London.

She herself is an artist and works in paper. On the left hangs a shirt she made out of water hyacinth paper and pheasant feathers, one of a series of symbolic representations she has
70 constructed. On the wall to the right of the shells is a drawing on vellum from a Coptic bible by an Ethiopian artist, and near it carved figures from West Africa.

Tribal rugs from Persia and Anatolia add
75 their colour and in front of the table with the skulls a set of saddle-bags originally used by yurt-dwellers in Kazakhstan find an alternative role on the floor. Mara has just spent several months in Kazakhstan, part of the former USSR,
80 advising craftspeople how to pick up the threads of their pre-Revolutionary skills, deliberately crushed in 70 years of 'socialist realism'. Their crafts were mummified, she says; instead of their symbolic patterns and native decorative arts
85 they had to make busts of Lenin or repres-entations of people driving tractors. 'Many of these crafts survived only in the more remote areas where old people kept them going because of dowry customs and so on. The younger ones
90 see them as living libraries of their past – please read them with us, they asked, so that we can earn our living through them again.' ■

Ena Kendall, *The Observer Magazine*

comprehension

A **Choose the best explanation for these words and phrases according to how they are used in the article.**

1 exotica (line 15)
   A beautiful or exciting sounds
   B curious or rare art objects
   C strange customs

2 sustains her (line 24)
   A carries her weight
   B supports her financially
   C strengthens her morale

3 fairly cramped space (line 30)
   A rather confined area
   B very uncomfortable quarters
   C quite limited scope

4 the navel of the world (line 31)
   A the dregs of civilization
   B the hub of the universe
   C the scourge of society

5 went down the plughole of grandiose bureaucratic enterprises (line 41)
   A was siphoned off by important local officials
   B drained away on account of inappropriate business deals
   C disappeared in extravagant official ventures

6 there is very seldom any of that aid visible (line 43)
   A we rarely see any concrete use made of the money donated
   B we often witness the money being put to inappropriate use
   C we are never given an opportunity to see how the money has been used

7 an alternative role (line 77)
   A another character to represent
   B an optional part to play
   C a different purpose in life

8 to pick up the threads (line 80)
   A to learn how to sew properly
   B to start where they left off
   C to repair damage done to

9 deliberately crushed (line 81)
   A purposefully squeezed
   B prudently conquered
   C wiped out on purpose

10 mummified (line 83)
   A shrivelled and dried up
   B respected and revered
   C forgotten and untalked of

B **Reference devices.** What do these underlined words and expressions refer to in the article?

1 by this (line 1)
2 their designs (line 9)
3 an example (line 16)
4 the fairly cramped space (line 30)
5 that aid (line 43)

6 producing it for (line 60)
7 helped them market (line 61)
8 a sample (line 64)
9 near it (line 72)
10 them as living libraries (line 90)

C **Discussion.** In small groups discuss the answers to these questions and be ready to tell the class what conclusions you reached.

1 According to Mara, what has been the Western attitude towards craft skills in the developing world? Do you agree with this point of view?

2 What is Mara's attitude towards people offering traditional skills in the developing world? Do you think her ideas will be effective?

summary 2

Write a summary of between 60 and 90 words describing the difference between Mara's attitude and the attitude of the West to traditional skills in the developing world.

p 41

In the Picture

A **A guide is showing a group of visitors round an art gallery.** Listen to the commentary about this picture and choose the best answer.

1 According to Burne-Jones, a painting
 A ought to be true to nature.
 B must have a clear moral point.
 C should play an instructive role in a modern industrial society.
 D need not have any practical value.

2 The story of the King and the Beggar Maid
 A was a well-known Victorian tale.
 B was popularized by a poet.
 C was brought to the artist's attention by his wife.
 D was taken up by novelists at a later stage.

3 According to the guide, the painter
 A wanted to portray the beggar very realistically.
 B copied parts of the painting from an Italian masterpiece.
 C had certain items in the painting made for him.
 D had difficulty in painting jewels.

4 The public who first viewed the painting probably
 A recognized Frances Graham as the model for the Beggar Maid.
 B realized how personal the painting was for the artist.
 C interpreted the painting without difficulty.
 D did not approve of the subject matter of the painting.

B **One of the visitors to the gallery stays to take a close look at the painting on the left.** Listen to the tape and say if the following statements are true or false.

1 In the shop there are posters of all the paintings in the gallery.   T/F

2 Laura does not want to see any of the modern paintings in the gallery.   T/F

3 Amelia is irritated by Edward's concern about her health.   T/F

4 Edward is pleased with the way the servants behaved.   T/F

5 Amelia is watching the last guests leave.   T/F

6 The housekeeper ensured that Amelia sat next to Captain Richardson.   T/F

7 Edward is jealous because Amelia has been seeing Captain Richardson secretly.   T/F

8 This is the first time that Edward has shown that he is jealous.   T/F

Ask your guide (Student A) about:

- the painter of the picture.
- what other works the artist has done.
- the artist's life.
- what the guide feels personally about the picture.
- what the various parts of the picture represent.
- how much the picture is worth and whether it is for sale.

C   Dialogue writing.

Work with a partner to make up a short dialogue based on this picture. Use relatively formal language, as in the example on the tape. When you have finished, perform your short dialogue for another pair or group in the class.

speaking

A   Role-play.

STUDENT A You work in a commercial art gallery and are giving a client (Student B) an individual guided tour. You discover, to your horror, that there is a new painting (see below) about which you know nothing, but in which your client is extremely interested. Invent answers to your client's questions but do not let him / her realize that you have no idea what you are talking about.

STUDENT B You are a wealthy visitor to the town and are having a private guided tour of the fine art gallery. You are particularly interested in the painting below, and want to know everything about it.

B   Picture discussion.

1   Which of the paintings in this unit do you prefer and why?
2   Do you find any of these paintings annoying / boring / sentimental / obscure?
3   Are there any other kinds of paintings that you prefer to these?
4   Do you find some kinds of art easier to appreciate than others?
5   How often do you go to art galleries and exhibitions?
6   Describe the kind of paintings, pictures or photographs you have at home.
7   What is Art with a capital A?

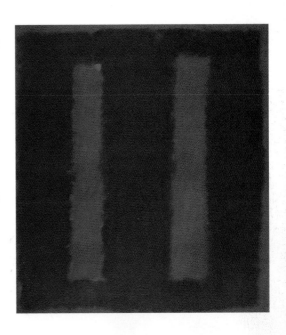

introduction

In the task-based composition, you may be asked to write a report or speech based on some factual information. Attention must be paid to information extraction and style.

sample composition

A **Look at the following composition title.** Mrs Jackson has received a bill and some terrible photographs from the official photographer at her daughter's recent wedding.

1 *Write a letter from Mrs Jackson to a friend who came to the wedding, explaining what has gone wrong and asking him / her to send any photos that he / she took. (200 words)*

2 *Write a letter of complaint from Mrs Jackson to the photographer. (150 words)*

B **Read the two letters.** What is wrong with them?

Dear Mrs Mills,

Thank you for your letter of 11 June. It gives me great pleasure that you were able to attend the wedding of our daughter and that you found it satisfactory.

My daughter and son-in-law will shortly return from their honeymoon, but unfortunately the wedding album has not yet been prepared. The reason for this is that the pictures which were taken by the official photographer were entirely unacceptable. Some of them were out of focus, others were poorly composed, and in one instance the image was obscured by the photographer's finger. The photographer therefore has been informed that his fee will not be paid.

I believe that you had a camera at the wedding, and I would be most grateful if you could forward any photographs you have to the above address so that an album of the guests' photographs can be compiled.

I look forward to hearing from you.

Yours sincerely,

Jane Jackson

Dear Mr Norton,

Thanks very much for your letter with the bill and the photos. I'm terribly sorry to have to say this, but I think they're absolutely awful! Some of them are completely fuzzy, some of them have got bits chopped off, and in one of them there's a great big finger in the way. I'm really upset, because when you go to all the trouble of hiring a so-called professional photographer, this isn't the kind of thing you expect, is it?

Anyway, I'm sending your bill back to you because you've made such an absolutely dreadful mess of everything, and I'm certainly not going to pay you a penny. What's more, I think you ought to do something to make up for it. I'm going to try and put an album together by using some of the photos that the guests took, and I think you ought to pay for the developing and enlarging. Is that OK?

Hope to hear from you soon.

Yours

Jane Jackson

exam tip

The question for the task-based composition will always say exactly what kind of writing is required – a letter, report, speech, etc. You must follow these instructions precisely or you will be heavily penalized.

C **Formal and informal vocabulary.** The main problem with the letters is that they are written in the wrong style. One element that contributes to style is vocabulary. Read the letters to help you find the formal and informal equivalents of the following words and expressions, as in the example.

Formal	Informal
out of focus	*fuzzy*
to compensate for	to make up for
(some) poorly composed	they've got bits chopped off
entirely unacceptable	absolutely awful
(can be) compiled	put something together
to forward	sending (your bill) back
I look forward	Hope to hear from you soon.

D Formal and informal styles. Vocabulary is only one element of style. Here are a number of other features that contribute to an overall style. Look at the letters and make notes about the differences between formal and informal styles. The first has been done as an example.

Features	Informal	Formal
1 Abbreviations and contractions	used extensively, for example, *I'm, they're, there's,isn't*, etc.	not used; the full form is necessary for example *has not, I would be*, etc.
2 Use of the passive and active		*much more common*
3 Use of the first person singular	*common, informal*	*less so, avoid I think*
4 Use of intensifiers (eg *really, absolutely*)	*like in speech*	
5 Use of phrasal verbs	*common*	*Latin words eg compensate compile*
6 Link words	*simple anyway*	*more formal but, ∴*
7 Set phrases and idioms	*speech*	
8 Rhetorical questions	*possible*	*best avoided + embedded q rather*
9 Expression of personal feelings		*kept out* *them direct*
10 Ellipsis (missing out words)	*oh*	*no*

writing task

Rewrite the letters in a more appropriate style.

Stage 1 General approach. Select a suitable style for each of the letters.

Stage 2 Brainstorming. Extract the relevant information for the two new letters and consider what new information you might like to include.

Stage 3 Organization. Which letter would these paragraphs be in, and in what order?

  a Mrs Jackson says she will not pay the bill and suggests some compensation.
  b She refers to the date and contents of the letter she has received.
  c She refers to seeing them at the wedding and mentions the honeymoon.
  d She explains the precise nature of her complaint.
  e She talks about her and her daughter's feelings about the photographs.
  f She asks for some other photographs to be sent.

Stage 4 Write each of the letters out in full using about 150 – 200 words each.

Stage 5 Checking. Take particular care to refer to your notes about formal and informal styles.

Overview 6

vocabulary

Choose the word which best completes each sentence.

1 I showed the painting to an expert who .... it at about £500.
   A costed   B estimated   C assigned   **D** valued

2 I'd like to buy that glass vase you have in the window – the one with the roses .... on the side.
   A inscribed   B tattooed   C designed   **D** etched *short tool*

3 According to the opinion polls, over 20% of voters in the .... General Election have yet to make up their minds. *duty on ya*
   A forthcoming   B future   C impending   D incumbent

4 He's a fairly pleasant child but he has a strong .... of stubbornness when he doesn't get his own way.
   A trait   B streak   C character   D mark

5 The room feels very .... now that we're having to store all my brother's furniture.
   A cramped   B pressed   C filled   D crowded

6 On reflection, the reviewer realized that he had been .... unfair in his harsh criticism of the play.
   A somewhat   B moreover   C anywhere   D whatever

7 The two children tried as hard as they could to .... a reconciliation between their parents.
   A bring about   B bring up   C bring in   D bring together

8 Anna is a very nervous child and she's very .... of strangers.
   A terrified   B frightened   C petrified   D horrified

9 By the time he had finished work and returned home, he was absolutely ....
   A exhausted   B tired   C weary   D weak

10 That was one of the best films I have ever seen – it was .... magnificent.
   A very   B fairly   C quite   D extremely

11 All through his life he remained .... resentful of the way he had been abandoned by his parents as a child.
   A fully   B seriously   C completely   D bitterly

12 The manager was very pleased with her last business trip, which had been a .... success.
   A whole   B complete   C full   D high

13 He decided to go ahead with the new business, although he was .... aware of the risk.
   A most   B gravely   C seriously   D fully

14 On returning home, Peter discovered .... his horror that the pipes had burst and the entire house was flooded.
   A by   B of   C at   D to

15 The museum guards were shocked to find that the painting on the wall was a copy and the .... had been stolen.
   A first   B original   C blueprint   D genuine

rewriting

For each of the sentences below, write a new sentence as similar as possible in meaning to the original sentence, but using the word given in capital letters. The word must not be altered in any way.

1 You'd be wasting your time trying to make him change his mind.

   POINTLESS ....

2 Peter inherited a large sum of money from his uncle.

   LEFT ... *was left* ....

3 The result of the match was a deep disappointment to the fans.

DEEPLY ....

4 The thieves apparently got into the museum through the roof.

SEEM. ....

5 She earns money from her paintings.

SOURCE ...... *her paintings* ....

6 Impressionist paintings are ridiculously expensive these days.

PRICE .... *is ridiculous* ....

7 My impression of him was that he was a very capable person.

STRUCK ...... *I was* ....

8 In her previous job, Mara was a picture restorer.

WORK ..... *used to work* ....

9 You can now buy these products at all large supermarkets.

SOLD ...... *are sold* ....

10 It is her father who is Italian.

HALF ...... *is half ... on his side* ....

to do

collocations

Intensifiers can be used with nouns and verbs, and follow similar patterns to the intensifier and collocation patterns in the Structure section. In the following sentences, choose the best answer.

1 Mary's having a terrible time at work because she absolutely .... her boss.
  A dislikes   **B** mistrusts   **C** loathes   **D** resents

2 It is just as well you didn't put your money in that company, because it would have been an absolute .... if you had.
  A mistake   **B** error   **C** miscalculation   **D** catastrophe

3 I .... understand your reasons for wanting to leave, but I still think there are one or two other points you ought to consider.
  A quite   **B** highly   **C** greatly   **D** terribly

4 When morning came, the scene of where the bomb had fallen was one of utter ....
  A disturbance   **B** damage   **C** disruption   **D** devastation

5 The news of his sister's death came as a(n) .... shock to him.
  A utter   **B** entire   **C** extreme   **D** great

6 I quite .... Mozart, but on the whole I prefer Bach.
  A adore   **B** love   **C** like   **D** idolize

7 After the crash, a number of people were taken to hospital with .... injuries.
  A great   **B** serious   **C** deep   **D** high

8 For many years, my sister .... regretted turning down the chance she had had to go to university.
  A bitterly   **B** highly   **C** entirely   **D** absolutely

9 If you managed to pass your driving test, it would be an .... miracle.
  A utter   **B** entire   **C** extreme   **D** absolute

10 The bank manager said that he .... appreciated that we were having problems, but there was nothing he could do to help.
  A greatly   **B** fully   **C** utterly   **D** largely

ONLY FLESH AND BLOOD

Reading

Rich and Poor

talking points

A Descriptions. Look at these photos. What connection do you think there might be between the young woman and the old woman in the large photo?

Combine the adjectives and adverbs on the left with the words on the right to describe them.

bushy	eyes
fair / dark / greying	moustache
shabbily / elegantly	hairline
receding	expression
straight / curly	eyebrows
worried	smile
staring	hair
attractive	dressed

What assumptions could you make about the character and personality of the people by looking at the photos?

B Speculating. We don't know what eventually happened to the people above, but we could hazard a guess from the photos. Use the photos to speculate on what might / could / must have happened to them.

reading

A The following passage is about the people in the pictures. Read it through quickly
to find out:

a what it is about.
b where / when the events take place.

Whatever happened to Baby Doe?

Leadville, Colorado, is one of the high places of American legend, the most famous of the silver towns of the 1880s, wiped out in the crash of 1893 and left desolate ever since. Like many other legends, it is rather shabby and down-at-heel, and needs a discerning eye to be appreciated.

In its heyday, the town must have been an odd mixture of vulgar opulence and Western austerity. The austerity is still evident in the fragile wooden houses most citizens live in, not very different from a century ago, and the grim weather of the high Rockies: Leadville is 10,000 feet high. The opulence is long gone, but the Tabor Opera House still stands, where Lily Langtry and Sarah Bernhardt performed, and where Oscar Wilde lectured on the aesthetics of Benvenuto Cellini. It was in the Leadville saloon to which Wilde was taken after his lecture that he observed over the piano the sign he made famous: PLEASE DO NOT SHOOT THE PIANIST. HE IS DOING HIS BEST. He remarked that this was the only rational method of art criticism he had ever come across.

Leadville tries to preserve its Western heritage while seeking some more lucrative substitute, without much success. It is a bare, windy place, even in midsummer, surrounded by spectacular mountains and the debris of mine workings. Tourism has not flourished, which is fortunate for tourists.

Leadville's charm is in its dilapidation.

The town's celebrity comes from the story of Horace Tabor and Baby Doe. He was a prospector and speculator who owned the general store there in the 1870s and acquired shares in a piece of land staked out by two German immigrants. He gave them a sack of provisions for the stake. It turned into the Matchless Mine, the richest silver mine in the United States apart from Constock in Nevada. Tabor bought up prospects all over Leadville, and was soon one of the richest men in the country, with a fortune estimated at more than $100 million.

Then he met Baby Doe. She was a girl of doubtful antecedents, from Wisconsin, luscious rather than beautiful, who had acquired and disposed of a husband and numerous protectors on her way to Colorado. She met and captivated the prospector millionaire, who was by now mayor of Leadville and one of the most prominent citizens of the state. She induced him to divorce his wife, Augusta, and to marry her.

The office of US senator was vacant at the time, and Tabor hoped for the position. He was defeated by another, and smarter, silver baron, but as a consolation prize was appointed to the last 30 days remaining of the previous senator's term. He went off to Washington for his moment of glory, and

there married Baby Doe, in a splendid ceremony in the Willard Hotel, a block from the White House. The wedding was attended by the President, Chester Arthur, and by all the other notables of the Republican Party. None of their wives came.

The Tabors spent $40 million in the next decade, living a life judged extravagant even by the other *nouveaux riches* of that extravagant decade. In 1893 the silver boom collapsed. The Sherman Act, which had made silver legal tender at a parity of 16:1 with gold, was repealed, and the Tabors were bankrupt.

They lost a huge mansion and their second opera house in Denver along with all their holdings in Leadville, including the opera house and everything they possessed – except the Matchless Mine, which was by then completely exhausted and closed. ■

The Tabor Opera House in Leadville

B Comprehension: reading for gist. In this type of passage the multiple-choice questions usually focus on understanding the gist or context, rather than on individual words and phrases. Look at questions **1** to **6**. They are based on what you might have found out by reading the passage through once. Answer them briefly by referring to the passage again if necessary.

1 What was Leadville like before 1893? *— strange — combin of osten wealth deprivn of NA West*

2 How did Oscar Wilde interpret the sign over the piano in the saloon? *logical comment on art*

3 What does the writer say Leadville is remembered for today? *Tabor & Doe*

4 Why was Horace Tabor's term as a senator short-lived? *failed US senater electi-ns — last 30 dys*

5 Why do you think none of the dignitaries' wives attended his wedding? *low opinion & last scato + bride*

6 Why did the Tabors become paupers? *1893 silv. boom collapsed*

C Multiple-choice questions. Now look at the multiple-choice options for questions **1** to **6** in **B**. Choose the best answer. Is it less / more detailed than yours?

1 A It was an abandoned, windswept place.
B It was badly in need of structural repairs.
C It was a place of great contrasts.
D It was shunned by the rich and famous.

2 A It meant the saloon was a violent place in which to perform.
B It suggested that music was not popular in Leadville.
C It requested customers to behave in a civilized manner.
D It gave a fair appraisal of the pianist's talents.

3 A Two of its more colourful inhabitants.
B Its disused silver mines.
C Its cultural heritage.
D Its depressing state of dilapidation.

4 A He was ousted from office by another silver baron.
B He returned to Leadville to take up the position of mayor.
C He had not been elected to the position in the first place.
D His marriage was frowned upon in high circles.

5 A They were otherwise engaged.
B The guest list was already too long.
C They disapproved of Baby Doe.
D They were snubbed by Baby Doe.

6 A They had squandered their money needlessly.
B Silver ceased to be a legal form of currency.
C The Matchless Mine had nothing more to offer them.
D They lost huge sums of money in Denver.

vocabulary

Similar but different. Choose the best word to complete each of the sentences below. The words labelled **A** are all in the passage. Find out what the other words mean by using a dictionary if necessary.

1 The collapse of the silver market left him financially . . . .
A desolate   B dejected   C destitute   D derelict

2 In times of . . . . unemployment figures usually rise dramatically.
A austerity   B severity   C sobriety   D gravity

3 The committee is happy to report that it has no . . . . to the construction of the new senate building.
A criticism   B objection   C disapproval   D censure

4 At his . . . ., the silver mine was left to his wife.
A heritage   B birthright   C inheritance   D bequest

5 The President was eventually . . . . by a military coup.
A disposed   B despised   C deposed   D dispersed

6 The pianist's excellent performance . . . . the audience.
A captivated   B captured   C capitulated   D capitalized

7 . . . . reports of the number of casualties in the disaster have caused widespread panic.
A Extravagant   B Exaggerated   C Excessive   D Extortionate

listening

You will hear someone talking on a radio programme entitled 'Whatever happened to ...'. Read through the prompts below then listen to what really happened to Baby Doe. Complete the information as you listen.

1 Horace tried to provide for his family by *hauling or iron labourer contractor*

2 After Horace's death, Baby Doe *...........................*

3 She became *wild eccentric figure ....*

4 She lived with her daughters *small squalid shack at ....*

5 One daughter *ran away died as a ....,*

the other *..................................*

6 Baby Doe ended her days *frozen death in blizzard 1935*

Structure

Too Many or Too Few?

talking points

changes in birth rate in 5 diff regions in 2 five-year periods 1960-90

cloze development
- verbs
- determiners
connectors
adjs / prepos / nouns

Look at the following table.
Can you explain what the figures show?
Can you remember how many different types of word are omitted in a cloze exercise? Read the following passage about population trends. The type of word missing is given. Can you supply the word?

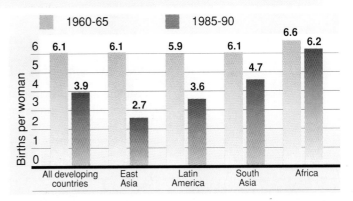

Today the most important population trends are the fast growth in the number of elderly people and the sharp drop in the number of teenagers leaving school.

The size of the elderly population is (**1**) *growing / growing*

5 (*verb*) because people are living longer and

(**2**) *fewer* (*adjective*) babies have been born.

In 1911, only 5 per cent of the UK population was older than 65. Today, the (**3**) *figure / proportion* (*noun*) is more than 15 per cent. Over the next decade the greatest

10 (**4**) *increase / rise* (*noun*) will be in people aged 75 and over. The drop in the number of school-leavers was

(**5**) *caused* (*verb*) by the fall in the birth rate

(**6**) *between* (*preposition*) 1964 and 1977. This trend is known (**7**) *as* (*preposition*) the

15 "demographic time bomb" – because demographers knew that, once the birth rate fell, there was (**8**) *no*

(*determiner*) way to stop it (**9**) *having* (*verb*) an explosive effect on the economy and on society 16 years later.

However, the impact may (**10**) *well* (*adverb*)

20 be short-term. According to some forecasters the UK's birth rate may soon become one of the highest in western Europe.

Companies have to (**11**) *take* (*verb*) into account the age of the population when they are deciding what goods to produce and when they are recruiting staff.

25 In Britain and most of Europe, the birth rate fell between the early 1960s and the mid 1970s. That (**12**) *meant* (*verb*) that, by the second half of the 1980s, the number of teenagers leaving school and looking for jobs each year fell sharply.

In 1986, there were 6.2 million people

30 (**13**) *aged* (*adjective*) between 16 and 24 in the labour force. By the turn of the century, this is likely to

(**14**) *have* (*verb*) fallen to 4.9 million. That means that companies who generally recruited many of their staff

(**15**) *straight / direct* (*adverb*) from school have had to think

35 of other ways of attracting workers.

At the other end of the age scale is the significant increase in the number of elderly people in the population. Over the

(**16**) *last / past* (*adjective*) ten years, several companies have (**17**) *grown* (*verb*) up which specialize

40 (**18**) *in* (*preposition*) building "sheltered accommodation" for elderly people – groups of houses or flats where there is a warden on (**19**) *duty* (*noun*) to give help. In the 1970s, these companies were virtually unknown. They have come into (**20**) *being / existence* (*noun*) because of

45 demographic change. ■

vocabulary

A Words which cause confusion. Study the list of similar words below. One of each group appeared in the passage. What is the difference between them? Use a dictionary if necessary.

1	migration	immigration	emigration	4	decline	incline	recline
2	inverted	converted	diverted	5	subtract	detract	attract
3	converse	inverse	reverse	6	inquire	acquire	require

Now choose one of the words above in its correct form to fit into each of the following sentences. They are in the same order as the words.

1 During the fifties ...emig.... from Britain to Australia was extremely popular.

2 The traffic was ...diverted.... because of the accident.

3 This car has four forward gears and one ...reverse....

4 I apologized for having to ...decline.... their invitation.

5 The fact that the music centre is second-hand does not ...detract... from the excellent sound reproduction.

6 I have recently ...acquired.... an old copy of Shakespeare's plays.

B Expressions 1. In the passage on page 89 we came across the expression *short-term*. Some compounds of *short* have a corresponding noun, verb or adjective form. Sometimes the meaning is the same, sometimes it is slightly different.

Complete the following table and explain the meaning of any corresponding forms.
(**NB** Not all the expressions have noun, adjective and verb forms.)

	Noun	Adjective	Verb
1	a short circuit	....	to short-circuit
2	....	short-changed	...short change...
3	....	....	make short work of
4	a short cut	....	...to cut short...
5	a short list	...short-listed...	....
6	...short hand...	short-handed	....
7	....	....	run short of
8	shortcoming	....	....
9	...ness...	short-sighted	....

Now use one of the expressions in its correct form in the sentences below.

1 Fewer than five candidates were ...short-listed... for the job.

2 I'm afraid your order cannot be processed immediately as we're ...short handed... at the moment.

3 There were only two applicants for the job so we ...made short work of... interviewing them.

4 Despite his ...short-comings..., I feel he will make a good doctor!

5 You have to be careful when shopping in open-air markets as you can often be ...short-changed....

6 We tried a ...short cut... but it took longer than the main road.

7 I'm afraid we've ...run short of... time – the meeting must end at 12.00.

8 His ...short-sightedness... prevented the company from investing in a market which was certain to be a success.

C Expressions 2. In the passage we came across the idiom *take into account* meaning 'consider'. Look at the following idioms with *take*, then match them to the explanations on the right.

1 *take pot luck*   a have a detrimental effect on
2 *take something amiss*   b choose which you would like
3 *take one's pick*   c be upset or offended by
4 *take someone down a peg or two*   d understand what someone is implying
5 *take its toll*   e cheat or deceive someone
6 *take someone for a ride*   f reduce an over-confident person to normal 'stature'
7 *take a hint*   g take a risk without prior knowledge

Now choose one of the expressions in its correct form to complete the sentences below.

1 We have several kinds of rose for sale, so you can ....*take your pick*................... .

2 She's so insensitive that even when you've made the same suggestion two or three times she still can't ...*take a hint*..................... .

3 He thinks he's the cat's whiskers. He needs to be ...*taken down a peg or two*.... .

4 The earthquake on the east coast certainly ..*took its toll*..................... .

5 I was really ...*taken for a ride*............... until he admitted he'd borrowed the uniform that morning.

6 You never know what the weather is going to be like here – you just have to ....*take pot luck*.................. .

7 Please don't ...*take it amiss*............... when I say that your last report needed a lot of reworking.

passive review

A Look at the following pairs of sentences. Is there any difference in meaning between the pairs of sentences? Which sentence in each pair sounds more natural and why?

1 a They will make a statement in Parliament tomorrow. *don't know who they are; omit if obvious*
   b A statement will be made in Parliament tomorrow.

2 a Someone murdered a man outside his house in Newgate last night. *statement more imp them who is doing it*
   b A man was murdered outside his house in Newgate last night.
crime more imp

3 a An expert in the field of information technology will give a talk.
   b A talk will be given by an expert in the field of information technology.

4 a We poured the liquid into a test tube and heated it. *experiment*
   b The liquid was poured into a test tube and heated.

NB Remember that the passive can be used for different shades of meaning and emphasis.

B Can you rephrase these sentences in two different ways? Begin as suggested below.

1 They say the Prime Minister is on the point of resigning. *typical of newspapers*

   a It ....*is said*.........................

   b The Prime Minister ....

2 They said the Queen was considering abdication.

   a It ....

   b The Queen.......................

3 They said the Chairman of the Board had absconded with the funds.

   a It ....

   b The Chairman.......................

Where might you see or hear sentences like those you have written?

C Sometimes other changes need to be made. When writing sentences in the passive, verbs may become nouns and adverbs change to adjectives. Rewrite the following sentence in two different ways. Clues have been given to help you.

1 They have not finally decided on whether to adopt the new project.

a No...*Final decision*...

CLUE Change *finally* to an adjective, *decided* to a noun, and supply another verb.

b It.............*whether*..

CLUE The word *on* will have to disappear.

D Often there is more than one verb to be changed into the passive. Rewrite these sentences using the prompts below.

1 The management are issuing redundancy notices and they will probably sack over half of the work force.

Redundancy notices..........*are being issued*.......................... and over half the work

force ....

2 They should have forced people to stop smoking, then they would have saved more lives.

If people...*had been*...

E Does the word order change the meaning of the following sentences? If so, how?

1 Plans were drawn up to take on extra staff in the 1980s.

2 Plans were drawn up in the 1980s to take on extra staff.

3 In the 1980s plans were drawn up to take on extra staff.

Rewrite the sentence below using the following prompts. Which one would change the meaning?

4 The leader of the opposition party gave the students a talk on 'The Politics of Power' in the nineteenth century.

a The students.....*were given*...

b A talk ....

c In the nineteenth century....*followed by either*.......................

F Can you remember which tenses sound awkward if used in the passive?

Transform the following sentences. When you have done so, decide which sentence is more appropriate, or whether they are suitable for different contexts.

1 They believe that the senator is well over seventy.

a It..*is*..

b The senator...

2 They thought the old lady had been living in an abandoned shack.

a It..

b The old lady..

3 The government has already closed down several coal mines and will close down more in the near future.

Several coal mines .... and more.......................

4 The aid agency issued a statement saying that they would send emergency food supplies to the famine-stricken area.

A statement .... that emergency food supplies

....

5 They will not officially declare independence until next year.

No ....

6 Yesterday someone handed in a petition, which 300 people had signed protesting about the proposed new motorway.

A petition, which .... yesterday.

7 Various charities gave large sums of money to the refugee fund.

a Large sums of money ....

b The refugee fund ....

Summary Skills

Who Depends on Whom?

talking points

Describe the pictures and explain what the people are doing.

Who looks after (**a**) the very young and (**b**) the very old in your society?

- mothers
- fathers
- childminders / babysitters
- staff in nurseries

- granny / grandad 'sitters'
- staff in old people's homes
- sons
- daughters

Are there any alternatives to the above options?
Where do you think the responsibility for feeding, clothing, and taking care of the very young and very old should lie?

writing headings

A **The study of the population is known as demography.** The following report is about the effects of demographic changes on our society. Read each paragraph and write a brief heading for it.

EXAMPLE Paragraph **1** *The relationship between demography and politics.*

DEMOGRAPHY

1 Demography, the size of population, the speed at which it changes and its age structure, is an important factor in determining how a country's economy will perform and what economic policies a government should pursue.

2 For example, in a country where the population is growing very fast, the economy has
5 to grow quickly if the income per head is not to fall. In a country like South Africa, where the population is rising by about 2.7 per cent a year, politicians are worried about generating enough extra national income to at least match that level of increase. In Britain, however, the population has grown by less than 2 per cent over the last 10 years. Therefore almost all the economic growth in Britain during that time has meant
10 higher average income per head, even if the distribution of income is unequal.

3 It is also important to know how many of the people in the total population will be economically active. Some will be children and therefore too young to work. Some will be elderly and will have retired. It is only the group in the middle – say between the ages of 16 and 60 or 65 – who are
15 available for work.

4 The very young, schoolchildren, students and people who have retired are known as the "dependent" population, because they depend on other people or the state for their income.

5 The relationship between the number of dependent people and
20 those who are of working age is known as the "dependency ratio": the greater the proportion of dependent people, the higher the ratio. This ratio is sometimes referred to as the "welfare burden"; it increases if more people stay on at school or go to college. It will also increase if people retire earlier and live for longer after they have retired.

6 Over the last 50 years, the dependency ratio in Britain has stayed roughly the same: as a percentage of the population of working age, the dependent population has been between 55 and 65 per cent.

7 But people are now living longer. In 1931, a man's life expectancy was 60. Now it is 73. So there will be more old people who will need pensions provided for them
30 through income taxes paid by those at work.

8 The dependency ratio is not a completely accurate measure of how many non-working people need to be supported by those with jobs. After all, not every man between 16 and 65 and every woman between 16 and 60 has paid employment. In many societies it is frowned upon for married women – particularly those with young children – to
35 have jobs.

9 Attitudes have changed in recent years. Yet the "participation rate" – the proportion of women of working age who do go out to work – is still much lower than that of men. In 1989, some 94 per cent of British men aged 25 to 44 were in the labour force; the proportion of women was 72 per cent. And only one woman in eight with a child
40 under five years old had a full-time job. ■

David Brindle and Ben Laurance, *The Guardian*

B Compare your headings to the ones below. Were they similar? Now match the headings below to the appropriate paragraphs, eg Paragraph **1** = **e**.

- **a** Age range of those capable of generating income
- **b** Drawbacks of relying on the dependency ratio
- **c** Participation of the female in the work force
- **d** Explanation of the term 'dependency ratio'
- **e** The relationship between demography and politics
- **f** The effects of longevity
- **g** Comments on the dependency ratio in Britain over the last half century
- **h** Definition of the dependent population
- **i** Illustration of the effect of demography on the economy

comprehension

Look at the comprehension questions below and the answers supplied. The answers are all unsuitable. In pairs, can you decide why they are not suitable and suggest answers of your own?

1 Explain the phrase *a factor in determining* (line 2). ANSWER A factor in deciding.

2 What is meant by *income per head* (line 5)? ANSWER Income per person.

3 What does *that level of increase* (line 7) refer to? ANSWER The rise in line 6.

4 Explain what politicians are worried about in South Africa. ANSWER The national income.

5 Explain the effect of the slower population growth in Britain over the last 10 years. ANSWER Because the population has grown by less than two per cent over the last 10 years, almost all the economic growth in Britain has led to higher income per person, although the distribution is not equal.

6 What is meant by the phrase *economically active* (line 12)? ANSWER Engaged in some kind of economic activity.

7 Explain the term *dependency ratio* (line 20). ANSWER The proportion of people relying on others.

8 Why is the dependency ratio referred to as *the welfare burden* (line 22)? ANSWER Because it is a burden on the welfare state.

9 What is the effect of increased life expectancy on the dependency ratio? ANSWER Disastrous.

10 Why is the dependency ratio not always an accurate measure of those who are not *economically active*? ANSWER Because women don't always work.

11 Explain the effect changing attitudes have had on the proportion of women going out to work. ANSWER None whatsoever.

Now check your explanations of why the answers are not suitable. (See page 215.)

summary

Look at this information summarizing paragraphs 1 to 5 of the report. It tells us how demographic changes affect the economy. Link the notes using the words suggested in italics, or provide alternatives of your own, to produce a coherent summary of 100–120 words.

1 Rapid increase in population / (*result*) decrease in income per capita / (*unless*) economy grows quickly.

2 More gradual increase in population / (*lead*) increase in income per head / (*although*) benefits not universal.

3 Vital to know numbers of economically active / (*since*) / young, old rely on above for support.

4 The dependency ratio / (*namely*) / relationship between economically active and dependants / can increase dramatically / (*if*) / more people go on to further education / or take early retirement.

5 Outcome / increased dependency ratio / heavy financial burden for state to bear.

You should now have a summary on *How demographic changes affect the economy* of between 100 and 120 words.

talking points

Consider the following points. Decide which are desirable / undesirable ways to help the poorer countries of the world. Give reasons for your opinions.

- sending food parcels, clothing, etc.
- sending gifts of money
- offering loans to be repaid
- providing technical expertise
- setting up small businesses
- ensuring political stability
- letting them solve their own problems
- providing fresh water for personal and agricultural use
- building factories to create jobs
- building good roads

Have you any ideas of your own to add to the list of ways to help?

listening

A **You will hear four different people talking about helping others.** As you listen to each speaker, make brief notes next to each heading in the grid.

	Speaker 1	Speaker 2	Speaker 3	Speaker 4
Possible identity of speaker?	volunteer	pop star		
Where / When speaking?	social occ	lifeconcert TV		
Type of help offered?	food, clothing	money for lo	loans for projects	sponsoring chld
Name of organization offering help?	Save Ch Fund	Helpline	World Bank	Action Aid
Effect of help?	beneficial	reasonable	disastrous	beneficial

B **Now listen again and tick the statements which reflect what the speakers say.**

Speaker 1
1 The expedition was a gruelling experience.
2 The main fund-raising was undertaken by a children's charity.
3 When we left, the children were in good hands.
4 Some of the children were brought back in lorries.

Speaker 2
5 The appeal remains open until midnight.
6 The proceeds will go to relieving hunger.
7 Supplies often do not reach target areas.
8 If you don't help, you won't have a clear conscience.

Speaker 3
9 The information given is supposed to be confidential.
10 Poor countries are subjected to a considerable wait before receiving help.
11 Forestry management plans have helped preserve parts of the Amazonian rainforest.
12 Major dam projects in India and China will provide work for thousands of people.

Speaker 4
13 We work for an organization fighting poverty.
14 We became interested in charity work after hearing an appeal on the radio.
15 We have adopted a child who will eventually return to her own community.
16 We have pledged to the charity a fixed monthly sum to be deducted from our bank account.

Can you rephrase the other statements so that they reflect what the speakers say?
Which of the methods of helping people mentioned on the tape do you consider to be the most practical?

vocabulary

A Expressions. Match the expressions with *help* on the left with the explanations on the right.

e	1	*help someone out*	**a**	no one can change the situation
c	2	*lend a helping hand*	**b**	take what you want
a	3	*it can't be helped*	**c**	assist someone willingly
d	4	*can't help doing / can't help oneself*	**d**	can't stop oneself doing
b	5	*help yourself*	**e**	assist someone in a difficult situation

B Rewrite the following sentences using one of the expressions above.

1 He's always ready to be of assistance, when we're busy on the farm.

....

2 Every time he opens his mouth, he says something tactless.

....

3 She's tried not to lose her temper so often, but with no success.

....

4 Have some olives.

....

5 We'll just have to make the best of this dreadful weather – there's nothing we can do about it!

....

6 When I was struggling to set up my small business, he provided tremendous backup.

....

Writing

Telling a Story

introduction

The narrative question in the composition paper may simply provide you with the title of a story. You will need to think of ways of interpreting this and of coming up with a good structure.

stage 1
general approach

A Make outlines of what the story could basically be about. When answering a question, try to think of two or three different outlines and then choose the one that you think is best. Look at the composition title and the following outlines.

Write a story with the title 'The Present'.

OUTLINE 1   Woman goes to a shop to get a special present; has considerable difficulty finding it; goes to a number of shops; discovers that she needs to go to London; goes to the city and finally buys it.

OUTLINE 2   Begin with life in the present – describe how people live now, cars, cities, etc. Compare with life in the past – 100 years ago. Predict what life will be like in the future, new inventions, ways of travelling, etc. Conclude.

OUTLINE 3   Lonely old woman at home – no relatives. Someone comes to the house with a present (though it isn't one yet); it turns out to be her birthday; gives her a present; very happy.

Discuss these questions with a partner:

1   Which outline would almost certainly guarantee a Fail grade? Why?
2   Which two outlines would answer the question?
3   Which outline has the greatest potential for emotional impact?
4   Which one would run the risk of being repetitive?

B   **As quickly as possible, write three outlines for the following composition, and then discuss your ideas with your partner.**

Write a story with the title 'The Surprise'.

stage 2
brainstorming

A writer is talking about the second stage of planning the composition called *The Present*, using outline 3 above. Listen to the tape and answer the questions.

1   The writer decides to establish that it is the woman's birthday because he wants to
   A stress her age.
   B provide motivation for giving the present.
   C emphasize her emotional state.
   D have an opportunity to describe the room.

2   The writer decides that the present should come from a stranger because
   A this fits in with the theme of the woman's loneliness.
   B the woman has no family or friends.
   C the stranger does not know it is her birthday.
   D the stranger can be a man.

3   The stranger finds out it is her birthday
   A because she tells them.
   B because they ask.
   C because they see a birthday card.
   D because someone else tells them.

4   The birthday card comes from
   A the stranger.
   B someone in the woman's family.
   C a friend.
   D the old woman herself.

5   The writer decided to make the stranger
   A a postman.
   B a delivery man.
   C a woman.
   D a child.

6   In the final version of the writer's story, the stranger
   A leaves the house to go and get the woman a present.
   B originally intended to sell something to the woman.
   C picks some flowers from the woman's garden.
   D is suspicious of the woman.

stage 3
organization

A   **Before writing the composition itself, arrange the ideas into sections.** These will normally correspond with paragraphs but, with direct speech, there usually have to be new paragraphs every time the speaker changes.

Arrange the following sections of the story into the correct order.

1 ......   **2** ......   **3** ......   **4** ......   **5** ......   **6** ......

a   The young girl comes into the room and looks around – sees the birthday card on the table and reads it.
b   Emily sees a young girl coming to the house – she offers to sell some violets and Emily goes to get some money.
c   Description of the old woman – Emily – of her face, hair, age, etc.
d   The girl leaves, and Emily's mood changes from loneliness to happiness.
e   The girl decides to give her the flowers as a birthday present, and says she will come back again one day to visit.
f   She opens the letter on the floor and reads the birthday card she has sent to herself – overwhelmed by feelings of loneliness. Goes to the window.

B   Read the following composition. Check that the order you chose for the sections matches the order in the story.

Emily walked slowly across the room towards the door, and glimpsed herself in the mirror. She noticed a loose strand of white hair, and immediately pinned it back. She was not expecting any visitors today, but wanted
5   to look her best just in case. She looked impassively at her pale, wrinkled face that eighty full years had changed so much.

The single unopened envelope lay on the floor. She bent down painfully to pick it up, slowly tore it open and read
10   the words inside, which had been written by her own frail and unsteady hand: 'To Emily, with all my love on your 80th birthday'. She clasped the card and held it close to her, struggling not to be overwhelmed by her loneliness.

15   She caught sight of a small child at the gate. It was a dark young gypsy girl, wearing a ragged dress of brown and red. Emily put the card on the table and went to the door.

'Can I help you, young lady?' she enquired.

20   'Do you want to buy some violets, Mam?' she answered with a confidence beyond her years. 'They're ever so

nice.' She held out a slender arm and Emily touched her hand. 'I'll just go and get my purse.'

While Emily was away, the young girl's curiosity drew her
25   into the front room. She looked at the old photographs on the walls, and then noticed the card on the table. She walked over to the table, read it, and then returned to the doorway to wait.

'Now, how much can I give you, young lady?' Emily asked.

30   'It's your birthday, isn't it?' the young girl replied, holding out a bunch of violets. 'You can have them for a birthday present. I'm sorry it's not very much, but it's all I've got. I've got to go now, but I'll come and see you again when we pass by.'

35   'Thank you, my dear, thank you so much.'

As Emily held the violets in her trembling hand and watched the young gypsy girl running down the path, tears welled up in her eyes at the girl's warmth and human kindness. As she noticed the scent of the
40   violets, it seemed to her that this small bunch of flowers was one of the finest presents she had ever received.

writing   **Write a composition.**

Stage 1   General approach. Select one of the outlines you wrote for the composition called *The Surprise*.

Stage 2   Brainstorming. Spend at least ten minutes working out possible details, and do not worry about the order for the moment.

Stage 3   Organization. Organize the ideas into paragraphs.

Stage 4   Write the composition, using about 350 words.

Stage 5   Check your composition carefully for grammatical mistakes.

exam tip   *You can check your composition once for grammatical mistakes as soon as you have written it. However, the best time to check it is after a little time has passed, so come back to it after you have written your second composition. In the final part of the exam, go back to the second composition and check that.*

Overview 7

vocabulary

Choose the word which best completes each sentence.

1 He was .... with an extraordinary musical ability.
   A ensured **B** entrusted **C** entreated **D** endowed

2 Not being able to find my phone number is a pretty .... excuse for not contacting me.
   A fragile **B** frail **C** feeble **D** faint

3 In the days before the widespread use of ...., having an operation must have been a gruelling experience.
   A aesthetes **B** aesthetics **C** anaesthetics **D** anaesthetists

4 Before their restoration, parts of the medieval building were in a state of ....
   A debris **B** dilapidation **C** devastation **D** destruction

5 All equipment must be sterilized and germ ....
   A vacant **B** free **C** vacuous **D** vacated

6 During the war, the black market in luxury goods ....
   A flourished **B** flowered **C** bloomed **D** blossomed

7 As his aunt's only beneficiary, he came .... a fortune on her death.
   A upon **B** across **C** into **D** up against

8 As he walked along the landing, he .... himself in the mirror at the top of the stairs.
   A glimpsed **B** glanced **C** gazed **D** glared

9 He .... so much harm on the nation during his regime that it has never fully recovered.
   A indicted **B** inferred **C** induced **D** inflicted

10 Please don't .... it amiss if I make a few suggestions for improvement.
   A think **B** assume **C** take **D** judge

transformations

Finish each of the sentences in such a way that it means the same as the sentence before it.

1 Experts say that the fall in the birth rate between 1964 and 1977 caused the drop in the number of school leavers.

   The drop ...... is said to have been caused ....

2 Those at work must pay for the welfare benefits in this country.

   The welfare benefits .... must be paid ....

3 Unexpected demographic changes have often proved population forecasts wrong.

   Population forecasts ....

4 They drew up emergency plans, later abandoned, to build new cities.

   Emergency plans .... later aban ....

5 They had to make plans for extra places in schools in the 1970s.

   Plans .... caused ..... had to ....

6 They say that they have partially repaired the damage caused by the lack of technical knowledge.

   The damage ....

7 They feel that the forecasters are doing an unsatisfactory job.

   The forecasters .... are felt to be ....

8 They dispose of any unsold perishable goods at the weekends.

   Any unsold ... per ... are disp ....

9 We gave the first scheme our approval.

   The first scheme ....

   Our approval ..... was given ....

100   UNIT 7

10   They say that Napoleon died from asbestos poisoning.

It . . . .

Napoleon . . . . *is* . . . *said* . . . .

blank-filling   *Fill each of the blanks in the following sentences with a suitable word or phrase.*

1   His fortune was . . . . . . *estimated* . . . . at well over half a million pounds.

2   The wedding was . . . . *attended by* . . . . about three hundred guests.

3   . . . . *In her* . . . . heyday, Baby Doe had been a rich and attractive woman.

4   Horace Tabor tried hard . . . . *to provide* . . . . for his family's needs.

5   He made . . . . *short work* . . . . of answering the pile of letters and was able to leave early.

6   The income . . . . *per* . . . . head here is much lower than in other European countries.

7   If you don't help us now, you . . . . . . *will never* . . . . forgive yourself.

8   He has . . . . *been charged* . . . . . . with murder.

9   The concert must . . . . *have been a* . . . . success, as they raised twice as much as they expected to.

10   She is thought . . . . *to h.* . . . . born at the turn of the century.

rewriting   *For each of the sentences below, write a new sentence as similar as possible in meaning to the original sentence, but using the words given in capital letters. These words must not be altered in any way.*

1   He's tried as hard as he can.

BEST . . . . . . *done his* . . . .

2   They have narrowed the many applicants down to three.

SHORT . . *-listed* . . . .

3   I'm not very keen on gold, I much prefer silver.

RATHER . . . .

4   He made an unsuccessful attempt to buy the company.

WITHOUT . . . . . *attempted to by* . . . .

5   The long-term economic forecast implies that prospects of recovery look bleak.

ACCORDING . . *to* . . . *long term* . . . .

6   They disapprove of smoking in this restaurant.

FROWNED . . . . . *is frowned upon* . . . .

7   When she sold the jewellery at such a low price she was cheated.

RIDE . . . . *taken* . . . .

8   We'd been thinking about helping them for some time.

BACKING . . . . . *giving them* . . . .

9   Under no circumstances would I have missed the concert.

WORLD . . . . . *have missed* . . . .

10   You'll just have to take a chance!

POT . . . .

WORDS SPEAK VOLUMES

Reading

The Tower of Babel

[handwritten: Bible 1611]

1 *[handwritten: Iraq Babel]* And they said Go to, let us build us a city and a tower, whose top may reach unto heaven. And the Lord said, Behold, the people is one, and they all have one language; and this they begin to do. Go to, let us go down, and confound their language, that they may not understand one another's speech. Therefore is the name of it called Babel; because the Lord did there confound the language of all the earth.

[handwritten: 1786 – distant past   Sir William Jones   First time Sanskrit Greek Latin]

3 The Sanskrit language, whatever be its antiquity, is of a wonderful structure; more perfect than the Greek, more copious than the Latin, yet bearing to both of them a stronger affinity than could possibly have been produced by accident; so strong indeed that no philologer could examine them all three, without believing them to have sprung from some common source, which, perhaps, no longer exists.

[handwritten: p 54]   *[handwritten: well]*   *[handwritten: elegantly]*

4 And frensh she spak ful faire and fetisly, After the scole of Stratford atte Bowe, for frensh of Paris was to hir unknowe.

[handwritten: As if she had been taught   her]

5 *[handwritten: Anglo Saxon]* Beowulf maþelode, bearn Ecgþeowes: 'Ne sorga, snotor guma! Selre biđ æghwæm, *[handwritten: Beowulf]* þæt he his freond wrece, þonne he fela murne.'

2 *[handwritten: late 20]* 'The Babel fish,' said the Hitch Hiker's Guide *[handwritten: p 54]* to the Galaxy quietly, 'is small, yellow and leech-like, and is probably the oddest thing in the Universe. If you stick a Babel fish into your ear you can instantly understand anything said to you in any form of language. The poor Babel fish, by effectively removing all barriers to communication between different races and cultures, has caused more and bloodier wars than anything else in the history of creation.'

talking points

A Language change. Read through the extracts, which are written in varieties of English dating back to the eighth century. Assuming that the oldest texts are the most incomprehensible, can you match the extracts to the dates?

- Circa 8th century   Text *5*....
- Late 14th century   Text *4*...
- Early 17th century   Text *1*...
- Late 18th century   Text *3*...
- Late 20th century   Text *2*...

B Look at the following questions, then compare your answers in groups.

1 Has your language changed more or less than English over the past 1200 years?
2 How well would you have understood someone speaking your own language 500 / 1000 / 1500 years ago?
3 Do you think someone 500 years in the future would understand your language as it is spoken now?
4 Does your culture have any myths or stories to explain the diversity of language?

2 main ideas — many mod lang related to e.o.
— proto Indo European only member of older family dec Nostratic

reading　　**A** **Read the following article.** What is the main difference between the language known as proto-Indo-European and Nostratic?

The Tree of Language

The first voice spoke, and the sounds faded on the drifting wind; yet those words that were uttered at the dawn of time have echoed through the centuries. Generations upon generations of languages have flourished, and though they may themselves have died, they have left daughter languages, which in turn have split up and developed into new tongues. The tantalizing goal that linguists have set themselves is to work out the family tree of the world's myriad tongues and to delve back into the distant past to find the original source of language itself.

It was Sir William Jones, writing in 1786, who first set this branch of scholarship in train. He noted that Greek, Latin and Sanskrit, an ancient language of India, were related in a way that could not be put down to chance, and that they must have 'sprung from some common source, which, perhaps, no longer exists'. The similarities were striking: the words *Jupiter* in Latin, *Zeus pater* in Greek and *Dyaus pitar* in Sanskrit all derive from the more ancient words *deiw-os* and *p'ter* meaning 'god' and 'father' respectively.

When linguists compare languages, they look for cognate words (ie words that are the same in different languages) and at sound shifts. For example, the English word *father* has links with *Vater* in German and *pitar* in Sanskrit, and this *f – v – p* pattern is repeated in many words. By examining these and other features, linguists can not only establish links between languages, but can also reconstruct the protolanguage from which later languages have derived.

The protolanguage that has been the most painstakingly researched is proto-Indo-European, which was spoken perhaps 7,000 years ago, and which is seen as the source of a vast array of modern and ancient languages. It shows how apparently diverse languages such as English and Gujarati in fact share a common ancestry.

Linguists have been able to reconstruct the vocabulary of proto-Indo-European, and the words themselves give a unique insight into ancient cultures. For example, it contains words for domesticated animals and crops, indicating that these ancient societies were agricultural. The word for the father of the gods, *Dyeu p'ter*, reflects too upon both their anthropomorphic religious beliefs and the patriarchal nature of their societies.

Proto-Indo-European started in Transcaucasus (not far from the site of the Tower of Babel itself), and then spread eastwards and northwards, round the Caspian Sea towards Europe (see the map below). As the mainly agricultural communities migrated and separated from each other, the language changed into different dialects and then daughter languages and, by about 4,000 years ago, proto-Indo-European had split into twelve distinct languages, not all of which survived.

The full description of proto-Indo-European may once have seemed an almost impossible task; but just as it was nearing completion, the certainties it offered vanished like a mirage. For some linguists now believe that proto-Indo-European is itself merely a branch of a much larger tree of ancient languages, and that it is possible to trace the roots of language even further into the past.

Two Soviet linguists, Illych-Svitych and Dolgopolsky posited the theory that Indo-European, together with five other language families, stemmed from a far more ancient language, which they called Nostratic, and which was spoken some 15,000 years ago. Work on the reconstruction of Nostratic vocabulary has uncovered some 1,600 roots, and in many ways the words speak volumes about the lives of those ancient people. Nostratic has many words in common with proto-Indo-European, but it is the differences that are far more significant. For example, Nostratic has no words for crops and does not distinguish between domestic and wild animals. It does, however, have words for hunting, and terms like *haya*, which refers to tracking and hunting an animal for several days. This suggests that Nostratic was spoken by hunter-gatherers long before the development of agriculture, and these cultural inferences are backed by archaeological evidence.

Not all linguists agree with the Nostratic theory, but most accept that the monogenesis of language is plausible. As the history of language is uncovered layer by layer, each discovery brings new insights into the past. It may indeed be that language itself was the critical factor in defining homo sapiens and in ensuring the survival of our species, perhaps at the expense of our then contemporaries the Neanderthals, who have long been extinct. ■

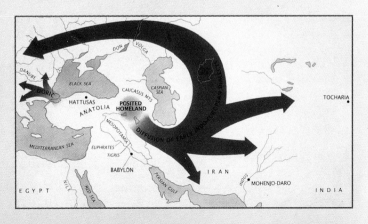

B Comprehension. Answer the following questions using your own words.

[handwritten: process of achieving it is complex & frustrating — long in turn has changed over cent]

1 Why is the goal that linguists have set themselves described as *tantalizing*?

2 What is meant by the phrase *the family tree of the world's myriad tongues* (line 14)? *[handwritten: historical rel between]*

3 What name was later given to the *common source* that Sir William Jones mentioned?

[handwritten: original —] 4 What is the meaning of the prefix *proto-* in the context of the passage? *[handwritten: Indo-European]*

5 In what ways does the vocabulary of proto-Indo-European shed light on the culture of its speakers? *[handwritten: — more farmers, culture male-dominated, religious beliefs reflection of how view of self]*

[handwritten: as farming commun moved] 6 What reason is given for the spread of proto-Indo-European?

[handwritten: it goes further back — original source] 7 In what ways has the theory of Nostratic undermined the theory of proto-Indo-European?

[handwritten: lack of words for crops, food wild animals - not look of other] 8 What specific features of Nostratic suggest it was spoken far earlier than proto-Indo-European?

9 What feature of language do the majority of linguists agree on? *[handwritten: — could be single source]*

[handwritten: primitive] 10 What does the writer imply about the role language played in evolution? *[handwritten: — in survival Neanderthals lack — extinction]*

[handwritten: discussion] **Talk about these topics, in groups.**

1 In the light of the passage, how accurate does the old story of the Tower of Babel appear to be?

2 Do you think it possible that there may have only been one language in the past?

[handwritten: h. work] 3 Look through the following list, and say which factors you think would tend to increase the speed at which a language changes into separate 'daughter' languages, and which factors would slow it down.

- strong central government
- isolation from other cultures
- literacy
- foreign tourists
- domination by a foreign power
- mass education
- television

4 Is it possible that in the future there may be only one language? What factors would enable this to happen, and what factors might prevent it?

Structure

Figures from Literature

cloze development

Dickens and his public. The following twenty nouns all appear in the critical appreciation of Charles Dickens. They are not in the right order. With the help of a dictionary if necessary, place them in suitable gaps in the text on the opposite page.

matter	diffusion
foray	dialogues
perception	success
characters	longings
novelist	abuse
responsiveness	range
culture	prophecy
relations	bread
love-affair	copyright
champion	adaptations

Young Dickens enjoyed a rocket-like ascent into the favour of the British reading public with the circulation of *Pickwick Papers* in 1836. He magnificently disproved a (**1**) prophecy that his fame would disappear just as quickly as it had come. He remained until his death 34 years later far and away the most popular (**2**) novelist the English-speaking world had ever known, so much so that Trollope declared that the (**3**) success of Dickens' books "has been so different from that which is expected of ordinary novels that it has resembled in its nature the sales of legs of mutton or loaves of (**4**) bread ".

Besides this tremendous "consumption" of the novels there was also a great (**5**) diffusion of them through innumerable dramatic (**6**) adaptations (nearly all completely unauthorised, the (**7**) copyright laws being then much weaker). Dickens's great comic (**8**) characters , like Mr Pickwick, gave huge delight and many phrases from their (**9**) dialogue passed into the language. But above and beyond such eager (**10**) responsiveness to his art there existed also what Dickens called "that relationship personally affectionate and like no other man's" which he enjoyed with the public. This had its basis in the widespread (**11**) perception of him as a great (**12**) champion of the poor and oppressed against all forms of injustice and (**13**) abuse of power.

Dickens' (**14**) love affair with the public was at its most intense during the sensationally successful Public Readings from his own works that he undertook throughout Great Britain (with one equally successful American (**15**) foray) during the last 12 years of his life. The story of his love-life and, indeed, of all his close emotional (**16**) relations with women, is a good deal more complex and disappointment-shadowed than that of his relations with the public.

Yet, out of his non-understanding and also his needs and fears, his disappointments and his (**17**) longings , Dickens created an extraordinary (**18**) range and variety of female characters who live in our minds and in our (**19**) culture , in all their strangeness and distinctiveness, in a way that no other female characters created by Victorian novelists do, no (**20**) matter how well those writers may have understood women. ■

language study

A Emphasis. Read the following sentences from the text.

1 *But above and beyond such eager responsiveness to his art there existed also what Dickens called 'that relationship personally affectionate and like no other man's' which he enjoyed with the public.*

2 *Yet, out of his non-understanding and also his needs and fears, his disappointments and his longings, Dickens created an extraordinary range and variety of female characters.*

Sentences like these are often more dramatic and emphatic than those which follow normal word order.

B The following section looks at different ways of creating emphasis.

1 Stress. In spoken English, it is possible to emphasize certain parts of a sentence simply by using stress. Underline the words you would stress in the following sentences to emphasize the information in brackets.

a I have read most of Dickens' novels. (but you haven't)
b I have read most of Dickens' novels. (you are wrong to say that I haven't)
c I have read most of Dickens' novels. (but not all of them)
d I have read most of Dickens' novels. (but I haven't read much by George Eliot)
e I have read most of Dickens' novels. (but not his letters or other writings)

exam tip

Sometimes you may wish to emphasize certain words or phrases when you are writing a composition. Do not use capital letters or underlining to do this. Instead, use suitably formal cleft sentences or other variations of the words to achieve the effect you want.

2 Cleft (ie divided) sentences can also help to convey emphasis.

a It is possible to emphasize certain parts of a sentence by using the word *It*. What difference of focus is there in each of the following pairs of sentences?

Dickens captured the imagination of Victorian England.
It was Dickens who captured the imagination of Victorian England.

Dickens devoted so much time to writing because his personal life was unhappy.
It was because his personal life was unhappy that Dickens devoted so much time to writing.

Dickens published Pickwick Papers in 1836.
It was in 1836 that Dickens published Pickwick Papers.

b *What*, meaning 'the thing that', can also be used to add emphasis. For example, the sentence *Critics have always admired Dickens' <u>style</u>* could be rephrased as follows:

What critics have always admired is Dickens' style.
or: *Dickens' style is what critics have always admired.*

c It is possible to focus on an action by using *what* + subject + *do* + *be* + infinitive with or without *to*. For example:

He wanted to popularize his books, so what he did was (to) travel round the country.

d The word *all*, meaning 'the only thing that', can be used in a similar way to **c** to emphasize that a particular action is the only one that is performed.

Our literature lessons were rather dull. All we did was read the books out loud round the class.

All + subject + verb + *be* can also be used to focus on the complement, as in:

I went to a bookshop to look for a first edition, but all I found was a second-hand paperback.

C **Practice.** Transform the following sentences.

1 I wasn't in the office yesterday, so you must have spoken to my assistant.

I wasn't in the office yesterday, so it must ....

2 I can't understand why you didn't come and see me earlier.

What...

3 The doctor said that I wasn't ill and that I just needed a good holiday.

The doctor said that I wasn't ill and that all ....

4 It was the busy main road that put us off buying the house.

What...

5 She hardly sees her husband. He spends his whole time working.

She hardly ever sees her husband. All he ....

6 She wouldn't have been upset if you hadn't lied about your past.

It...

7 He stole a Mercedes because he knew he would never be able to afford one.

He knew he would never be able to afford a Mercedes, so what ....

8 I've no idea why she's crying. I just smiled at her.

I've no idea why she's crying. All ....

9 What I find irritating is his arrogance.

It...

10 I didn't realize we had been at school together until he mentioned his surname.

It was only ....

vocabulary

A Negative prefixes. In the passage above there was the word *innumerable*. The prefix *in-*, like *ir-* before 'r', *il-* before 'l', and *im-* before 'm', 'p' and 'b' can mean 'no', 'not', 'without' or 'non'. Match the adjectives on the left to the explanations on the right.

b **1** *inauspicious*   **a** not suitable
e **2** *implausible*   **b** not favourable
i **3** *inadvertent*   **c** cannot be damaged / hurt
j **4** *immutable*   **d** not fit to be eaten
f **5** *incessant*   **e** not credible
a **6** *inappropriate*   **f** never stopping
h **7** *incoherent*   **g** cannot be erased
g **8** *indelible*   **h** cannot be understood
k **9** *illogical*   **i** not intentional
d **10** *inedible*   **j** cannot be changed
c **11** *invulnerable*   **k** not logical
l **12** *irreverent*   **l** showing no respect

Which of the adjectives can be used in modern English without a prefix? For example, *auspicious* and *plausible* are acceptable but *cessant* is not.

B Expressions. Here are some idioms connected with reading and words. One word from each expression is missing, but the correct explanation is on the left. Fill in the blanks with the correct words from below.

mince   in   for   lost   perfect   take   lines

1 regard something as being known   ...take... it as read

2 understand what is implicit but not necessarily explicit   read between the ...lines...

3 verbatim   word ...for... word

4 briefly   ...in... a word

5 to know the lines of a speech by heart   word ...perfect...

6 speak freely or directly   not to ~~be lost for~~ mince words

7 not know what to say   ...lost... for words

Now complete the following sentences using the idioms on the right, making any necessary changes.

1 My interview with the policeman took longer than I had thought because he wanted to copy down my statement ...word for word... .

2 My answer, ...in a word..., is no.

3 I'm extremely angry with you and I'm not going to ...mince... . I thought your behaviour was absolutely disgraceful.

4 ...Reading between the lines..., I sensed that she was trying to tell me that she was having problems at home.

5 He read the speech again and again until he was absolutely sure that he was ...word perfect...

6 When she was told she had won the prize she was ...lost for words..., and tears welled up in her eyes.

7 I don't think we need to put 'Informal' on the invitations – most people will ...take it as read...

Reading between the Lines

Read the introductions to the reviews of these four books. Decide which book you would most like to read and explain why. What are the ingredients of a 'best seller'? *NB*

1 Polish king who lost his castle and his country

Elected royalty had its problems, concludes **J. H. Plumb**

THIS is a remarkable book, not only for the story it tells; even more impressive is the skill with which it is told. The complexities of Polish history are immense, as entangling as the Amazon delta and could so easily be too daunting for the average reader.

THE LAST KING OF POLAND
by Adam Zamoyski
Jonathan Cape £25, 550 pages

pyre for burning corpse

3 A great civic builder

James Joll on the work of the Victorian architect Alfred Waterhouse

ACCORDING to a recent poll, Alfred Waterhouse enjoys a greater reputation than any of his fellow goths and the emergence of the Natural History Museum, one of his finest works, from decades of grime has reinforced his popularity with the public.

ALFRED WATERHOUSE
1830-1905: BIOGRAPHY OF A PRACTICE
by Colin Cunningham and Prudence Waterhouse
Oxford £80 + illustrations

beginner or novice

2 Fire Power

IN the ancient philosophies of China, India and Greece, fire was regarded as a living spirit, one of the primal elements, of which the world was composed. In certain of these civilisations the ancient philosophy of fire still survives – in the Hindu funeral pyre, for example, as compared with our hygienically out-of-sight cremations.

FIRE AND CIVILISATION
by Johan Goudsbloom
Allen Lane £20, 247 pages

play with words

4 Travels with the literati

Mark Cocker has come up with what sounds like a good subject after his workmanlike tyro biography of Richard Meinertzhagen. *Loneliness and Time* sets out to be a study of – a meditation on the function of – British "travel writing" in this century.

LONELINESS AND TIME
by Mark Cocker
Secker & Warburg £17.99, 294 pages

How does each newspaper title compare with orig of book
Why newspaper should have written under

Read the article on page 109 and decide which sentence best sums up the overall point the writer is trying to make.

ok, but narrow

A There is nothing wrong with the teaching of reading in the early stages of education.
B The reasons put forward for the poor teaching of reading are unfounded.
C Unless we widen the scope of our reading materials, reading standards are unlikely to improve.
incorrect **D** Special training is needed to teach younger pupils how to read.

These words and phrases appeared in the article. Try to explain them in your own words according to how they are used in the text.

p 5⁹⁰

1 hopelessly deficient in their command of English (line 9)
2 The latest panic was prompted by ... a dubious test (line 14)
3 No wonder it was castigated for intellectual sloppiness (line 17)
4 illuminate reading problems (line 20)
5 contrary to much printed panic (line 41)
6 grapple with ideas (line 49)
7 hit a text (line 57)
8 baffled when it does not (line 59)
9 In the articulation of argument (line 79)
10 inhabit (line 92)
11 require a clear thread of reading tuition (line 103)

Fact and reading fiction

THE notion that reading is one of the most important keys to educational success is agreed by all: newspaper critics, devoted teachers and parents. But
5 what is happening to standards? Employers are critical: "It is a great surprise and disappointment to us to find that our young employees are so hopelessly deficient in their command of
10 English." Many may long for the golden days, but that quotation *was* from those days – 1921! The complaints of today are remarkably like those of the past.

The latest panic was prompted by a
15 very limited study by a group of educational psychologists using a dubious test. No wonder it was castigated for intellectual sloppiness. Yet there are many detailed research
20 studies that illuminate reading problems. In May it was shown that the more lead, aluminium or zinc in a child's body as tested by hair or saliva tests, the lower the reading scores. Did that get widely
25 reported?

Other research focused on left- and right-handedness. Fascinatingly, the researchers found that there is a connection between reading skills and
30 skill with the use of the left or right hands: children with either a very strong right- or a very strong left-hand skill are likely to have poorer reading skills. Did that get widely reported?
35 The same fears are repeated often:

"But are they being taught to read?" The worries appear to be misdirected. Yes, there are serious doubts about whether the present curriculum is helping
40 effective reading, but it is not the early stages that are weak. Nor is it, contrary to much printed panic, because of too little teaching of phonics. It is because we stop developing reading skills except
45 in the teaching of literature. We are extraordinarily good at teaching fiction. Reading for learning is something different but equally important. This is how we grapple with ideas, arguments
50 and the discourse of Higher Education.

Fiction, marvellous as it is as an art form, is a poor training for the reading of non-narrative. The story carries the reader along and stimulates the
55 understanding of the text without too much conscious effort. When those pupil-readers hit a text explaining facts or arguments, they expect the same thing to work and are disappointed and baffled
60 when it does not.

This is partly due to sentence length and structure: the average sentence in fiction (according to one US computer analysis) is as low as 11 words, whereas
65 in learned and scientific writing sentences average 21 words. They are often of a different structure to those in stories, with far more subordinate clauses. The paragraphs are also
70 different: fiction keeps rolling. Non-

fiction writing has ideas followed by arguments, followed by examples, before returning to a second argument. Seeing the structure of a non-narrative
75 paragraph is to see the pattern of the argument and reading fiction will not help a pupil develop this skill.

The words used are equally different. In the articulation of argument,
80 "signal words" are very important: *however, despite, accordingly, although, since, while.* Those last two confuse pupils. They have met them mostly as words concerned with time. In non-
85 narrative, however, they demonstrate the argument.

The key conceptual words are often derived from Latin or Greek, and our curriculum rarely gives access to even a
90 modest understanding of their meanings and sentence patterns. Science and medicine inhabit a world-wide "constructed" vocabulary, derived from the ancient western world. The
95 relationship between the spelling of words like "haematology" and how young people come to pronounce them requires further study.

What is certain is that our pupils will
100 not have access to higher education without specific reading tuition in non-narrative. From primary to secondary, all our curriculum plans require a clear thread of reading tuition.
105 Most reading for learning is non-fiction; our best higher reading teaching is through literature. It is this mismatch between need and offer that is at the heart of the difficulties of learning to
110 read and reading to learn. The reading aspect of the curriculum starts well but needs development and broadening during a pupil's education.

Michael Morland, *The Guardian*

---

summary 2

A In the article, the reader is exposed to the following points.

A Suggested explanations as to why students find reading difficult.
B Fallacious arguments as to why this is so.
C Suggestions as to how we can deal with the problem.

Read the passage again and underline the information which could be included in each section, labelling each piece of information **A**, **B**, or **C**. You should be able to find nine points for **A**, two points for **B** and two for **C**.

B Now link the nine points you marked A above to form a paragraph. Write about 90 to 100 words on why pupils find reading difficult. Remember to use the connectors introduced on page 66.

'If they can't
understand
English, just
shout at them
a bit louder'

speaking

A **Work in groups to discuss the answers to these questions.**

1 Describe the men in the picture and what is going on.
2 Have you had any personal experience of such behaviour by foreigners visiting your country?
3 How, in general, do people react to foreign tourists who try and speak your own language?
4 What reception would you get if you travelled abroad and could only speak your own language? Would you get different reactions in different countries?

B **Ranking.** Your class has decided that, having reached such a high standard of English, it is time to start learning a completely new language. In pairs or small groups, list the following criteria in order of importance so that you have a framework for selecting your next language.

lang in which people of diff nat. can commun.

- total number of native speakers
- literary tradition
- usefulness in business and commerce
- simple to learn

- usefulness as lingua franca
- economic and political power of host nation(s)
- attractiveness of host nation(s) as tourist destination
- prevalence of the language in entertainment / media

Having decided which criteria are important, which language would you choose?

C **Read the following situation.** You are called in to advise the countries of the English-speaking world on the adoption of a common foreign language that all the countries would teach in their schools. Which of the following languages would you suggest and why?

- Esperanto (an artificial, simple and totally regular language)
- Latin
- Japanese

- French
- Spanish
- your own language (if it is not one of the above)
- another language

listening 1

Wordwatch. Say if the following statements are true or false.

1 *Wordwatch* is a department in a large publishing and broadcasting company. T/F
2 The *Guide* was developed as a result of the company's publishing activities. T/F
3 Amanda says the furore over the 'split infinitive' is relatively recent. T/F
4 According to Amanda, the *Guide*'s advice on split infinitives is controversial. T/F
5 Amanda says that the *Guide*'s advice on the use of the words 'fewer' and 'less' has changed to reflect current usage. T/F
6 The interviewer says *Wordwatch* might be accused of being too liberal in its approach to language. T/F
7 Amanda says that *Wordwatch* aims to set an internationally acceptable standard of English. T/F
8 According to Amanda, the *Guide* takes a very progressive and liberal approach to language. T/F

listening 2

Word games. Listen to the passage and choose the best answer.

1 Oliver's attitude towards Christmas is that
   A the same films tend to get shown every year.
   B it has not changed fundamentally.
   C none of the old traditions are kept up.
   D the atmosphere has changed.

2 One feature of the drawing game that Emily describes is that
   A there need to be six players.
   B the contestants do not need to be good at drawing.
   C players need to have an extensive vocabulary.
   D no talking is allowed until the picture is finished.

3 In the 'I like' game described by Janet, the connections are
   A based on spelling.
   B not necessarily linguistic.
   C statements which have to be true.
   D based on the meanings of words.

4 In the last game that is described, the players
   A have to stop as soon as a word has been spelled.
   B can only add a letter to the beginning or end of the set.
   C are allowed to use the letters in a set in any order.
   D must think of words that begin with the set of letters.

picture charades

A Introduction. Match the following words and phrases to the drawings below.

a blank stare   *a brainstorm*   *hairy chest*

1

2
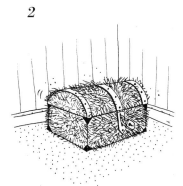

3

Now work out what the following pictures represent.

4

5

6

skeleton key
to kill time
a fairy tale   background
to look like drowned rat
a stuffed shirt
p 61

couch potato
slipped disc
storm in a T-cup
mother tongue
time bomb

B Game. Follow the rules of the game as explained in the listening passage. There are two teams, **Team A** and **Team B**.

TEAM A and **TEAM B.** Choose some expressions that you have learned in the book so far, or use the suggestions supplied by your teacher, which revise idioms and expressions from previous units.
Copy each idiom or expression onto a separate piece of paper. When it is the other team's turn, give one of the players an expression to draw. Do not allow him / her to show the piece of paper to other members in the team. If the team can guess the word from the player's drawing within two minutes, they gain a point. If not, you gain a point.

introduction

In Unit 1, you studied the simplest style of writing an argument. It consisted of an introduction, a number of paragraphs for the proposition, a number of paragraphs against the proposition, and a final paragraph that drew a balanced conclusion.

The topic-based structure, however, is more complex, and therefore needs additional linguistic features to make the argument crystal clear to the reader. You need to identify a number of important issues that the question raises and discuss each of these in turn before coming to the conclusion.

sample composition

Assess the following composition in terms of relevance, ideas and organization.

The best international language would be an artificial one. Discuss.

Firstly, what do we mean by best? And what is the point of an international language anyway? The answer is communication, business, making travel easier, making education widely available.

What artificial languages are there? Esperanto and a few others. What are their advantages? They are easy to learn, but who for? If they are based on western languages, they are still very difficult for the Japanese, so would they be international anyway? A language needs a nation. Without it it will wither and die. What is wrong with languages like English, French, Spanish which are already widely spoken? Partly that they are difficult to learn, with their spelling, irregular verbs and so on. However, they have a large number of speakers already.

How are you going to persuade people to learn this new language? Who is going to do it? Nobody. People follow trends. If everyone is learning Russian, everyone else will. It's also impractical because language is changing, almost daily. There are new words, words change their meaning, slang develops, words are borrowed from other languages. What are the

problems of not having an international language? There is considerable expense, as at the United Nations with all its interpreters, and a lack of communication between people, misunderstandings, and difficulty with trade and travel.

But language is also a part of culture – its people, traditions, even modes of thought. This would be lost if everyone learned a single language. The language choice would inevitably change anyway. At various times in the past it has been Latin, then French. Now it is mainly English.

It is a misconception based upon the idea that language is a static thing that can be regulated. There may be a role for simplifying some of the more bizarre aspects of real languages, simpler spelling or writing for example, but these tend to develop naturally. An artificial language is a language without a heart. Esperanto may have lots of 'works of literature' translated but these are not the real thing. One of the real incentives of language learning is to be able to use it as a means of communication.

link words

A Read the composition on page 113, which is the result of using the notes from the same brainstorming session. This time, the information has been selected and organized and the sentences are more complex.

Match the topics of each of the paragraphs with the following headings:

a the relative difficulty of learning artificial and natural languages
b final decision as to whether an artificial language would be better than a natural one
c qualities needed by a language in order to be successful
d the current status of artificial and natural languages
e practical considerations of adopting an artificial international language

B Complete the composition by filling in the missing words from the following list.

while   whereas   just as   also   because   therefore   at first glance
despite   unlike   however

There is and always has been a need for an international language, and historically languages have competed with each other for this role. The current leader in the field is English, with other European languages following behind, but artificial languages such as Esperanto are nowhere in sight.

(1) *At first glance* ...., this might seem surprising, as the advantage of artificial languages is that they are supposed to be simple to learn. (2) *Unlike* ...... natural languages, there are no irregular verbs, the grammar is extremely simple, and the vocabulary has a large number of words that appear to be easy to learn. However, (3) *while/whereas* ...... this may be true for speakers of European languages, it is by no means true for speakers of a language like Japanese, which is entirely different. Artificial languages are therefore not suitable for everyone, because they are based only on European languages.

There would (4) *also* .... be practical problems if an artificial language was chosen as an international means of communication. There is no official organization or government that could make such a decision, (5) *because* ...... as far as languages are concerned, success breeds success. Most people want to learn a language such as English, Spanish or French that is already widely spoken, and popular languages

continually attract new learners. It would (6) *therefore* ...... not be realistic for governments to impose an artificial language with almost no speakers, because people would simply refuse to learn it.

Ultimately, (7) *however* ...., the main problem with an artificial language is related to the nature of language itself. An artificial language is simply a set of words with no heart, no native speakers and no traditions, (8) *whereas/while* ...... a living language is dynamic. Living languages can change and develop. They have literary traditions and are capable of growing and adopting new words and ideas. Languages are aggressive too, and take over and kill off minority ones, (9) *just as* .... English has almost eliminated Gaelic. In these circumstances, an artificial language could never hope to survive.

To sum up, although the current international languages are not ideal, there is no evidence that artificial languages would be any better. (10) *Despite* .... their deceptive simplicity, it would be almost impossible to make everyone learn one, and it would probably not survive unchanged anyway. It is possible that English will continue to dominate and may one day be a completely international second language, but whatever happens, the process will be determined by the speakers, and will not be under political control.

writing

Write a composition of about 350 words on the following:

Discuss the view that television is making literature increasingly irrelevant in the modern world.

Stage 1 General approach. Choose the topic-based mode, as in the example above.

exam tip

You can use direct questions when you are planning your composition, but do not use them when writing the composition itself. Your job is to answer the questions, not to ask them.

Stage 2 Brainstorming. Ask yourself as many questions about the topic as you can and jot down any thoughts you have in any order.

Stage 3 Organization. Re-read the title carefully. It is about television and literature, not about whether or not television is a good thing. Sort your main topic thoughts into three or four areas that will form the basis of your composition.

Stage 4 Writing. Imagine the reader is not as intelligent as you. Make your argument as clear as possible. Begin each paragraph with a strong, clear statement like the sample composition.

Stage 5 Checking. Concentrate in particular on the first sentence of each paragraph.

- purpose of lit - why it is relevant (develops the intellect) broadens exp
- purpose of lit taken over by TV. - passing time + entertainment intellect
- purpose of lit not been taken over by lit - active dev intellect

Overview 8

Choose the word which best completes each sentence.

1 Linguists have discovered that Nostratic and proto-Indo-European have many words in

. . . .

A relation   **B** affinity   **C** common   **D** conjunction

2 I have told her that I am not going to go ahead with my plans . . . . she may think.

A whether   **B** whatever   **C** however   **D** despite

3 The best way of writing a composition in a foreign language is to try and write . . . . thinking in your own language.

A unless   **B** except   **C** without   **D** apart from

4 Recent EC legislation is aimed at removing trade . . . . between member states.

A barriers   **B** walls   **C** boundaries   **D** fences

5 The tabloid newspapers, which are engaged in a . . . . war, are all trying to print the most sensational stories to improve sales.

A press   **B** paper   **C** trading   **D** circulation

6 However good Schoenberg . . . . have been, I still find his modern music very difficult to appreciate.

A could   **B** may   **C** should   **D** would

7 There are very few artists who have . . . . much material success in their own lifetimes.

A enjoyed   **B** disposed   **C** possessed   **D** realized

8 No . . . . how hard he tries, he always seems to make the same grammatical mistakes.

A importance   **B** effect   **C** matter   **D** question

9 Doctors advise people who are deficient . . . . Vitamin C to eat more fruit and vegetables.

A from   **B** of   **C** in   **D** for

10 Life expectancy in the third world is relatively short, ... in the western world it has increased substantially.

A whereas   **B** unlike   **C** however   **D** contrary

11 Although he spoke slowly, I found it difficult at times to follow the . . . . of his argument.

A spool   **B** track   **C** thread   **D** path

12 I copied down . . . . the directions that he gave me.

A verbatim   **B** by word   **C** by heart   **D** finely

13 The professor noticed that the student's essay . . . . a strong resemblance to an article he had seen published in a journal.

A bore   **B** held   **C** carried   **D** contained

14 The murder weapon was eventually found after a . . . . search of the field, which lasted several days.

A vigilant   **B** particular   **C** painstaking   **D** circumspect

15 The similarities between all three crimes were such that they could not be . . . . down to chance.

A set   **B** put   **C** laid   **D** taken

Fill each of the blanks in the following sentences with a suitable word or phrase.

1 If you read between the . . . . lines, you'll see that he's trying to tell us that he is being bullied at school.

2 No ...*wonder*.......................... angry with you; after all, you did take his car without even asking him.

3 Excellent as *he was* ~~*had been chosen*~~ ...... a player, he made a very poor manager of the football club.

4 The factory manager asked all the employees to see if they could come ...*up...with*..... .... some ideas as to how the problem could be solved.

5 He is ......*far a away*............... away the most successful pop singer of his generation.

6 No ....*matter*.........*how*......... organized I try to be, I never seem to be able to find the documents I need.

7 It .....*was...as*................... an actor that Ronald Reagan first became famous.

8 I'd forgotten my key so what I ....*did...was*..................... to go round to the neighbours to borrow theirs.

9 I think you can ....*take it as*............... read that you ought to wear formal dress – after all, it is a wedding.

10 As ....*far...as*................. am concerned, you can come home whenever you like.

transformations

Finish each of the following sentences in such a way that it means exactly the same as the sentence before it.

1 Mrs Thatcher was known as the 'Iron Lady'.

It ....

2 Monday was the day when the letter arrived.

It.....*was Mon that I ~~on~~ Mon when*.....................

3 Many school leavers speak English inadequately.

Many school leavers do not have an...*ad ~~text~~ command*.......................

4 Although the papers claim that they are going to get divorced, they are not.

Contrary....*to what the papers claim*....................

5 His memory gradually failed as he grew old.

The older...*he got*...............................

6 Vitamin intake and intelligence are not connected.

There.....*is no connection*........................

7 The fire led to the setting up of a public enquiry.

As a ....

8 You will still have to pay the mechanic even if the car cannot be repaired.

Whether.....*the car is*.............................

9 It was his lack of confidence that surprised me.

What ..*surprised*.................................

10 We would have had a nice party if he hadn't behaved so badly.

It was his...*bad behav*...............................

9

THE CALL OF THE WILD

Reading

Wild Men and Beasts

talking points

Look at the picture then answer the questions.

cave

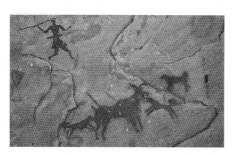

- Can you describe the picture?
- What does it depict?
- Where might it be found?
- How old do you think it is?
- What does it tell you about the people who painted it?

reading

p b 3

A **Fernand Braudel's writing technique is described as *pointilliste*.** This technique blends together myriads of separate details from different people's lives, to give an overall picture of the world these people inhabit. How many detailed descriptions can you find in the extract on page 117?

B **Reference devices.** What do the words underlined refer to in the passage?

1 <u>They</u> are the main thing (line 2) *civilizations*
2 And <u>each</u> has its own plants (line 17) *culture*
3 the civilized who might wish to escape <u>there</u> (line 32)
4 <u>This</u> was all too true (line 55) *empty castle / castman forest*

5 <u>They</u> were flanked by (line 62)
6 <u>its</u> mountains (line 98)
7 <u>they</u> multiplied (line 104)

short-sighted / unable to look beyond

C **Comprehension.** In small groups, discuss the answers to the following questions.

1 What is the author's implied criticism in seeing *only the civilizations* of the world?
2 Why might a civilized view of ancient peasant agriculture be somewhat different from reality?
3 What atmosphere does the writer create with his references to man and animals? *romantic*
4 Why should both the hunter and the hunted flee what they saw? *fear; kill or be k.*
5 In what way could the wolves be considered indicative of social conditions?
6 How successful is the *pointilliste* technique? *take reader into past – recreate*

400 animals

vocabulary

A **The words on the left appeared in the passage.** Think of the difference between these words and those on the right, then choose one to complete the sentences below.

a expended *spent time money energy*   expanded *increase in size*   **e** domain *under rule, inf*   dominion *in control of authority*
b invading *enter – subtle*   pervading *pervading*   **f** roamed *ramble wonder*   combed
c lurked   larked   **g** aroused *awakened*   arose
d flanked *both sides*   franked *off stamp*   **h** lapse *trans*   collapse

Furtive

1 The index was ...*expan*... to include all the reference notes.
2 The ..*inve*.... army crossed the frontier under cover of darkness.
3 A strange dark shape ..*lurk*..... in the shadows.
4 The President was ..*flank*.... by two bodyguards.
5 The North Pole is the ..*domain*... of the polar bear.
6 They ..*comb*... the countryside in vain but they found no trace of the missing vehicle.
7 The dispute ..*arose*.... when rival armies laid claim to the same territory.
8 After the ..*collapse*... of the negotiations, conciliation is unlikely.

slight error / slip

The Saga of Man and Animals

It is always very tempting to see only the civilizations. They are the main thing. Besides, they expended a vast amount of skill on rediscovering their former selves, their tools, costumes, houses, practices, even their traditional songs. Their museums are there to be visited. Every culture has its own distinctive features: Chinese windmills turn horizontally; in Istanbul, the scissors have hollow blades, and the luxury spoons are made of wood from the pepper plant; Japanese and Chinese anvils are different from ours; not one nail was used to build the boats on the Red Sea and the Persian Gulf, and so on. And each has its own plants, domestic animals (or at any rate its own way of treating them), its characteristic houses, its own foods. The mere smell of cooking can evoke a whole civilization.

However, not all the beauty of the world nor all the salt of the earth was contained in the civilizations. Outside them, encircling their frontiers and sometimes even invading their territory, lurked primitive life, and the empty, echoing wastelands.

Here was played out the saga of man and the animals, the golden legend of ancient peasant agriculture, a paradise in the eyes of the civilized who might wish to escape there from the constraints of urban life.

Wherever human settlement is sparse, wild animals multiply, even if the land seems poor or useless. They are to be found wherever man is not. Travellers' tales are full of savage beasts. One seventeenth-century account describes tigers prowling round Asian villages and towns, and swimming out into the Ganges delta to surprise fishermen asleep in their boats. The ground around the mountain hamlets in the Far East is still cleared even today to keep the man-eaters at a distance. No one feels safe after nightfall, not even inside a house. One man went out of his hut in a small town near Canton and was carried off by a tiger. A fourteenth-century Chinese painting represents an enormous tiger painted pink, like some pet monster, amongst the flowering branches of fruit trees. This was all too true throughout the Far East.

Siam consisted of the valley of the River Menam; its waters were alive with rows of houses on piles, bazaars, families crowded on to boats; on its banks stood two or three towns, including the capital. They were flanked by rice fields and then by great forests where the water penetrated vast expanses. The rare patches of forest that were permanently free from water harboured tigers and wild elephants (and, according to Kämpfer, even chamois). There were lions in Ethiopia, North Africa and Persia. Crocodiles swarmed in the rivers of the Philippines, wild boar on the coastal plains of Sumatra, India and the Persian plateaux; wild horses were regularly hunted and lassoed, north of Peking. Wild dogs howling in the mountains of Trebizond kept Gemelli Careri awake. The wildlife of Guinea included small cows which were treated as game.

However, both hunter and hunted took flight at the sight of bands of elephants and hippopotamuses, 'sea-horses' that ravaged 'the fields of rice, millet, and other vegetables' in the same regions. 'One sometimes sees troupes of three or four hundred at a time.' And in the vast expanses of southern Africa, which stretched empty and unpopulated north of the Cape of Good Hope, there could be seen alongside the very few men 'who lived more like beasts than human beings', many 'savage' animals – lions and elephants said to be the biggest in the world.

The whole of Europe, from the Urals to the Straits of Gibraltar, was the domain of wolves, and bears roamed in all its mountains. The omnipresence of wolves and the attention they aroused make wolf-hunting an index of the health of the countryside, and even of the towns, and of the character of the year gone by, a lapse in vigilance, an economic setback, a rough winter, and they multiplied. ●

B All these words appeared in the passage. In the context of their meaning in the passage, which are natural, geographical features and which are man-made?

1	blades (l. 11)	4	frontiers (l. 25)	7	hamlets (l. 45)	10	banks (l. 60)	13	cape (l. 89)
2	anvil (l. 14)	5	wastelands (l. 28)	8	piles (l. 59)	11	plains (l. 72)	14	straits (l. 96)
3	gulf (l. 16)	6	delta (l. 43)	9	bazaars (l. 59)	12	plateaux (l. 73)		

C The writer refers to many animals – generally and specifically. Match the animals on the right with his descriptions on the left then decide which animals match our modern concepts of these words. Some descriptions may be used for more than one kind of animal.

1	wild animals	a	tigers	g	horses
2	savage beasts	b	elephants	h	dogs
3	man-eaters	c	chamois	i	cows
4	monster	d	lions	j	hippopotamuses
5	game	e	crocodiles	k	wolves
6	sea-horses	f	boars		

D Expressions. *To play out* is used in the passage to mean 'to act out'. Match the following expressions with *play* to the explanations on the right.

e	**1**	*child's play*	**a** keep someone in suspense
b	**2**	*foul play*	**b** dirty dealings / murder
g	**3**	*play havoc with*	**c** pretend to co-operate with
f	**4**	*play down*	**d** involve yourself in a dangerous situation
d	**5**	*play with fire*	**e** a very easy task
a	**6**	*play cat and mouse with*	**f** pretend something is less important than it is
h	**7**	*play it by ear*	**g** throw into confusion
c	**8**	*play along with*	**h** act according to the situation

E Now use an expression with *play* in its correct form to complete the sentences below.

1 I don't agree with his policies but I'm going to *play along with* them for now.

2 Although the death looked accidental, the police suspect *foul play* .

3 As we have no idea what's going to happen, we'll just have to *play it by ear* .

4 The torrential storms *played havoc with* the summer sports programme last year.

5 Using a computer is *child's play* , once you know how!

6 I wouldn't get involved in that deal if I were you – you'd be *with fire* .

7 Why don't they tell us what's going to happen to the department and stop *cat a m* us.

8 The disastrous effects of the government's new policies have been *played down* .

Structure

The Struggle for Survival

cloze development

A Look at the diagram. The missing words are given below but the letters are in the wrong order. Can you unscramble them to complete the information? One of the words is used twice.

thach   rebed   dial   defe   sourvinorac   roverbihsou

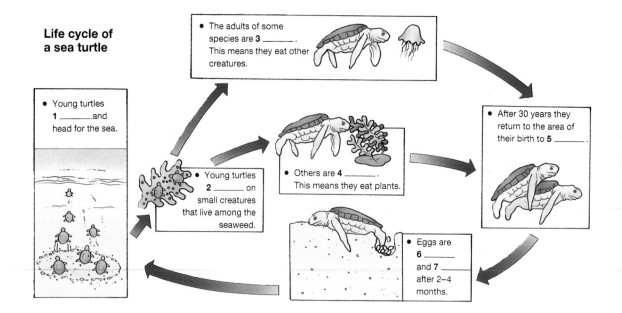

Life cycle of a sea turtle

- Young turtles **1** _____ and head for the sea.

- Young turtles **2** _____ on small creatures that live among the seaweed.

- The adults of some species are **3** _____ . This means they eat other creatures.

- Others are **4** _____ . This means they eat plants.

- After 30 years they return to the area of their birth to **5** _____ .

- Eggs are **6** _____ and **7** _____ after 2–4 months.

B Read the following passage about turtles. The very first underlined word is wrong because it should be *Unlike* instead of *Dissimilar*. Can you correct the other underlined words?

Dissimilar many other species of turtle, the red-eared terrapin (*Chrysemys scripta elegans*) is not rare. In fact, four to five million hatchlings are extorted annually from American farms. About 200,000 been sold in the United Kingdom.

5 It is ranked that as many as 90 a cent of the young terrapins die in their first year as of the poor conditions in which they are kept. Those which survive may live for twenty years and arrive the size of a dinner plate. At this staging they require a large tank with heat and specialized lighting.

10 Terrapins conduct salmonella bacteria which can poison people. This is why the sale of terrapins was banished in the United States in 1975. They are still, although, exported to the United Kingdom.

Modern turtles come from a very antique group of animals
15 that lived more 200 million years ago. At this time dinosaurs were just beginning to establish them.

Different types of turtles own interesting features: some box turtles are known to be lived for over 100 years, since other species of turtles can remain underwater for other than
20 24 hours. And the green turtle is the most prolific of all reptiles, laying as many as 28,000 eggs each year.

If unwanted pet turtles are unleashed into the wild, many will die and those which subsist will threaten the lives of native plants and animals.

vocabulary

A Adjectives. Choose one of the following adjectives to complete the sentences below.

non-native   wanted   mature   common   sparse   general   modern

1 The black rhino is no longer a .... sight in Africa.

2 *Human Resources* is a .... term of reference used instead of *personnel*.

3 Although she is a .... speaker, her English is almost perfect.

4 When the green turtle is .... it lays up to 28,000 eggs annually.

5 Encyclopaedias provide .... rather than in-depth knowledge of a range of subjects.

6 It is important to ensure that every child in the community feels .... and needed.

7 The population of some parts of Canada is ...., largely due to the inhospitable terrain.

Now find an adjective in the passage which means the opposite of those above.

B Expressions. Here are some idiomatic expressions connected with fish, ducks and water. Match them to the explanations on the right.

1 *other fish to fry*
2 *a fish out of water*
3 *plenty more fish in the sea*
4 *a big fish in a small pond*
5 *water off a duck's back*
6 *take to it like a duck to water*

a something that has no effect
b an important figure in a small organization
c out of your depth, in the wrong place
d other people or things to choose from
e like or become familiar with straight away
f more important things to do

C Complete the following sentences using one of the expressions above in its correct form.

1 She was upset when her boyfriend left her, but I assured her there were . *plenty* ....

2 I know it's not a huge corporation to work for – but it's better to be *big* ....

3 He wants me to spend all my time doing paperwork but I have ... *other* ....

4 Mark's getting on very well with his horse riding – he ... *taken* ....

5 He hates his new job. It's such a different field. He feels like ... *out* ....

6 She never listens to our suggestions – what we say is ... *water* .... to her.

conditional variants

A **Which of the following different types of conditional sentences refer to:**

- an impossible present situation?
- an imaginary past situation?
- a universal truth?
- a possible situation?
- a theoretically possible but highly unlikely situation?

1 If you are looking for a large specialized tank, you will find one in the pet shop up the road.
2 **a** If zoo animals were released into the wild, many would die.
   b If I were a turtle, I wouldn't want to lay my eggs on a crowded beach!
3 If we had visited the wildlife refuge, we would have seen some extremely rare animals.
4 If turtles are kept in unsuitable conditions, they die.

B **The sentences in A illustrate four types of conditional you already know.** Now look at sentences **1–5** below. Discuss the differences in structure and meaning between these sentences and those in **A** above. *1st*   *2nd (advice)*

2nd (unlikely) *3rd im past*

1 If your daughter wants a pet snake, she would be better off not buying a poisonous one.
2 If I were rich, I wouldn't have had to ask for money to buy my own horse. *3rd imag past*
3 If you had checked that the hotel accepted dogs, we wouldn't be without a bed for the night! *}*
4 If I had had a pet turtle when I was younger, I'm sure I would want to try and protect the *2nd* species today. *3rd imag past*   *2nd (theo poss)* *unlikely*
5 If you have bought an animal, you should look after it carefully.
   1st with (pres per)   *instead of would*

C **Sometimes *if* can be used with, or replaced by, other structures.** Consider the following:

1 **a** What does the use of *should* suggest in this sentence?
   Should you require / If you should require any further information, do not hesitate to contact me immediately.

   b Complete the following sentences, making any necessary changes.

   If help is needed urgently, dial 999.

   Should you . . . .

   If . . . .

2 **a** What does the use of *were to* + infinitive suggest in this sentence?
   If I were to give you a pet crocodile, what would you do with it?

   b Change the sentence below in the same way.

   If I disappeared tomorrow, what would you think?

   If I . . . .

3 **a** What is the effect of *Had I* in the following sentence?
   Had I known what hard work it was going to be, I wouldn't have bought them a pet.

   b Complete this sentence.

   I didn't realize how widespread rabies was in that country, so I didn't have an injection against it.

   Had . . . .

4 **a** Notice the expressions:
   If it hadn't been for (the fact that)   *Had it not been for*
   If it weren't for   *Were it not for*
   But for

   When do we use these structures?

   EXAMPLE *If it hadn't been for the fact that I had already booked the tickets, I would have cancelled the trip.* (As I had the tickets, I didn't cancel the trip.)

b Write similar sentences using this information. Think about the meaning of the sentences!

The traffic was terrible. I was late.

If it hadn't . . . .

He's partially deaf so he finds it difficult to communicate on the telephone.

Were it . . . .

D Other uses of *if*.

1 a What word follows *if* in the sentence below?
If . . . . I lived by the sea. I love the sea air.

b Transform the following sentence in the same way.

I wasn't very patient with my old dog when he was ill.

If . . . .

2 a What word could we use before *if* here for emphasis?

. . . . *if I had stayed up all night, I still wouldn't have finished the work.*

b Transform this sentence in the same way.

There's no point in my trying to please him. He still shouts at me.

Even . . . .

3 a Although the sentence below looks like a conditional, it is different. Why? What is the meaning of *if* in this sentence?
If the bell rang, she would race to see who was at the door.

b Transform this sentence in the same way.

During exam time he always revised all night.

If . . . .

4 a What is different about this sentence?
I should be most grateful if you would / could phone the office as soon as possible.

b Transform the following sentence in the same way.

Please send me a copy of your brochure.

I should . . . .

5 Other expressions can have a similar function to *if*, eg *Supposing (that)*, *Provided (that)*, *Unless* or *As long as*. Complete the sentences below, using one of these expressions. Think carefully about the meaning!

a . . . . security checks are carried out, accidents will be frequent.

b . . . . you won a huge sum of money, how would you cope with the sudden wealth?

c . . . . security checks are carried out, there should be little danger of accidents.

6 Often, mixed conditional sentences involve deduction and reasoning.

EXAMPLE *If he were going to stand for the presidency, he wouldn't have divorced his wife.*
(But he did divorce his wife, so he can't be going to stand for the presidency.)

Make a similar sentence based on this example.

He can't be at home. He promised he would phone as soon as he got back.

If . . . .

E **Now transform these sentences.** Remember you may need to make several changes.

1 It's a pity the weather was so bad last week. We could have gone camping.

If it .. *hadn't* .. for the fact that .. *the weather* ....

2 The dog was always barking at passers-by but the owner's answer was to assure them that the dog was harmless.

If .... *the dog barked* .... the owner .. *would assure* ....

3 Why didn't you tell me about the party? You know I like going to parties!

Had .. *you told me* ....

4 What a shame we didn't go by air! Think of the saving in time!

If only .. *we had gone* ....

5 Please send us a copy of your directory.

I should ....

6 A successful interview means that you will be offered a job.

Provided .. *that* ....

Unless .. *it is   you won't* ....

7 He can't be a policeman. I've never seen him wearing a uniform.

If he .. *were* .... , I .. *would* ....

The Law of Nature

talking points

Look at the pictures below.

- Describe the animals and their habitat.
- Zoos and safari parks have recently come in for a lot of criticism. Why?
- Can you think of any benefits to wild animals of being kept in a zoo or a safari park?
- What problems do wild animals face living in their natural habitats?

summary 1

A **Read the following article about zoos and people's attitudes to them.** The article contains seven paragraphs. Summarize each paragraph with a short sentence.

EXAMPLE   Paragraph **1** *Although we realize the limits of our own freedom, we are reluctant to believe that total freedom does not exist in the animal kingdom.*

The comfo...
of the cag...

Michael Robinson, The Guardian

1 ANTI-ZOO critics use a common script: "Animals in zoos are imprisoned without trial". However, "Man is born free" is sheer anthropological romanticism and we all know it, but we now apply this dictum to animals, where "Born free!" is even more unreal.

2 That mass killer, the lion, not only slaughters prey on a huge scale but also indulges in infanticide. Urban humans have become insulated from the reality of struggle and death that characterizes all life in the wild. Most of us see the biological world only in the censored electronic imagery of television. As a consequence, we imagine that the word freedom has biological significance, and fantasise about a peaceful kingdom. We think wild animals are free, happy, unstressed, stimulated and fulfilled.

3 A moment's reflection shows that this attitude is a ludicrous perversion. Life in the wild is a constant struggle for survival.

3 Reproduction in all b... handful of species is... beyond common be... profligacy is biologica... sation for the dreadf... which young perish in... (even our own). These... not die easily, in the... euthanasia, but are torn... starve to death, or waste in disease. And, of course, as animal behaviourists realise, there is another unfreedom.

4 Apart from the stress of food-finding and predator avoidance, inner compulsive drives lead to the competitive stress of territoriality or pecking orders. Such is the power of these that we coined the term "rat race" to characterise human competitive stress. Another source of irrational confusions about zoos is simple misinterpretation of behaviour and basic natural history. For example, people think that a solitary cat in a zoo is unnaturally lonely, when in nature it only consorts with its own species for a brief and violent

public institutions.

6 The allure of the animal world is indubitable. Take as an example the United States where more people go to zoos and aquariums than go to all field sports combined.

7 Ultimately, we must preserve habitats wherever we can, and restore the damaged ones. Zoo education can motivate the first process and zoo science can help the second. The careful husbandry of small populations that zoos have developed is a recipe for dealing with shrinking wild populations. Zoos may have been Victorian in their flowering but they are as essential to our future as Victorian free education. ■

Now compare your answers with those of a partner.

B **Points of view.** Some paragraphs contain differing points of view, others do not. Which paragraphs put forward both sides of the coin?

comprehension   **Underline ten expressions that you would ask someone to explain if you were testing comprehension.**

EXAMPLE   a common script (paragraph **1**)

When you have finished, see if you can explain your partner's expressions and vice versa.

summary 2

A **Arguments for and against.** The writer lists the arguments against zoos which some people put forward, then he refutes them. In note form, list the arguments he mentions and how he refutes them.

	Arguments against	Refutation
EXAMPLE	*animals helplessly locked away*	*not free to begin with*

B **Linking information.** Now join both parts of the argument using some expressions from the list below.

in contrast   *whereas in reality*   *notwithstanding (the fact that)*   *it is a fact that*
nonetheless   *despite the fact that*   *the opposite is true*

Remember that while link words are important, it is planning and organization that will determine whether your summary is a good one or not.

C **Summarizing part of a passage.** Summarize the arguments **against** the idea of zoos based on the writer's portrayal of anti-zoo critics. Make your summary between 60 and 80 words then compare your work with a partner's. Do the arguments sound convincing?

Listening and Speaking

Back to Nature

talking points

Look at the following picture.

SAFARI HOLIDAYS

- Can you describe the picture?

- What is it trying to show?

- Why is it ironical?

- What kind of picture might you have expected to go with the caption?

- What would be the advantages and disadvantages of a holiday of this kind? Would it appeal to you?

listening

A Listen to a radio programme about safari holidays and fill in the missing details in the chart below.

Recommended location	For those who want	Holiday company	Length of holiday	Cost of holiday	Time to go
Masai Mara Kenya	1 to *see ove...* 2 to *...on.com*	Windsor Safari	3 *15 days*	4 *1,183*	Dec to Mar
Ngorongora 5 *Crater* Tanzania	6 *sheer spectacle* 7 *see black rhino*	Bales Tours	14 days	8 *2,095*	X
South Luangwa 9 *Nat Park* Zambia	10 *see game*	11 *Teachers world*	15 days	£2,341	July to Sept
Kruger Park South Africa	12 *see small group in 4x4*	Southern Africa Travel	X	13 *265 a night*	X

bb

B Now listen to the tape again and complete the following information.

1 People have been encouraged to experience a safari holiday by *wildlife TV* .

2 According to the *doom-mongers*, in Kenya *game is disappearing* .

3 A camel safari in Kenya is recommended as being *tranquil calm comf* .

4 The accommodation at Ngorongora, Tanzania, is in *lodges* situated *on crater* .

5 Cut-price holidays are now available in Zambia because *reports of drought* .

6 The safari in South Luangwa is different as it can only be done on *foot* .

7 The geography of Kenya differs from that of South Africa in that *has open plains not bush* .

8 Luxurious private reserves on the edge of the Kruger are frequented by *V.I.P.s* .

C **What a difference a letter makes.** Look at the picture below. Which consonant is missing? In **1–15** below, the words on the left all appeared on the tape. What is the difference in pronunciation and meaning between those on the left and those on the right?

Graham Rawle's **LOST CONSONANTS III**

(88) The charity walk had attracted an unexpectedly large crow

1	track	tack
2	kinds	kids
3	world	word
4	first	fist
5	baby	bay
6	three	tree
7	coast	cast
8	part	pat
9	shores	sores
10	camps	caps
11	quiet	quit
12	boasts	boats
13	fine	fin
14	plains	plans
15	made	mad

speaking

exam tip

Think aloud and explain why you approve / disapprove. The examiner cannot assess you on silence!

Expressing preferences. In the interview you may be asked to select items from a list and explain your reactions and attitudes towards the items you have either selected or rejected.

The holidays described in the listening all involve animals. Look at the list of leisure activities connected with animals, decide on one that you might enjoy, and explain why.
Why would you not enjoy some of the other options?

- pony trekking
- greyhound racing
- equestrian gymkhana
- bull fighting
- fox-hunting
- deep sea fishing
- falconry

ADVICE After talking about the activity you have chosen, think about the issues behind some of the other options, such as the campaign against blood sports and the unfair exploitation of animals by man. Talk about one of these in relation to the second part of the question.

Writing

Describing an Ideal

introduction

You may be asked in an examination for a description of an ideal house, parent, pet, or something similar. In many ways this is a straightforward composition. However, its disadvantages are that it is more difficult for you to demonstrate the full range of your writing abilities.

stage 1
general approach

Which of the three approaches below would be the most suitable for answering this question?

Describe the ideal pet for a young child.

OUTLINE 1 general introduction about pets – description of your childhood pet – its looks, personality, etc.; adventures you used to have – when you got it, how long you had it, who looked after it – problems and difficulties you used to have – what happened to the pet in the end

[handwritten: interesting – but irrelevant; your topic, not experience, leads to rambling]

OUTLINE 2 take a number of examples and discuss advantages and disadvantages – dogs, cats, hamsters, rabbits; discuss problems of keeping dogs in cities – mess on pavements, etc.; problems of what to do if the animal gets lost; cost of keeping an animal; conclude by pointing out that many people don't like animals

OUTLINE 3 general introduction; purpose of giving a pet to a child – emotional and educational – characteristics of an animal that would make a good pet, ie good nature, practical considerations, such as where child lives, parents, etc.; conclude with short list of choices

[handwritten: most promising]

stage 2
brainstorming

Work out a list of ten points that would be important to mention in the composition. When you have finished, check to see whether they have been covered in the sample composition on page 127.

stage 3
organization

Read the sample composition and match the headings to the paragraph notes below.

Introduction   Paragraph 2   Paragraph 3   Paragraph 4   Conclusion

a Characteristics of animal – safe, relatively docile; neither too demanding or energetic, nor too difficult for child to control. . . . .

b Broad outline of what approach will be taken in composition – will look at three main areas – child's needs, characteristics of an ideal pet, practical considerations, leading to choice in conclusion. . . . .

c Practical considerations – where child lives – role of parents, who will inevitably do a great deal of the caring, paying, etc. . . . .

d Choice – depending on where child lives, small dog or cat, possibly hamster. . . . .

e Child's needs – purpose of giving pet mainly educational – teach to care, give sense of responsibility – also fun for child – also emotional, good for child to form bond with animal. Ideal pet needs to be suitable for these aims. . . . .

sample composition

A Read the following composition. As you read it, think about what is wrong with the style of the underlined sections.

In deciding what pet would be ideal for a young child aged about five or six, we need to look at three main areas. Firstly, it is important to define what educational and emotional needs we would be ideally trying to meet;
5 secondly, we need to look at the characteristics of the kind of animal that would be suitable for a child; and, thirdly, we have to bear in mind a number of practical considerations that would affect the choice of an ideal pet.

10   As far as the first point is concerned, the first main aim of giving a child a pet would be to provide him or her with a valuable educational experience. The child would have to learn to care for the animal, to feed it and generally develop a sense of responsibility. Therefore the
15 ideal pet would place certain demands on a child, but would not be too demanding or time-consuming. The other main aim would be to provide the child with an emotional experience, and an ideal pet would offer a child friendship, companionship and fun. These aims point to a cat or dog.
20 Cats or dogs would depend on a child. Cats or dogs could interact with a child. These aims rule out certain pets. An example of the kind of pet these aims rule out is a goldfish. Goldfish are not sufficiently engaging.

As regards the pet itself, it would need to have
25 certain clearly defined characteristics. It would above all have to be safe and entirely reliable even under extreme provocation, because there would inevitably be moments when the child and pet were alone together. This would rule out certain breeds of dog. Certain breeds of dog are
30 unpredictable. Certain breeds of dog are capable of aggression. Pit-bull terriers are an example of this. There are other important characteristics as well. The pet would need to be manageable. This again rules out certain breeds of large dog. Certain breeds of large dog may be
35 delightful as puppies. Certain breeds of large dog quickly become too boisterous. Certain breeds of large dog quickly become uncontrollable.

There are numerous practical considerations that would affect what kind of animal would make an ideal pet.
40 For example, a great deal would depend on whether the child lived in the city or in the country, as some animals require far more space than others. Much would depend too on the parents. This is because they would inevitably do a great deal of the caring. The parents would assume
45 the ultimate responsibility for the well-being of the animal. The preferences of the parents would need to be taken into consideration.

An ideal pet for a child would therefore be something like a small dog, a cat, a rabbit or even a hamster, as any
50 of these would be capable of meeting the child's needs and would be perfectly safe, and the final choice would depend on the family circumstances and the individual preferences of the child and the parents.

B Sentence synthesis. Look at the following extracts from the composition where the sentences were entirely inappropriate in terms of their repetitiveness and lack of complexity. Rewrite each set of sentences to form one complex sentence.

1 These aims point to a cat or dog.
Cats or dogs would depend on a child.
Cats or dogs could interact with a child.
These aims rule out certain pets.
An example of the kind of pet these aims rule out is a goldfish.
Goldfish are not sufficiently engaging.

EXAMPLE *These aims point to an animal such as a cat or dog, which would depend on and could interact with the child, and they rule out pets such as goldfish, which are not sufficiently engaging.*

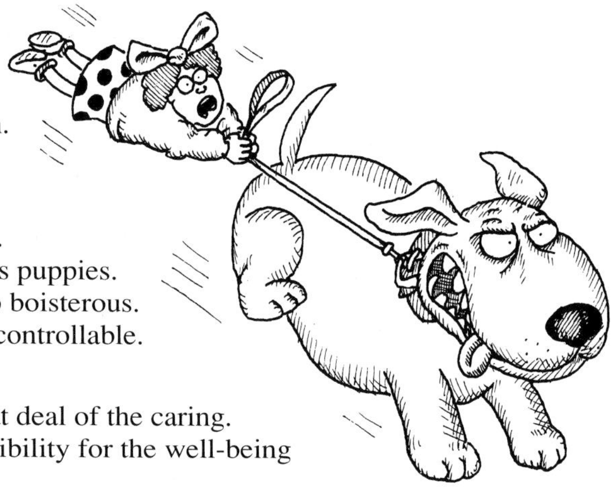

2   This would rule out certain breeds of dog.
   Certain breeds of dog are unpredictable.
   Certain breeds of dog are capable of aggression.
   Pit-bull terriers are an example of this.

[handwritten: pt8]
[handwritten: whichare]
[handwritten: such as]

3   The pet would need to be manageable.
   This again rules out certain breeds of large dog.
   Certain breeds of large dog may be delightful as puppies.
   Certain breeds of large dog quickly become too boisterous.
   Certain breeds of large dog quickly become uncontrollable.

[handwritten: which, while they]

4   Much would depend too on the parents.
   This is because they would inevitably do a great deal of the caring.
   The parents would assume the ultimate responsibility for the well-being
   of the animal.
   The preferences of the parents would need to be taken into consideration.

[handwritten: pt8]
[handwritten: they because]

C   Conditionals. One of the difficulties in writing about any hypothetical
situation is the use of extended conditionals (the repeated use of conditionals throughout
the paragraphs).
Look at these extracts from the sample composition.

As regards the pet itself, it would need to have certain clearly defined characteristics.
(Here the conditional is being used because the text is focusing specifically on the 'ideal' and
hypothetical pet.)

… as some animals require far more space than others.
(Here the present is being used because the text is focusing on something that is always true, and
is not talking only about an ideal pet.)

In the following extract, based on the title *Describe your ideal home*, choose whether each verb
would be better in the present tense or in the conditional.

The most important feature of my ideal home would
be / is its position – it would have to be / has to be in
the country, preferably in a small village, because
peaceful surroundings would be / are essential for me.
5 I would love / love a big garden too, where I could grow
/ can grow flowers and where the children could play /
can play safely. It would be / is an old house too,

perhaps made of stone and with a thatched roof,
because I think older houses would have / have much
10 more character than modern ones, even though they
would be / are sometimes a little less easy to look
after. Inside it would have / has a lot of interesting
features such as old fireplaces and beams, which
would make / make it feel warm and safe.

writing task

Write a composition of about 350 words on the following topic.

Describe the conditions in an ideal zoo or wildlife park.

Stage 1   General approach. Think about zoos and safari parks, the needs of the animals, the
requirements of the public in terms of safety, etc. At the end say whether you think
the concept of keeping animals out of their natural surroundings is a good idea or not.

Stage 2   Brainstorming. Jot down any ideas or thoughts that spring to mind related to the subject.

Stage 3   Planning. Read the question again carefully before you select the relevant thoughts from
stage 2 and work out a more detailed structure.

Stage 4   Writing. Pay particular care to present and conditional sentences, and aim to write well-
synthesized sentences.

Stage 5   Check your work carefully.

Overview 9

vocabulary

Choose the word which best completes each sentence.

1 .... of bees can be seen in the orchard in the summer months.
  A Troupes   **B** Herds   **C** Flocks   **D** Swarms

2 The complaints he received were like water off a duck's ....
  A feathers   **B** wings   **C** back   **D** body

3 In these remote regions the saga of men and animals was played ....
  A along with   **B** havoc with   **C** down   **D** out

4 The small box .... a tiny live terrapin.
  A contained   **B** comprised   **C** consisted of   **D** included

5 Whenever he had an important decision to make, he .... a cigar, supposedly to calm his nerves!
  A had lit   **B** would have lit   **C** would light   **D** would be lighting

6 .... for the fact that he was working abroad, he would willingly have helped with the project.
  A If it had been   **B** If it hadn't been   **C** Had it been   **D** Hadn't it been

7 It is often difficult to .... from young children exactly what their fears are.
  A cajole   **B** entice   **C** tempt   **D** elicit

8 The tiger .... round the village in search of prey.
  A prowled   **B** lurked   **C** roamed   **D** stalked

9 I'm opting out of the .... race and going to live on a small farm in the countryside.
  A horse   **B** dog   **C** rat   **D** cat and mouse

10 In some countries there have been widespread demands for the .... of seal hunting.
  A extinction   **B** extermination   **C** annihilation   **D** abolition

transformations

Finish each of the following sentences in such a way that it means exactly the same as the sentence printed before it.

1 It's a pity that the TV packed up. We can't watch the football now!

If the TV ....

2 What a shame I can't speak French. I had to find an interpreter.

If I ....

3 Provided that you leave a forwarding address, we will be able to contact you.

Unless...

4 Unless you save some money, you will never be able to buy a car.

Provided that ....

5 Those terrapins which survive their first year may live to be twenty.

Should ....

6 If he told you he loved you, what would you say?

If he were ....

7 In the event of your failing your driving test, would you take it again?

Supposing that...

8 I know he didn't remember my birthday. Look, he hasn't given me a present!

If he...

9 Whenever he felt depressed, he went for a long walk across the hills.

If...

10 There was no point trying to telephone him as he never answers the phone after midnight.

Even if I ....

blank-filling

Fill each of the blanks in the following sentences with a suitable word or phrase.

1 Nowadays smoking is .... in many public places for safety reasons.

2 Many zoos are .... with closure.

3 Eggs are laid and .... after two to four months.

4 Some animals are now being bred in captivity and .... at a later stage into the wild.

5 If .... the species will soon be endangered.

6 If I were .... marry me, would you accept?

7 Had I ...., I would have arranged to take you out for dinner.

8 .... their continental neighbours, the British are extremely fond of drinking tea.

9 The panda is wrongly .... a cuddly, gentle animal.

10 Life in the wild is a constant .... survival.

rewriting

*For each of the sentences below, write **two** new sentences as similar as possible in meaning to the original sentence, but using the words given in capital letters. These words must not be altered in any way.*

1 Many species of wild life are threatened with extinction.

VERGE / DANGER. ....

2 Pandas need a special diet, without which they perish.

PROVIDED / UNLESS ....

3 He liked the new job straight away.

DUCK / EASE. ....

4 She felt uncomfortable in the huge hotel.

FISH / PLACE. ....

5 We would like a copy of your new prospectus.

GRATEFUL / KIND ....

6 I don't see any point in trying to save endangered species.

WORTH / WASTE ....

7 No smoking on the underground.

BAN / PERMIT. ....

8 It is roughly estimated that some turtles lay 28,000 eggs a year.

GUESS / AVERAGE. ....

9 I regret shouting at him.

ONLY / WISH. ....

10 The customs of the people no longer seemed strange.

FAMILIAR / USED. ....

| Reading | **Family Values** |

talking points

Parent profile. A baby has been found abandoned on the steps of a church, and the mother has disappeared. You have been asked to form a committee to decide who should adopt the child. Your aim is to provide a profile of the ideal parents. Discuss the following criteria and mark the ideas as to how important they are, on a scale of 1–5 (5 = vitally important, 1 = irrelevant). Then compare your notes with other students.

The adoptive parents should:
- both be under 35.
- be a couple, ie the child should not go to a single-parent family.
- have some professional experience of dealing with children, ie as teachers, nurses, etc.
- have other children in the family.
- both be in full-time employment.
- be of the same racial group as the child.
- be either in the middle-income bracket or rich.
- be married.
- not adhere to any minority religious group or cult.

reading

A Read the following article from the American magazine *Time* and answer these questions.

1 What crime were Mr and Mrs Marrero arrested for?
2 Why did Mr and Mrs Marrero behave in the way they did?
3 What is their daughter's attitude to the crime her parents committed?

THE URBAN JUNGLE
At the End of Their Tether

A Bronx couple win sympathy for trying to beat the mean streets

In New York City parents are usually arrested for trying to kill their children, not for trying to save them. So when police were tipped off that a couple in the Bronx were keeping their daughter chained to a radiator, they moved in, figuring that they would be rescuing the girl and preventing a tragedy. Maria and Eliezer Marrero were hauled off in handcuffs; bail was set at $100,000, a sum fit for a murderer; and their daughter Linda, 15, landed in a foster-care center in the nearby borough of Queens.

None of this would be especially remarkable, except that by the end of the week fewer people were praising the courts for saving the child than were defending the natural rights of parents to lash their children to radiators. As the Marreros tell it, they had tried everything to keep Linda in

school, off drugs and out of the local crack house. When all else failed, Eliezer, a building superintendent, went down to the local hardware store and bought a 4.5 meter chain. If the Marreros could not drive drugs from their door, they could at least lock their daughter behind it.

They wound up in a court-room that has seen parents who threw their children out windows, dipped them in boiling water, beat them with electrical cords. The Marreros, who had never had any trouble with the law, were accused of unlawful imprisonment and endangering the welfare of a child. There was an irony in that charge, since it was being leveled at parents

driven to despair as they watched their daughter seduced by the ghetto's most beguiling drug. "We are not criminals," said Maria. "There was nothing else to do."

As the story unfolded in the tabloids, it forced other parents to wonder whether, given the same choices, they might not have done the same thing. Friends and
50 neighbors were accustomed to seeing Linda in chains – including, the girl claims, the police themselves. Linda and her brother told reporters that she had called the police back in the summer and that when officers
55 came to investigate, they found her locked up. Their response was to tell her mother, "Good job. Just keep her away from the phones." "They told me I was a lost case," Linda recalls.
60 To hear her story, they may not have been far wrong. She dropped out of school in sixth grade after throwing a teacher down the stairs, and started selling crack at 13. In 1989 she was placed in a home for troubled
65 girls but fled after the first day. So her parents sent her to live with her grandfather in Puerto Rico. But when she returned to New York, she began staying out all night with a dangerous crowd. One time she
70 disappeared for three weeks and was

"My mother preferred seeing me here, chained, than dead in an alley"

returned, bruised and beaten, by two gun-toting drug dealers demanding money that they said she owed them.

Maria and Eliezer say they had
75 petitioned the city for help. They called the welfare agencies and urged the courts to intervene. City officials admit that children like Linda fall through the cracks. "We really haven't faced this before," said
80 Marjorie Valleau, spokeswoman for the Child Welfare Administration. "I'd be hard pressed to name a specific program that specializes in the children." Which left the parents to their own meager resources.
85 "They said what I did was cruelty," said Maria. "But when I begged them for help, they denied it to me. How can they say I was cruel?"

Last week, Linda seemed to have
90 reached the same conclusion. "My mother preferred seeing me here, chained, than dead in an alley," she said, lending a whole new meaning to the notion that parents need to set limits for their children. She even said
95 she would be willing to be chained again. "As long as I'm with them, I wouldn't mind."

After two nights in jail, Maria and Eliezer returned home as heroes. Linda,
100 meanwhile, had left the foster-care center and turned up in a local crack house. She said she had not been doing drugs – she just went to see her friends, dance, listen to music, as though this were a natural place
105 for a teenage girl's pajama party. "I'm desperate now," her father told the Daily News after he tracked her down. "I'm going to the hardware store to buy another chain." ∎

Nancy Gibbs, Time Magazine

B **Multiple-choice questions.** Choose the best answer, according to the article.

1 The police came to arrest Mr and Mrs Marrero as a result of
  A a phone call from Linda.
  B information from an unnamed source.
  C complaints from the neighbours.
  D a report by the Child Welfare Administration.

2 The charge of 'endangering the welfare of a child' is described as ironical because Mr and Mrs Marrero
  A had not committed any offence.
  B had locked up their own child.
  C were acting in their daughter's best interest.
  D were protecting her from armed drug dealers.

3 After being away from home for three weeks, Linda came home because
  A she had been beaten up.
  B she wanted more money from her parents.
  C drug dealers wanted her parents to pay her debts.
  D she had nowhere else to go.

4 While her parents were in jail, Linda
  A invited some friends home for a party.
  B ran away from the foster home.
  C got into trouble with the police.
  D stayed with friends in a different part of the city.

C **Comprehension.** Answer the following questions as fully as possible in your own words.

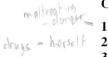

1 What misapprehension were the police under when they came to arrest Mr and Mrs Marrero?
2 What principally were the Marreros trying to protect their daughter from?
3 What does the use of the word *local* in the phrase *local crack house* imply about the problem of drug abuse in the city (line 101)? widespread, not far away
4 What does the writer imply by saying that Linda's case lends *a whole new meaning to the notion that parents need to set limits for their children* (line 92)? extreme situation - shocking
5 What does the writer imply by the phrase *as though this were a natural place for a teenage girl's pajama party* (line 104)? sarcastic crack

British and American spelling

The main differences between British and American spelling are listed below.
Read the text about the Marrero family again to find examples of the following differences.

1 Many words which end in *-tre* in British English end in *-ter* in American English.

   EXAMPLE **GB** theatre, metre; **US** theater, meter

   Find an example in paragraph 1. . . . .

2 Words that double a final *-l* in an unstressed syllable in British English do not do so in American English.

   EXAMPLE **GB** travel – travelled, unravel – unravelled; **US** travel – traveled, unravel – unraveled

   Find an example in paragraph 3. . . . .

3 Many words ending in *-our* in British English end in *-or* in American English.

   EXAMPLE **GB** colour, favour; **US** color, favor

   Find an example in paragraph 4. . . . .

4 Verbs which can end in either *-ise* or *-ize* in British English end only in *-ize* in American English.

   EXAMPLE **GB** categorise, categorize, realise, realize; **US** categorize, realize

   Find an example in paragraph 6. . . . .

exam tip

Both British and American spelling are acceptable for the Cambridge Proficiency exam, but a mixture of both is not.

Structure

Social Change

listening

A **Social change.** You will hear an interview in which a journalist discusses her reaction to a recent report about social change in Britain. Listen to the tape and say whether the following statements are true or false according to the journalist being interviewed.

1 The divorce rate alone is responsible for the decline of the nuclear family. T/F
2 A relatively small proportion of mothers have full-time jobs. T/F
3 People are paying much more attention to the views of feminists and the Left. T/F
4 There is little awareness of the enormous changes taking place in society. T/F
5 Television is almost entirely responsible for creating the myth of the nuclear family. T/F
6 The advertising industry has been quick to respond to changes in society. T/F
7 The majority of people would benefit if the nuclear family was not seen as the norm. T/F
8 It would be best to ignore some of the changes that are taking place. T/F

B **Explain the meaning of the following words and phrases as they are used in the interview.**

1 a traditional nuclear family
2 Mr and Mrs Average
3 two point four children
4 soaps
5 Kelloggs Cornflakes families
6 wall-to-wall cornflakes
7 single room supplements

cloze development

In the following passage, there are twenty mistakes. Read the passage carefully and correct all the words so that the passage makes sense.

GET THAT RIDICULOUS FAMILY OUT OF HERE!

Lies, damned lies and awkward statistics temper the mood of the week as we see the latest snapshot of the country with the publication of *Social Trends 22*. For as their

1 statistics chronicle when are probably the most rapid social

2 5 changes from British history, we are surrounded by forces

3 who will say green is white, if necessary, in order to deny

4 the evidence through the figures.

5 Basically what the survey tells us is that: marriage is in

6, 7 steep fall, divorce the highest outside Europe, remarriage

8 10 declining further more. Single persons living alone now

9 account of more than a quarter of all households, lone-

10 parent households are at the rise, and although the majority

11 of parents stay still married, an astonishing 28% of babies

12 are now born without wedlock.

13 15 Put all these in and you may be shaken, if not stirred.

14 But then consider the greatest extraordinary figure of all. The percentage of households now living Kelloggs

15 Cornflakes style, with a married husband and stay-at-home-

16 with-the-kids wife, is actually little a fraction over seven per

17 20 cent, but around 1.4m of our 19.5m households.

In 1979, when the first statistics became available, the figure stood at nearly 12%, and since then there has been a

18 persistent upward trend. It means, in other words, the dear

19 little nuclear reactor, which was born of – and for – the

20 25 industrial revolution, had gone. It did not even last 200 years. RIP. ∎

present perfect simple and simple past

A Look at the following extracts from the listening comprehension and cloze passage.
For each of the extracts discuss the reasons why the present perfect or simple past was used.

1 … the most surprising figure that has come to light is that only 7% of all households comprise a traditional nuclear family …

2 I've always known that Mr and Mrs Average and their 2.4 kids were something of a myth …

3 Marx and Engels were very unenthusiastic about it …

4 In 1979 … the figure stood at nearly 12%, and since then there has been a persistent downward trend …

B Right or wrong? Many of the following sentences may look grammatically incorrect, but in fact only three are absolutely wrong. Work out which they are, and discuss the contexts and meanings that make the others acceptable.

1 Since his father owned Kilman and Co, he worked there.

2 My sister is a doctor since she left university.

3 When have you ever helped with the washing up?

4 Gee, I'm sorry, Jane's not here – she just went out.

5 My parents have gone to America for their silver wedding anniversary.

6 Shakespeare has been a towering figure in English literature for centuries.

7 This will be the last time that I have helped her.

8 I'm sure that I have seen you somewhere before.

9 I've lived abroad for 11 years and in England for 16.

10 I've done my homework a few days ago.

perfect tenses

A Read through the following sentences and put the verbs into the past, present or future perfect (active or passive).

1 You might as well take the parcel tomorrow – the post office .... (close) by the time you get there if you go now.

2 You will like Clare, she is one of the nicest people I .... (ever / meet).

3 Do you realize that next Friday is 18 August, and then we .... (know) each other for exactly four years?

4 My brother .... (change) so much since our last meeting that I hardly recognized him.

5 The garden looks so much better now that all that rubbish .... (take away).
[handwritten: has been taken away]

6 Let's meet up after I come back from my holiday – we'd better not say Monday 19th, because
I .... (only just / get back). What about the following Thursday?
[handwritten: will only just have got back]

7 She was horrified to discover, on returning home, that her entire flat .... (ransack).
[handwritten: had been ransacked]

8 I found my first few weeks at the office very tiring because I .... (never / have)
a full-time job before.
[handwritten: had never / haven't done / had]

9 I tell you I am completely innocent – I .... (not / do) anything. You've got the
wrong man.

10 I blushed profusely; .... (I / never / find) myself in such an embarrassing position
before.
[handwritten: I had never found]

B **Discussion.** Discuss what significant changes have taken place over recent years in the following
areas. Agree on the three most important changes in each area, and when you have finished,
compare your responses with others in the class.

- family life
- relationships before marriage
- the quality of life
- the workplace
- the behaviour patterns of the younger generation
- society as a whole as a result of all these developments

present perfect
simple and
progressive

A **Read through the following sets of sample sentences and answer the questions.**

1 The present perfect progressive can be used to talk about finished activities of which some
evidence still remains. Discuss the difference in meaning between the following sentences.

I've been playing squash with Jim; that's why I'm so hot. *[handwritten: result]*
I've played squash with Jim. He's a terrible cheat. *[handwritten: exp.]*

2 The present perfect progressive can emphasize that a single activity or action which started in
the past is still going on and has not finished. Discuss the difference in meaning between the
following sentences.

Jess has been writing her thesis; she's over halfway through. *[handwritten: not finish]*
Jess has written her thesis. She's very relieved.

3 The present perfect progressive can be used to talk about a series of repeated actions that have
carried on up to the present. Discuss the difference in meaning between the following sentences.

I've been phoning her, but I think she must be out.
I've phoned her, but I think she must be out.

4 The present perfect progressive can suggest that an action or activity is temporary rather than
permanent. Discuss the difference in meaning between the following sentences.

Jack has been living with us since he came to England. *[handwritten: short-term]*
Jack has lived with us since he came to England. *[handwritten: now member of house]*

5 Which of the following two sentences seems to be an exception to the rules above? *[handwritten: been to]*

He doesn't want to come with us because he's already been skiing twice this year. *[handwritten: gone + come back 2, contradict]*
He's exhausted because he's been skiing all day. *[handwritten: = pres perf simp, time rule 3, to go skiing, vb 1, repeated]*

Which sentence contains the present perfect simple of *to go skiing*?
Which sentence contains the present perfect progressive of *to ski*?

6 Stative verbs (see Unit 2) are not normally used in any progressive tense, so are rarely found in
the present perfect progressive. However, the verbs *mean* and *want* can be used in this tense.

There's something I've been meaning to tell you for ages.
This is a problem I've been wanting to talk to you about for a long time. *[handwritten: exception]*

B **Complete the following sentences.** Put the verbs into either the present perfect simple or present perfect progressive.

1 Look at you – you're covered in mud – what on earth ...... *doing* ...... (you / do)? [*have you been*]

2 This is my favourite coat, and I ...... *have had* ...... (have) it since I left school.

3 Since the offices at the front of the building were damaged by the bomb, quite a few of us ...... *have been working* ...... (work) in the corridor.

4 The car's nearly ready, madam; the mechanic .... (change) [*has changed*] the oil and ...... *has checked* ...... (check) the brakes, but he ...... *hasn't completed* ...... (not / complete) all the paper work yet.

5 I ...... *have been learning* ...... (learn) Spanish at evening classes for the last month, but I'm not much good.

6 Well, of course I'm angry, what do you expect? I ...... *have been sitting* ...... (sit) here waiting for you for over an hour.

7 I ...... *have been meaning* ...... (mean) to have a talk with you about a problem that I ...... *have known* ...... (know) about for some time.

8 Because of pressure of work at the office, Jack ...... *has been getting* ...... (get) home late recently.

British and American English

A **Grammar and vocabulary.** Here is an example of a grammatical form that would be correct in American English but incorrect in British English.

Gee, I'm sorry, Jane's not here – she just went out.

Read through the following sentences and decide whether they show features of American English or British English, based on their structure and vocabulary.

A 1 Do you promise that you'll write me every day when you're away?
A 2 Prime Minister Major met with the President at Camp David last Sunday.
A 3 The baby's diaper is fine – I just changed it.
B 4 Hello? Is that the operator? I'd like to make a reverse charge call to Tokyo.
B 5 He works at the off-licence from Monday to Friday, and as a postman at the weekends.
A 6 My sister was real mad when her jewelry was stolen, and she's never gotten over it.
A 7 The patrolmen were told to look out for a man wearing black suspenders and blue pants.
B 8 My boot and bonnet were damaged in the crash and the bumper was dented.
B 9 The latest rise in gas prices will lead to higher heating bills.
A 10 You find alumni from that school almost anyplace you go.

Find examples in the above sentences of the following:

a differences in vocabulary ....

b differences in the use of prepositions ....

c differences in the use of tenses and verb forms ....

d differences in spelling ....

e differences in the use of adverbs ....

B **Discussion.**

1 How major are the differences between American and British English?
2 In the future, do you think the various varieties of English will become more homogeneous or mutually incomprehensible?
3 Do you find an American or a standard British accent easier to understand? How easily can you tell the difference?
4 In your own language, how informative is a person's accent? Does it tell you where they come from, how well educated they are, what class they are, etc.?

DON'T CALL ME AND I WON'T CALL YOU

Jim Shelley with the chilling story of one man for whom the party line's over ....

My name is Jim Shelley and I am an addict... With these words I began to break the spell, began to conquer the problem, the problem of my addiction, my telephone frenzy.

From waking to the darkest, deepest hours of night, I wait to be phoned, I want to phone.

It started socially I suppose – a few calls each day. It seemed harmless, just innocent chat. Soon it was frequent use, then compulsive calling, until, finally, habitual addiction – phone fever.

Gradually, it began to affect my work. I was spending all of my lunch-break phoning. Within weeks, I was arriving at work early, to start the day with some phoning. During the day, I would disappear for a quick fix, a swift hit.

People ask why I became an addict. I suppose it was boredom, insecurity, attention-seeking. My counsellor says it was really a cry for help. I think any other excuses (pressure of work, disturbed childhood, alcoholic parents) are just excuses: I have to take responsibility for the problem.

The only time I felt alive was when I was on the phone. I was charming, warm, generous and handsome; everyone liked me and I actually liked them. I had no misgivings and no inhibitions. Life's pressures disappeared. In no time, my best relationships were phone relationships, I became inept at the social graces. I was more at home talking to people who were like me, addicts. I developed a hatred of other users – particularly people who were phoning a lot at home, or in their jobs, people who were rich enough to phone whenever they liked. Stockbrokers and telephonists were the worst.

I spent days waiting for the phone to ring. I got agitated. In my mind I heard the first ring, heard the silence break. I concentrated on that sound, tried to make it real, but no call came. In the end, I would ring someone. Then someone else, telling myself "just one more", but in the end, ringing everyone. In really low moments, I would call international. Peak rate. I felt I belonged to the world.

Slowly things began to deteriorate. I was calling people and leaving messages to guarantee enough calls to see me through the day. I would arrive at friends' homes and before the door was closed, head straight for the phone with the words, "Is it OK if I just use the phone...?" Some nights, I thought I could hear the phone ringing downstairs. I would leap out of bed and race down, only to find it hadn't rung at all.

I'd end up lying there, wondering whether the phone had become unplugged. What if all my calls were going to crossed-lines? Being intercepted? What if the exchange had been hit by a power cut?

The panic attacks and paranoia grew so bad I would ring people and ask them if they'd been trying to ring me. I stopped going out in case people called. I had a business line and a private line installed. I borrowed money and bought an Ansaphone. I bought a pager and a portable. I bought a car to put my carphone in. As my addiction worsened, I no longer spoke to people at work. I became hostile and violent when colleagues attempted to stop me from phoning in an attempt to get me to do work. Finally, my superior took action. I hit him (with the phone) and ended up slumped in a corner, sobbing, clutching the Yellow Pages. I was dismissed and offered redundancy or one week's free calls, which I accepted.

My body had begun to suffer. My head tilted to one side, from the hours of cradling the phone on one shoulder. One ear was inflamed and bruised. The other was no longer as strong at actually hearing. I was always tired. Phone bills littered my room like dirty needles, red reminders of the extent of my habit. Piles of spent phone cards lay among them. No one would contribute to the bills – they knew I was "using" more than I said.

Finally I was arrested for destroying a call box that had not only taken my last £1 coin, but had cut me off mid-call, leaving me hanging, high and dry.

As a result, a counsellor was appointed. I haven't had a phone in the house for three weeks. It's several days since I used a phone box. I'm trying to cut down on television – people on TV are always making calls, answering the phone. I stay away from stations and airports.

The first thing I have to do every day is to tell myself I do not need phones, that I am a fine human being, loved by my friends and family and that I am an addict. At least I can say it: my name is James Shelley and I am an addict.

••••••••••••••••••••••••••••••••

F **1** Jim's addiction resulted in his not turning up for work.   T/F
F **2** Jim blamed his background for his addiction.   T/F
T **3** Jim lived in a fool's paradise on the phone.   T/F
T **4** Jim was unable to relate to people unless he talked to them on the phone.   T/F
T **5** If he got really depressed, he would make expensive calls.   T/F
F **6** Jim's phone never stopped ringing.   T/F
T **7** He invested his non-existent funds in all types of phone technology.   T/F
F **8** After his dismissal Jim was given one week's redundancy money.   T/F
F **9** Jim was attacked and injured by one of his colleagues.   T/F
F **10** Jim now makes phone calls only to friends and family.   T/F

comprehension

Explain the meaning of the following words and phrases which all appeared in the article.

1 to break the spell (line 3)
2 my telephone frenzy (line 5)
3 a quick fix, a swift hit (line 20)
4 no misgivings and no inhibitions (line 34)
5 inept at the social graces (line 37)
6 peak rate (line 55)
7 deteriorate (line 57)
8 the panic attacks and paranoia (line 78)
9 a pager and a portable (line 85)
10 slumped in a corner, sobbing, clutching the Yellow Pages (line 93)
11 cradling the phone (line 99)
12 cut me off mid-call, leaving me hanging, high and dry (line 111)

summary

A Improving a summary. Read this summary of the passage. It is too long and rather repetitive in places. Can you reduce each paragraph by one half (or more) of its length? Decide which expressions you could omit, condense or change. Some clues are provided. The first is done for you.

1 Jim Shelley's addiction to making phone calls cannot be attributed to the many excuses he can invent for it. It is due to the fact that when on the phone he feels he is at his best, so he feels that he alone is responsible for his habit.

EXAMPLE *Jim Shelley feels more confident when using the phone and blames his addiction not on invented excuses but on himself alone.*

2 He began to hate anything or anybody that prevented him from indulging in his favourite activity. He started imagining that the phone was ringing and he became obsessed with the idea of making sure that he would receive enough phone calls from other people.

CLUE Use *any obstacle which ... took steps to ensure.*

3 When his colleagues at work tried to break him of his habit, he treated them as enemies and became abusive, reacting in such a violent manner that he was made redundant and lost his job.

CLUE Use *to cure him ... his violent reaction.*

4 His addiction caused physical side-effects, for example, his hearing in one ear was impaired and the other ear became inflamed and bruised. Eventually the police arrested him after he had wilfully destroyed a phone box because he had lost a one pound coin in it.

CLUE Use *He suffered ... in his ears ... was arrested for.*

5 After receiving psychiatric help from a counsellor, he can now freely admit that he is a phone addict yet feel that he is able to control his addiction.

CLUE Use *After counselling ... his addiction is.*

B In 60 to 80 words summarize the psychological and physical effects of Jim's addiction before he was eventually sent to a counsellor. Use the paragraphs you wrote above to help you.

talking points

Relationships. In a recent survey, men and women were asked what qualities they considered most important in partners with whom they intended to spend the rest of their lives. Which table do you think shows the responses from men and which shows the responses from women?

w

1	sense of humour
2	faithfulness
3	loving nature
4	consideration
5	= intelligence
5	= physical attractiveness
7	reliability
8	practicality
9	hard-working character
10	strong will

m

1	sense of humour
2	consideration
3	faithfulness
4	reliability
5	hard-working character
6	loving nature
7	intelligence
8	practicality
9	= physical attractiveness
9	= tenderness

— most sign diff in res?
— do you agree with res
— any qualities you wouldn't ask for
— that you would ask for

listening 1

A journalist is interviewing the director of a Marriage Guidance Centre. Listen to the tape and complete her notes.

NB not order script

Interview with director of a Marriage Guidance Centre

Basic set-up
There are (1) ...160... centres in the country.
Each centre is responsible for (2) ...funding..., number of (3) ...employees...
and size of (4) ...waiting... lists.
Headquarters is at (5) ...Rugby....
This centre has (6) ...38... counsellors, and does
(7) ...busiest... interviews a year.
It is the (8) ...busiest... centre outside London.

Training
Possible candidates are sponsored (9) ...locally....
Then candidates are sent to HQ for national (10) ...selection....
Successful candidates then go on a residential (11) ...training...
course.
Course funded by (12) ...Home Office....

Qualifications required
Formal: (13) ...none....
Other: (14) ...warmth..., openness, awareness, intelligence

Areas of work
1   (15) ...relationship... counselling (main part of centre's work).
2   (16) ...sex therapy....
3   Preventive work (17) ...in schools....
4   Work for local (18) ...firms....
5   (19) ...work... for (20) ...theological... colleges.

listening 2

A **Listen to a second interview, this time with one of the counsellors from the organization.** Say whether the following statements are true or false according to the counsellor.

1 The romantic state of being madly in love is only a phase in a relationship. T/F
2 In the 'hangover' phase, one sees people as they really are. T/F
3 Statistically, marriages between teenagers have very little chance of success. T/F
4 It is extremely important for couples to have similar backgrounds and interests. T/F
5 Most people subconsciously want the same kind of relationship as their parents. T/F
6 A sense of humour is of less importance than respect for your partner. T/F
7 Communication will help ease stresses and strains in a relationship. T/F
8 Communication means mainly the ability to express one's thoughts and feelings. T/F

B **Vocabulary.** Explain the meaning of the following words and expressions that were used in the second interview.

1 a first flush
2 dizzy passion and excitement
3 the love hangover
4 seeing someone warts and all
5 pointers
6 statistically speaking
7 deep-rooted ideas
8 make a mountain out of a molehill
9 coping with bereavement
10 bottle things up

reading

Sonnet 116. Read this sonnet by William Shakespeare then, in pairs, answer questions **1–6** below.

SONNET CXVI

Let me not to the marriage of true minds
Admit impediments. Love is not love
Which alters when it alteration finds,
Or bends with the remover to remove:
O, no! it is an ever-fixed mark,
That looks on tempests and is never shaken;
It is the star to every wandering bark,
Whose worth's unknown, although his height be taken.
Love's not Time's fool, though rosy lips and cheeks
Within his bending sickle's compass come;
Love alters not with his brief hours and weeks,
But bears it out even to the edge of doom.
  If this be error, and upon me prov'd,
  I never writ, nor no man ever lov'd.

1 What is the main message of this sonnet by Shakespeare?
2 What is the meaning of the words *Love is not love / Which alters when it alteration finds*?
3 In which line does Shakespeare give a definition of what he means by true love?
4 What effect does time have on love?
5 How certain is Shakespeare that he is right?
6 Do you agree with the feelings that are being expressed in this sonnet?

introduction

The question. The question in the argument composition may be based on the 'true or false' format, asking whether a proposition is true or whether you agree with it. You have already seen examples of this kind of question, eg *The best international language would be an artificial one* (Unit 8) and *Conventional medicine has little to learn from alternative medicine* (Unit 1).

A different style of question is the 'steps and measures' composition title, which asks you to analyse a problem and suggest what steps should be taken to solve it. Look at this example:

In many industrialized countries, juvenile crime is at record levels. Why is this so and what can be done about it?

question interpretation

To help you work out how to interpret the question, consider the following points.

a What does the question take for granted?
b What could you mention in an introductory paragraph?
c What problem would you be faced with if you decided to take issue with the opening statement?
d How relevant would it be to mention organized crime syndicates such as the Mafia?
e What do you need to do before you suggest solutions to the problems?
f What could you mention in your conclusion?

analyse what causes are

summarise reason/ how effective they are

sample composition

The paragraphs in the sample composition are in the wrong order. Match them to the following headings which are in the correct order.

a Introduction and illustration of the premise
b Analysis of the causes of the problem
c Suggestions for solutions based on the analysis
d Conclusion, including comments on the feasibility of the suggested solutions

links between 3 + 4

1 *d* To sum up, juvenile crime is a sign that there is something wrong with society. Young criminals are not inherently bad, they are reacting to the conditions in which they find themselves. It is only when these conditions have been improved that crime rates will fall. To do this is expensive, and requires more spending on employment, welfare and education, but to do nothing would lead to a further deterioration in social order and would be a false economy.

2 *a* Juvenile crime is not new, but the crimes *social environ* committed by young people today are far more common and serious than they were in the past. In a city such as New York, for example, it would not be considered extraordinary if someone were held up at gunpoint by a twelve-year-old or assaulted by a gang of teenagers.

3 *c* The problem of juvenile crime can therefore only be solved by removing those factors that cause it. Governments need to spend more on welfare benefits, but, more importantly, they need to create employment so both parents and children feel that they are part of society and can contribute towards it and benefit from it. Improvements in education are vital as well, so that children from even the

most disadvantaged homes have a base and can be given encouragement and the opportunity to succeed in life. Governments can do little to stop the decline in the traditional family, but improved social conditions might allow more families to stay together. *→ to family*

4 *b* Before one can suggest a solution, it is necessary to analyse the problem and to see what has caused the explosion in juvenile crime. There are three main causes. Firstly, the social environment in which many young people find themselves in the inner cities plays a major role. Poverty and unemployment can create a sense of alienation, and a child who thinks that he has no hope of achieving the wealth and happiness that other people have will often become frustrated and violent. Secondly, an inadequate education system may also be partly to blame. If a child feels he is not valued and is a failure, he will be prone to boredom and open to bad influences. Finally, the decline of the nuclear family and of traditional moral values may also play a role, and a child who grows up without the support of caring, loving parents may not develop a sense of responsibility or consideration for others. *difference of problem with family life*

timed writing task

Write a composition of approximately 350 words on the following subject.

In many cities, it is no longer safe to walk through the streets at night. Why is this so and what could be done to improve the situation?

After completing **stages 1** to **3**, allow yourself one hour to write and check the composition.

Stage 1 General approach. Work out an overall plan of how you intend to approach the question, and decide which parts of the question should have the most prominence in your answer.

Stage 2 Brainstorming. Think of as many ideas as you can about why violent crime has increased. Who are the attackers? What do they want? Why do they attack innocent passers-by? What do the police do? What role is played by unemployment, greed, drug abuse, poverty, laziness? Are punishments strict enough? Could the government do more? Should ordinary citizens do more? If you live somewhere that is safe, what is it that makes it safe? What makes other places dangerous? etc.

Stage 3 Organization. Organize your thoughts, and filter out those that are less important than others, or which are not strictly relevant. Think about the points you want to make within each paragraph and the order they should come in. As a general rule, rank your ideas in order of significance, and begin with the most important ideas.

Depending on what you have worked out, here are two possible structures:

Introduction	
Paragraph 2	cause 1, cause 2 and cause 3
Paragraph 3	solution 1, solution 2 and solution 3
Conclusion	

OR

Introduction	
Paragraph 2	cause 1 and solution 1
Paragraph 3	cause 2 and solution 2
Paragraph 4	cause 3 and solution 3
Conclusion	

exam tip

In a formal argument like this, try and avoid the use of personal pronouns. Do not say, for example, 'I don't think there are any easy solutions to this problem'. Instead, make your sentences impersonal and present these ideas as facts, eg 'There are no easy solutions to this problem.'

Stage 4 Timed writing. Try and illustrate your points with examples. As with the sample composition, you do not need to give actual cases or precise statistics. Try and avoid anything too dramatic, as you are aiming at a fairly detached, academic style that is not over-emotional. Try and avoid direct questions to the reader. Remember to time yourself, and leave yourself at least five minutes for **stage 5**.

Stage 5 Checking. Focus on sentence length and link words. Make sure that your sentences are not too long. Check that you have not repeated the same link word too often.

Overview 10

vocabulary

Choose the words which best complete the following sentences.

1　It's much more expensive if you use the phone at .... rate.
　　A　high　　　　　B　busy　　　　　**C** peak　　　　　D　heavy

2　The politician gave a press conference to deny the charges that had been .... at him.
　　A　targeted　　　**B** levelled　　　C　accused　　　　D　blamed

3　Fearing for his life, he .... the muggers for mercy.
　　A　pleaded　　　B　petitioned　　　C　urged　　　　**D** begged

4　I am sorry to have bothered you – I was under the .... that you wanted me to call you.
　　A　mistake　　　B　miscalculation　　C　misconception　　**D** misapprehension

5　I am not convinced that financial advisers always act in their clients' best ....
　　A　advantage　　**B** interest　　　C　intention　　　D　result

6　Many children who get into trouble in their early teens go on to become .... offenders.
　　A persistent　　B　insistent　　　C　consistent　　　D　resistant

7　Race relations in this country are unlikely to improve until people overcome their ....
　　feelings of hostility towards foreigners.
　　A　interior　　　B　internal　　　C　inverted　　　**D** innate

8　The real test of your relationship will come when you start to see your new boyfriend ....
　　and all.
　　A　faults　　　　B　spots　　　　C　moles　　　　**D** warts

9　It's a shame they didn't pick you, but it doesn't .... out the possibility that you might
　　get a job in a different department.
　　A rule　　　　B　strike　　　　C　cancel　　　　D　draw

10　When facing problems, it is important to keep a sense of ....
　　A proportion　　B　introspection　　C　relativity　　　D　comparison

exam tip

The correct answers are usually right because of one or more of the following: a grammatical pattern (see question 2 – only A and B can be followed by 'at'); the precise meaning of the distractor (see question 3); a collocation or 'set phrase' (see question 8).
When answering difficult questions, look for clues relating to these three elements to eliminate the most obviously wrong distractors; then select one of the remaining options rather than leave a blank.

blank-filling

Fill each of the blanks in the following sentences with a suitable word or phrase.

1　He's very homesick, because it's the first time he ...*has been away*... from home.

2　The water in the washing machine must have been much too hot – these jeans
　　...*have shrunk*... so much that I can't even get into them.

3　That was one ...*of the best programmes*... I have ever watched.

4　If ...*you have done / finished*... the work the boss gave you for this morning already, you'd better
　　go and ask her for some more work to do.

5　What on ...*earth have you been doing*...? You're absolutely covered in oil.

6　If it doesn't rain in the next couple of days, we ...*will have had*... the longest
　　period of drought since records began.

transformations

Rewrite each of the following sentences so that it means the same as the sentence printed before it.

1　Basically, a couple's happiness depends on their ability to communicate.

　　Basically, the more ...*a couple can communicate the happier they are will be*...

2 I'm trying to eat fewer fatty foods.

I'm trying to cut ...*down on fatty foods*...

3 That is the most shocking story I have ever heard.

I have ...*never heard such a shocking story*...

4 This is my brother's first solo flight in a glider.

This is the first time ...*that my brother has flown solo in a glider*...

5 We will not see each other again before I go.

This will be the last time ...*we see each other before I go*...

6 The train left before he got to the station.

By the time ...*I got to the station, the train had left*...

7 The school was founded ten years ago.

It is ten ...*years since the school was founded*...

8 The house looks better since the repainting was done.

The house looks better now ...*that it has been repainted*...

rewriting

*Each pair of sentences below can be rewritten **with the same phrasal verb but with a different meaning**. Rewrite each of the sentences and replace the underlined words with a phrasal verb using the particle shown.*

1 a He must learn that behaving like that is quite unacceptable.

ON ...*is (just) not on*...

b Do you know whether or not the party has been cancelled?

ON ...*is (still) on*...

2 a Could you explain that again – I can't quite understand what you're trying to say.

AT ...*getting at*...

b I'm not surprised he called you a terrible nag – you're always criticizing him for the slightest thing.

AT ...*getting at*...

3 a Do you think that people are attracted to partners who remind them of their parents?

FOR ...*go for*...

b They had the dog put down because it suddenly attacked a child for no reason.

FOR ...*went for*...

4 a The mower's not working – could you get a mechanic to come and have a look at it?

DOWN ...*has broken down*...

b The latest round of peace talks have collapsed amidst bitter recriminations.

DOWN ...*have broken down*...

5 a I had to throw the milk away because it was sour.

OFF ...*had gone off*...

b At first we got on really well, but then we found we were no longer attracted to each other and we broke up.

OFF ...*had gone off*...

THE HARD SELL

Supply and Demand

talking points

If these products suddenly became difficult to obtain, which would you be prepared to pay the most money for and why?

sugar   salt   coffee / tea   rice   water   petrol   soap   chocolate tickets to see your favourite pop group

exam tip

Do not waste time focusing on non-essential information, eg why these things would have become difficult to obtain. Focus on the task in question, justifying your choice of products.

reading

A Read the following article and explain what the title *Tulipomania* means.

TULIPOMANIA
one of the earliest and weirdest strains of moral epidemic

THE tulip, Dr Mackay tells us, was introduced from Constantinople to western Europe, and particularly to Holland, in the middle of the sixteenth century. It became increasingly popular among the rich until, by 1634, "it was deemed a proof of bad taste for any man of fortune to be without a collection of them".

By then, the middle classes had decided that they too could not be seen without tulips, and paid increasingly outrageous prices for them. At a time when you could pick up a suit of clothes for 80 florins[1], people invested 100,000 florins buying 40 roots. Tulips became so valuable that they had to be sold by the *perit*, "a small weight less than a grain".

Some tulips were more valuable than others, but none was as prized as the *Semper Augustus*. In early 1636, there were only two of these in Holland: one went for 12 acres of land; the other for 4,600 florins, a new carriage, two grey horses and a complete set of harness.

Newcomers to Holland sometimes paid for their ignorance of the mania. A sailor, arriving at a wealthy merchant's house, was offered "a fine red herring" for his breakfast. He was partial to onions and seeing a bulb very like an onion on a counter, he slipped it into his pocket and headed off to the quay to eat his breakfast. He was found, quietly sitting on a coil of rope, finishing off his 3,000-florin *Semper Augustus*.

Up to now, the tulip market still had a semblance of order. However extraordinary prices had become, it was driven by the pursuit of a relatively rare commodity. In 1636, however, tulip exchanges were set up in the stock markets of several Dutch cities, and the speculators moved in in earnest. According to Dr Mackay: "The stock-jobbers, ever on the alert for a new speculation, dealt largely in tulips, making use of all the means they so well knew how to employ to cause fluctuations in prices."

By judicious trading as prices ebbed and flowed, many people grew rich. "A golden bait hung temptingly out before the people, and one after the other they rushed to the tulip-marts, like flies around a honey-pot. Everyone imagined that the passion for tulips would last for ever... The riches of Europe would be concentrated on the shores of the Zuyder Zee, and poverty banished from the favoured clime of Holland." Everyone, "even chimney-sweeps and old-clothes-women" dabbled in tulips. People sold their houses at ruinously low prices to buy tulips. Lawyers, "tulip-notaries", appeared to make their bit from the trade.

The rich, for their part, were no longer inclined to put such valuable commodities in their garden, preferring to join in the trade, and it was not long before some of them realised that the market had lost all logic. They started to sell, and panic soon spread through the market. Buyers who had agreed to pay so many florins when tulips were delivered in six weeks' time, refused to pay because the price had fallen in the meantime. As sellers demanded the full amount and buyers refused to pay, defaulters were announced by the hundred. Substantial merchants were reduced almost to beggary, "and many a representative of a noble line saw the fortunes of his house ruined beyond redemption".

There was an attempt to bring some order to the market as it crashed around the tulip holders' ears. They lobbied the government, which told them to agree a plan between themselves. Eventually, after much bickering, it was agreed that all contracts made at the height of the mania, before November 1636, would be declared null and void, and that those made after that date should be nullified by the purchaser paying 10 per cent to the vendor.

This displeased both sides, and The Tulipomania collapsed in disorder. "Those who were unlucky enough to have had stores of tulips on hand at the time of the sudden reaction were left to bear their ruin as philosophically as they could," Dr Mackay says. "Those who had made profits were allowed to keep them; but the commerce of the country suffered a severe shock, from which it took many years to recover."

[1] *Foreign coin of gold or silver.*

B Multiple-choice questions. Choose the best answer to the questions below.

1 According to the passage title, the strange phenomenon Tulipomania was
A an insane craze.
B an intense fixation.
C a mental obsession.
D an ethical disease.

2 By 1634 the possession of tulips was thought to be
A a sign of bad taste.
B a dissipation of wealth.
C a status symbol.
D a display of one's popularity.

3 An unfortunate sailor who had never been to Holland before
A paid 3,000 florins for what he thought was a tulip bulb.
B was tricked into eating an expensive tulip bulb.
C stole 3,000 florins from a wealthy merchant's house.
D consumed what he thought was an inexpensive onion.

4 Throughout 1636 tulip prices
A decreased rapidly.
B rose and fell dramatically.
C increased sharply.
D remained for the most part steady.

5 Why did the tulip market eventually collapse?
A The poor could no longer afford to buy tulips on the open market.
B The rich undermined confidence in the market for tulips.
C There was not enough money in circulation to meet the demands of the market.
D Producers could no longer supply enough tulips for the market.

6 The government eventually decided that
A contracts made before November 1636 would be honoured.
B contracts made after November 1636 would be entitled to compensation.
C those with unsold supplies would be compensated.
D those who had made a profit would be taxed.

7 What is the main point the writer is making?
A It is often difficult to supply the market with the commodities it demands.
B Man's acquisitive nature can create ridiculous artificial demand for commodities.
C Commodities in short supply always create excessive pressures on the market.
D Buying and selling is an extremely inexact science.

vocabulary

A Find words or expressions in the article which mean the same as the following. They are all connected with buying, selling, or losing money.

1 trader *merchant*
2 something in great demand but short supply *rare / commod*
3 places where shares are bought and sold *exchange / stock*
4 those prepared to take a high risk with investment
5 those dealing in shares *speculators*
6 astute buying and selling *judic trading*
7 those unable to honour their debts *default*
8 extreme poverty
9 buyer *beggar*
10 seller *purchaser*

B These verbs all appeared in the article:

traded dabbled fluctuated crashed ruined went for spread made

Choose one in its correct form to complete the sentences below.

1 One tulip bulb ...*went for*... thousands of florins plus a carriage and horses.

2 In the late 1920s the stock market ...*crashed*... leaving thousands of people destitute.

3 When the company started selling all its shares, panic ...*spread*... through the stock market.

4 The price of coffee ...*fluctuates*... according to the season.

5 The company ...*traded*... with organizations abroad, which resulted in its expansion.

6 He's no expert but he occasionally ...*dabbles*... in stocks and shares just for fun.

7 Often huge profits were ...*made*... by those trading in tulips.

8 She was financially ...*ruined*... when her business collapsed.

C **Expressions.** It says in the article, you could *pick up a suit of clothes for 80 florins.*
What does *pick up* mean?
Look at the sentences below. They all contain an expression with *pick*. Can you explain
what the expressions mean?

[handwritten margin notes: singled out, victimise, learned, collect, become infected, no enthusiasts little, select, start fight, move slowly, start again with what's left]

1 He was *picked out* from three hundred contestants to represent his country in the Olympics.
2 Stop *picking on* me – the accident wasn't my fault.
3 I soon *picked up* the language when I went to live in Germany for three months.
4 Can you *pick up* the flowers from the florist's?
5 Don't come too near me – I think I must have *picked up* a bug somewhere!
6 She sits and *picks at* her food – she never seems to enjoy anything.
7 Why don't you go shopping in one of those big chain stores? They have more to *pick and choose* from.
8 Small children like to *pick a quarrel with* each other.
9 They *picked their way* carefully through the thick undergrowth.
10 Well, he's left me, so I'll just have to *pick up the pieces* and make the best of a bad job.

D **Now use one of the expressions above in its correct form to complete the sentences below.**

1 Learning how to drive a car properly is not something you can ....*pick up*...... overnight.

2 He's such a bully – always ..*picking on*.... anyone smaller than himself!

3 After the floods wrecked their home they just had to ....*pick pieces*.. and start their lives all over again.

4 I'm working late tonight so can you .*pick up*........ the car from the garage? They should have finished the service by then.

5 They *picked their way*.. through the snow and ice and managed to reach the village by nightfall.

6 Even when he was at school, the heavyweight champion was always trying to .*pick quarrel*.... with other boys on the smallest pretext.

7 Stop .*picking at*....... your vegetables – think about all those people who have hardly anything to eat at all.

8 She was *picked out*.... as being one of the most promising newcomers on the stage for years.

Structure	**Selling your Wares**

talking points

A **Why would / wouldn't you buy goods from the following people?**

- a person in the street
- a 'telephone' salesperson
- a mail order catalogue
- a door-to-door salesperson

B **What do you understand by the following?**

- a charity shop
- a jumble sale
- a car boot sale
- a pawnbroker

- hire purchase
- interest free credit
- plastic money
- discount prices

Which do you consider to be potentially beneficial / undesirable ways of raising, spending or saving money?

cloze development

A **Read the following extract about someone who is remembering what he did in his youth.**
He is using American English and a rather fragmented style (eg *mornings* instead of *in the mornings*, and *seemed* instead of *it seemed*) as he recalls his experiences as a door-to-door salesman.
The 20 words on the right have been taken from the extract and printed next to the line from which they have been omitted. Show where you would insert the words using a /. The first gap has been marked for you.

exam tip

Remember to check that your chosen answer fits with the information, vocabulary and structure before and after the gap.

I sold funeral insurance to North Carolina black people.
I myself am not black. Like everybody / who was alive fifty-nine
years ago, I was young then, you know? I still feel bad
about what went on. My wife says: Telling might help.

5   Lately, worrying over this takes a percentage of my sleep
right off the top. So I'm telling you. OK?
   I did it to put myself through college. I knew it wasn't
right. But my parents worked at the cotton mill.
I went everything they earned before they earned it.

10 I grew in one of these employee row-houses. Our place
stood near the cotton loading-ramp. Our shrubs were
always tagged with fluff blown off stacked bales. Mornings,
the view might show six white, wind-blown hunks, as big as cakes.
You didn't understand you'd steadily breathed fibres –

15 not till, like Dad, you started coughing at age forty and died
at fifty-one. I to earn everything myself. First I tried
peddling the *Book of Knowledge*. Seemed like a good
thing to sell.
   I attended every training. The sharp salesman showed us how

20 to let the 'T' volume fall open at the Taj Mahal. Our company
had spent little extra on that full-page picture. In a living-
room the size a shipping crate, I stood before my seated
parents. I practised. They nodded. I still remember,
'One of the finger takes us from "Rome" to… "Rockets"!'

25 Before I hiked off with my wares, Mom pack a bag-lunch then
wave from our fuzzy porch. 'Jerry? Say "Please" and "Thank
you very much". They like that.'
   Other sales kids owned cars. I had to walk from house to
house my sample kit; twenty-six letters' worth of knowledge

30 gets heavy pretty fast. My arms and back grew stronger but
my spirits sort of in. Our sales manager assigned me to the
Mill district – he claimed I had inside ties. The only
thing than facing strangers door-to-door is finding people
you know there.

35 Grinning, they'd ask me in. Mill employees opened their ice-
boxes, brought me good things. I chattered my whole
memorized. Neighbors acted proud of me. But I felt like
a circus dog and stuffy teacher, mixed. Like a crook. When I
finished, my hosts, said this book-set sure sounded great.

40 Then they admitted what we'd known along – they just couldn't
afford it. I'd spent forty minutes ignoring this. They looked
troubled as I backed out, smiling. 'Hey,' I called. 'You'll
save for the down payment. You'll get "Knowledge" in time –
it'll mean more to you.' Then I knocked at the next door.

45 I stood for an empty house. ■

1	else
2	pretty
3	somebody
4	only
5	through
6	up
7	such
8	had
9	session
10	a
11	of
12	flick
13	would
14	lugging
15	caved
16	worse
17	routine
18	sighed
19	all
20	praying

B Passage interpretation. What did the writer feel about his job as a door-to-door salesman and what problems did he encounter?

direct / reported speech

A These examples of reported speech, and of direct speech without punctuation, appeared in the passage.

He claimed I had inside ties.
My hosts said this book-set sure sounded great.
They admitted they just couldn't afford it.

What changes would you have to make to these sentences to write what the speakers actually said?

B Reported questions require other changes. Look at this sentence:

She would ask me in.

What might she have said?

How would you report the following questions?

'Have you ever sold books before?'
'How many books did you sell?'

C Remember to eliminate unnecessary expressions connected with direct speech. You can do this by using reporting verbs to convey added meaning or emotion.

EXAMPLE *'Yes, it's true – I can't remember whether I told them or not.'*
He admitted that he couldn't remember whether he had told them or not.

Report the sentences below, using one of these reporting verbs:

announced   whispered   explained   confessed

1 'Now to mend the fuse, first you unscrew this part.'

Paul . . . .

2 'Psst! Guess what? My father's just won a lot of money!'

Sally . . . .

3 'OK. Fine. You're right. I did it.'

The thief . . . .

4 'I'm not going to marry him – so there!'

Rebecca . . . .

D What happens to the tenses in the reported sentences when a statement is still a fact or still true, when certain modals or conditional forms are used, or when the reporting verb is in the present?

1 'We're negotiating terms at the moment.'

The President says that they . . . .

2 'I might pop round this evening.'

She said she . . . .

3 'If I were younger, I would learn how to use a computer.'

He says . . . .

4 'Would you mind not smoking in the library?' the teacher asked the students.

The teacher asked the students if . . . .

E *Suggest* **often presents problems.** Are these phrases correct?

He suggested me that...
He suggested me to go...

When should *suggest* be followed by *-ing* and when should it be followed by *that (you)* + simple present / simple past / *should*?

Report the following sentences using the prompts given.

1 'Let's have a barbecue,' said the students.

The students suggested ....

2 'Why don't you have a barbecue?' said Tim to his mother.

Tim suggested..

3 'We could try that new place for dinner,' said Bill.

Bill suggested ....

4 'If I were you, I'd do that essay again,' said the teacher.

The teacher suggested ....

F **Some reporting verbs can be followed by a gerund.**

EXAMPLE *'I never copied from my fellow students.'*
He denied copying from his fellow students.

Some can be followed by a preposition and gerund.

EXAMPLE *'I'm sorry I forgot to phone you.'*
She apologized for forgetting to phone me.

Other verbs can be followed by an infinitive.

EXAMPLE *He agreed to let me have a discount on the TV.*
She promised not to divulge her source of information.

Complete the sentences below using either the gerund or infinitive, in the positive or negative form. In some examples you will need to supply a preposition.

1 He insisted (do) the job himself.
2 She objected (have) to write the report again.
3 The teacher warned the children (cross) the busy road by themselves.
4 Those students were inquiring (take) an English course.
5 The company workers criticized the management (comply) with the new safety regulations.
6 The doctor admitted (make) a mistake with the prescription.
7 She threatened (sue) the company for neglecting safety precautions.
8 She complained bitterly (have) to get up so early in the morning.
9 The old man pleaded (be set) free from his prison cell.
10 The opposition leader urged the members of parliament (vote) against the unpopular tax bill.

What do you think the speakers actually said in the above examples?

G **In reported speech, remember to change words that relate to the present only when circumstances change.**

What would you put instead of the following?

today   yesterday   tomorrow   at present, now   this, these

here and now   next week   last week   a year ago

*reporting verbs
and accompanying
adverbs*

A Report the sentences below using one of the verbs in the list to replace *said*.

muttered   boasted   protested   conceded   denied   announced

EXAMPLE *'No, I haven't misappropriated company funds,' he said.*

He denied that he had misappropriated company funds.
He denied misappropriating company funds.

1 He said, 'Well, maybe I have not put as much effort into the job as I could have done.'

He ....

2 'I most certainly did not steal the money,' he said.

He ....

3 'I'm going to have a baby,' she said.

She ....

4 'Honestly, I really did do the homework myself,' said the student.

The student ....

5 'I am the greatest gymnast ever,' said the gold medal winner.

The gold medal winner ....

6 'I need to go to the bathroom,' said the little boy under his breath.

The little boy ....

B Which of the following adverbs could be used in sentences 1–6?

proudly   angrily   grudgingly   pompously   defiantly   discreetly

Can you read the actual words of the speakers in sentences **1–6** to convey the tone of the adverb you have chosen?

Summary Skills

After-Sales Disservice!

talking points

A Look at the following cartoon. What is it trying to show?

How successful is it in making its point?

B Simulation. You are buying an expensive computer and can select **one** of the following after-sales services **free**. Which would be the most useful?

- a two-year hardware replacement guarantee
- updated software for two years
- a visit by an expert to instruct the purchaser in how to use the equipment
- a computer course at the place of purchase running over six months
- a computer magazine delivered to a place of your choice for two years
- a permanent telephone help line

exam tip

Do not spend too much time making your choice. Remember to 'skim' read and make a decision quickly. You can always refer back to the other points after you have started speaking.

Asking questions to focus on information. Read the following article and the sample questions for the first two paragraphs below. Then continue writing purely factual questions of your own for paragraphs **3** to **9**.

A Hard Lesson follows the Soft Sell

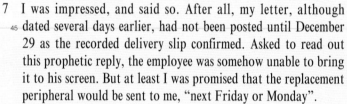

1 This is an account of an experiment to test after-sales service in the computing world. It is also an unremitting tale of woe.

2 The saga begins at the end of November last year when, needing some extra equipment for a computer, I placed an order with a specialist company for the goods. The add-on duly arrived but proved not to be working properly.

3 This, in itself, was not a terrible event. Electronic goods can become temperamental when shunted through the postal process and are normally promptly replaced. Less reasonable, however, was the fact that the gadget had arrived together with a sheet of paper detailing several facilities which were featured in the manual but NOT implemented in the model I had received. In fact I, and everyone else who had placed a similar order, had been sent a pre-production unit for the full price of the advertised item.

4 For a computer journalist this was no real problem. A quick call to the company's public relations firm would certainly have produced immediate apologies and the required product. But, on the basis that this is not a route open to most users, I decided to proceed more conventionally, returning the goods and requesting both a full working model and an explanation.

5 An initial telephone query to the company had resulted in the claim that most customers would not mind (which translates as "would not notice") the missing features and anyone who did could always send it back for replacement. My letter (recorded delivery) pointed out that to expect the recipients of substandard goods to go to the added expense of having to post them back in order to get what they had paid for was adding insult to injury.

6 It was a detailed and courteous letter from an unsatisfied customer. Over a month later it had received no reply. A telephone call to the managing director (still as from an aggrieved customer) established that he was in a meeting from which he would never emerge and that it was necessary to speak to an official who expressed shocked surprise that I had not received a reply to my original letter. Their computer showed, he said, that the reply was sent out on December 28.

7 I was impressed, and said so. After all, my letter, although dated several days earlier, had not been posted until December 29 as the recorded delivery slip confirmed. Asked to read out this prophetic reply, the employee was somehow unable to bring it to his screen. But at least I was promised that the replacement peripheral would be sent to me, "next Friday or Monday".

8 Several Fridays and Mondays duly arrived. The goods, however, did not. Suppressing the temptation to end the experiment, I wrote again to the invisible managing director requiring, within a week, the return of my property plus reasonable compensation for expenses incurred, lost interest on my money over some three months and the amount of time spent trying to sort out the situation.

9 Ten days later, silence having continued to prevail, I received another telephone call, this time from the company's public relations firm. They knew nothing of the problem, having called to ask me if I was interested in a new computer program. At this point my resolve weakened and I revealed all. The result was predictably rapid. The vanished add-on arrived by courier the next morning. A week later came a deeply apologetic letter from the managing director together with some software in lieu of compensation.

EXAMPLES **Paragraph 1**   What is the article about?
Paragraph 2   What happened when the extra equipment arrived?

Compare your questions with those of another student. Did you focus on the same areas of information?

comprehension

A **Explain the meaning and the implication of the following as they are used in the article.**

1 unremitting tale of woe (line 2)
2 become temperamental when shunted through the postal process (line 8)
3 adding insult to injury (line 28)
4 a meeting from which he would never emerge (line 33)
5 this prophetic reply (line 47)

6 Several Fridays and Mondays duly arrived (line 50)
7 silence having continued to prevail (line 57)
8 my resolve weakened (line 61)
9 I revealed all (line 61)
10 in lieu of (line 64)

B **Read the conclusion of the article below and find words and phrases which mean the same as the following.**

1 those at fault
2 sad story
3 became a casualty of
4 moved their attention away from the most important thing

5 a very serious mistake
6 cheated
7 to be prolonged tediously
8 slow moving

p 83

The names of the guilty parties have been left out of this sorry saga because it is a small company, producing some admirable products, which fell victim to a common problem of success in the computing industry. The sheer volume of that
70 success took the management's eye off the ball – which is the service given to customers – while it developed its range. In an industry this competitive, that can be a fatal error.

Computer goods must meet the same standards as other consumer products, and unless you agree in advance to buy a
75 product with some features missing, you have been short-changed if that is what you get. If the company will not either refund your money or replace the goods immediately, do not follow my example and allow correspondence to drag on indefinitely. Report the matter to the local Trading
80 Standards Office – always a good way of getting a quick response from an otherwise sluggish business. ■

summary

p 83

Write a summary of between 60 and 80 words summarizing how the company dealt with the writer's problems.

1 stated on phone
2 no reply first letter
3 e

| **Listening and Speaking** | **A Foot in the Door** |

talking points

Try your hand.

1 Could you persuade someone to buy something from you?
Try to sell a partner one of the following:

- a new-style felt-tip pen
- a foreign language course on tape
- double glazing
- an everlasting battery

Remember you must:

- sound convincing.
- answer any questions your partner may ask about the product.
- stress the quality of the product.
- emphasize its value for money.

2 Analyse your success.

Was your partner tempted to buy what you offered?
What kind of arguments did he / she put forward for not wanting the product?
How could you have been more persuasive?

listening

A The ten-point plan, part 1. Listen to someone training a new recruit to a firm selling water purifiers. She is explaining a ten-point plan. Listen to the tape and take notes on the following points.

1 The plan operates on a scale of...

2 It's a strategic approach to ....

3 If you follow the plan, you...

4 Preparation: **a** identify...

　　　　　　　　　　b prepare necessary..

5 Wear ....

6 For the water test take ....

7 You should appear..

Check your answers to the points above before doing the next exercise.

B The ten-point plan, part 2. Now listen to the rest of the tape, which is a detailed description of the ten-point plan and fill in the missing information below.

THE TEN-POINT PLAN

TIME SCALE
ONE HOUR

2 mins

5 mins

10 mins

15 mins

30 mins

35 mins

40 mins

50 mins

1 hour

PREPARATION
• Customer • Paperwork • Location • Appearance • Kit • Attitude •

1 ....

Husband and wife • Don't **2** .... •
Objections at door • Introduction •

ICE BREAK

3 .... • Identify problem • Needs and wants •

4 .... • Qualify company •

ASK QUESTIONS

How long have you lived here? • Do you work locally? •

5 ....? • How long have you been thinking about ...? •

6 ....

Stage management • Watch **7** .... • Price condition •
Prime Finance • Re-establish needs and problems •

DEMONSTRATION

Collect Dem-kit • Show product — features and benefits •

8 .... (Water test) •

QUALIFY

Product • Decision **9** .... •

PRICE

Keep selling • **10** .... closing • Confident price •

CLOSE

11 .... • Use many closes, orders gained after 4th no.

12 ....

Go through customer's copy • Reassure • Recommend • Tell them what happens next •
Change subject • **13** .... • (See again on installation date) •

vocabulary

A **Homonyms.** The word *scale* has at least three different meanings.

1 a coating that forms on metals when heated or rusted, eg the scale on the inside of a boiler.
2 a thin, flat, overlapping covering on many fish and reptiles.
3 the proportion that a map bears to what it represents, eg a scale of one centimetre to one kilometre.

The following words appeared on the tape. Can you find another meaning for each one? You may be able to find more than one!

1	smart	**3**	sole	**5**	scene	**7**	stage	**9**	trial
2	break	**4**	set	**6**	pitch	**8**	demonstration	**10**	deal

B **Expressions.** Here are some idioms connected with trade, buying and selling. Complete the idiomatic expressions on the right so that they correspond with the explanations on the left. Here are the missing words.

around   bankrupt   bulk   wall   even   bad   stock   good   credit

1 something worth buying   **a** a . . . . buy

   something not worth buying   **b** a . . . . buy

2 go to different shops and compare goods or services
   before making a decision   to shop . . . .

3 make neither a profit nor a loss   to break . . . .

4 buy large quantities at a cheaper price   to buy in . . . .

5 not available at the moment   out of . . . .

6 a business fails   **a** it goes . . . .

                                                                                           b it goes to the . . . .

7 to delay payment of goods, eg by using a plastic card   to buy on . . . .

speaking

A **Look at these advertisements then answer the questions below.**

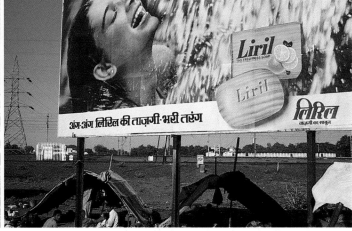

What are they advertising? Who are they aimed at? What image are they trying to create? What issues might they raise?

B **Which of the following statements do you agree or disagree with?** Explain why.

'Advertising should be banned as it persuades people to buy goods they do not need and often cannot afford.'
'Advertising provides information and stimulates trade.'

One of the features of the task-based question is that you may be given very little information on which to base your answer. This means that you will have the difficulty of thinking of suitable ideas, but it has the advantage of allowing you to keep to areas of vocabulary about which you feel confident.

Look at the following example:

You have been asked to write a report on the Book Club that your company's marketing department has recently started. Read through examples of complaints you have received, and make recommendations as to what improvements should be made. (About 350 words)

   a 'I received a bill from you for £2,339,126.99. What on earth is going on?'
   b 'Love the prices, hate the titles. Do you have much call for *Cattle Diseases in Botswana 1962–65*? But I'd be happy to pay for something worth having.'
   c 'What's the point of a catalogue with no blurb and no pictures?'
   d 'You recently sent me 25 copies of the same book. Do you think I'm a bookshop?'
   e 'You could have told me there were no pictures in this cookery book before I ordered it.'
   f 'I get your leaflet every month, but the choice of books you offer is so dull! Can't you do better?'

The title. This will specify what kind of composition is required – business letter, report, speech, informal letter, newspaper article, etc. Which of the above does the sample question ask for?

General themes. Before starting to write, you need to analyse each comment carefully to see what problems it mentions and what possible solutions it raises. Your aim is to extract general themes from specific complaints. Study each complaint and ask yourself a series of questions about it. For example, the first complaint might lead to the following:

- Is the bill reasonable? *No.*
- Why is it so high? *Probably a computer error – possibly a typing error.*
- What effect do errors like this have? *Create a bad impression – disorganization.*
- How can this kind of thing be stopped? *Check programs, improve management and possibly introduce training scheme for staff.*
- Have there been any similar complaints? *Yes – 25 copies of same book sent to customer.*

Now ask and answer questions about complaint **b**. When you have finished, compare your ideas with a partner.

Paragraph planning. If possible, do not write one paragraph about each point, as you may end up with a long list of short and disconnected paragraphs.

Your brainstorming session will have helped you to isolate a number of key problem areas which can be the basis of your paragraphs. Read the sample composition and note down the main problem area the paragraph is discussing, and which of the complaints (**a–f**) are referred to.

Paragraph 2	Main problem area	Mentioned in complaints ....
Paragraph 3	Main problem area	Mentioned in complaints ....
Paragraph 4	Main problem area	Mentioned in complaints ....

Language focus. Notice that the composition does not simply re-present the language from the quotations. Look through the sample and find what words or phrases were used to express the following:

- … so dull.
- the choice of books …
- Cattle Diseases in Botswana 1962–65
- blurb
- your leaflet …
- a bill for £2,339,126.99
- … sent me 25 copies … .

ACE BOOK CLUB

This report contains the results of the enquiries into the administration of the Ace Book Club following a number of complaints by members.

The most serious failing is that the variety and
5 range of titles on offer is not adequate. Low prices in themselves are not enough to generate demand and the sales policy should be re-examined. Efforts must be made to offer members a range of much more popular books at the best
10 discount possible, and specialist titles that have not sold well should be phased out entirely, however attractive the price.

The catalogue and other publicity material is not fulfilling its function. Although the distribution
15 and mailing are being carried out efficiently, the material is not creating demand. The catalogue should be rewritten and adequate information should be given about each title so as to stimulate interest. It should have illustrations
20 in full colour, and the cover of each book should be featured. If a particular title is being promoted heavily, samples of inside pages should also be shown where appropriate.

There were also a number of complaints about
25 grossly inaccurate invoices and multiple deliveries that suggested the possibility of problems with the computer program. My enquiries have shown that there is nothing wrong with the computer. The mistakes were
30 the result of typing errors by temporary secretaries who had been employed to cover for permanent staff. This policy should be stopped, and two secretaries from accounts should be retrained so that they can cover for absent staff
35 when necessary.

The above recommendations will be discussed in full at the next meeting on 24 June, but please feel free to contact me before then if you have any queries or if there are any other
40 suggestions you would like to make.

---

writing task **Write a report of about 350 words on the following subject.**

You have been asked to write a report for the manager of a team of young door-to-door salesmen who sell a variety of household cleaning products. Using the comments from local residents, make recommendations as to what should be done to improve results.

'It's all just rubbish – I mean, who wants to go on buying dusters week after week?'

'They look so scruffy. I can't imagine ever letting one of them into my house.'

'The fellow who came the other day was so surly and rude I asked him to leave even though I actually could have done with a couple of drying-up cloths.'

'You've got to be so careful these days with all these con men around.'

'There are always things we need but they never seem to have any of them.'

'I asked him if you could use the polish on furniture and he didn't have a clue.'

Stage 1 General approach. Use the model given in the sample composition as a basic outline.

Stage 2 Extracting information. Read the instructions and comments carefully. Try and identify the areas of weakness that each comment highlights.

Stage 3 Organization. Make sure that each of your main paragraphs follows the pattern of firstly identifying the problem and then suggesting answers.

Stage 4 Writing. Try and use your own words when discussing some of the problems. Remember that the style of the report needs to be fairly formal or neutral even if the style of the prompts is informal.

Stage 5 Checking. Read through your composition looking for one specific type of error.

Overview 11

Choose the word which best completes each sentence.

1 The outgoing president .... victory to his opponent.
   A admitted   **B** conceded   **C** claimed   **D** confessed

2 She .... agreed to go with him to the football match although she had no interest in the game at all.
   A apologetically   **B** shamefacedly   **C** grudgingly   **D** discreetly

3 He suggested .... a jumble sale to try and raise money for the scouts.
   A me to hold   **B** me that I held   **C** holding   **D** to be held

4 He had repeatedly warned the children .... playing too near the canal.
   A of   **B** with   **C** about   **D** for

5 After .... all his available resources in the venture, he was horrified when it failed miserably.
   A trading   **B** dabbling   **C** dealing   **D** investing

6 I'm afraid the supplies you requested last week are out of ....
   A order   **B** range   **C** sight   **D** stock

7 I believe Danish is a very difficult language to pick .... quickly.
   A out   **B** up   **C** at   **D** on

8 He insisted .... buying me a new suitcase to replace the one he had lost.
   A of   **B** about   **C** on   **D** in

9 'Well, the fact is – I took the money from the safe!' .... the bank clerk.
   A apologized   **B** regretted   **C** confessed   **D** entreated

10 He manages to get .... his monthly salary in a couple of weeks.
   A over   **B** through   **C** by   **D** round

Finish each of the following sentences in such a way that it means the same as the sentence printed before it.

1 'Let's go and have a pizza, shall we?' she said to her children.

She...

2 'I passed my driving test first time!' said Sam.

Sam boasted...

3 'Don't tell anyone or you'll be sorry,' Mary warned her friend.

Mary...

4 'Look! I'm telling you that I didn't break that window,' protested the youth.

The youth...

5 'If I were you, I'd tell your parents about it,' Anne said to Susie.

Anne suggested..

6 'Been waiting for a bus long?' the old man in the queue asked me.

The old man..

7 'I'm going to change the wheel on the car myself,' insisted Julia.

Julia insisted...

8 The manager asked, 'Have you made up your mind about the job?'

The manager wanted..

9 'You stole my gold bracelet!' she said to me bitterly.

She...

10 'Would you mind not mentioning the incident?' the secretary asked me quietly.

   The secretary . . . .

blank-filling   *Fill each of the blanks in the following sentences with a suitable word or phrase.*

1 He . . . . me of taking the car without his permission.

2 She . . . . to punish her son unless his behaviour improved.

3 The shop assistant asked the customer . . . . the receipt for the goods.

4 When the currency was devalued, panic . . . . throughout the country.

5 When the stock markets . . . . in the 1920s, millions of people were financially ruined.

6 He lost everything but he's trying to . . . . the pieces and start all over again.

7 The little girl promised that . . . . a lie again.

8 The policeman looked around the room and said, '. . . . . earth is going on here?'

9 You . . . . me you couldn't come to the concert before I ordered the tickets!

10 I asked the clerk . . . . sign the back of the cheque before I paid it in.

rewriting   *For each of the sentences below, write a new sentence as similar as possible in meaning to the original sentence, but using the words given in capital letters. These words must not be altered.*

1 The business is hardly making a profit at the moment.

   EVEN . . . .

2 Nowadays goods are often acquired but not paid for immediately.

   CREDIT . . . .

3 'Don't drink anything alcoholic if you're going to drive home!' said the father to his son.

   URGED . . . .

4 We never purchase small quantities as we would make less profit.

   BULK . . . .

5 'Please don't take my money, it's all I've got,' said the old woman to the intruder.

   PLEADED . . . .

6 Selling antiques made him a little extra money.

   DABBLED . . . .

7 The new manager blames me for everything that goes wrong.

   PICKING . . . .

8 They sold the car for £1,500.

   WENT . . . .

9 Books on animal diseases in Outer Mongolia are not exactly best sellers.

   CALL . . . .

10 We shall have an in-depth discussion about these recommendations at the next meeting.

   FULL . . . .

TAKING LIBERTIES

The Killing Fields

Discuss the following questions with another student.

1 Can you think of any countries where it is or was illegal to do the following?

a to criticize the government.
b to drink alcohol.
c to belong to a religious group.
d to travel without a permit.
e for a woman to drive.

f to get divorced.
g to be an intellectual.
h to be an atheist.
i to eat snake on a Sunday.
j to have more than one child.

2 How safe is your present system of law and government from being taken over by extremists?
3 Has your country ever been under totalitarian rule? What brought this about, and how did it end?
4 How would you react under a totalitarian government?

A Read the article below and answer the questions on page 161.

Journey to the front lines

The following morning the exodus began. Huoy and I packed the mosquito net, the mats and the clothes into bundles once again and attached them to the shoulderboard. Another journey. The Khmer Rouge said we were going to the 'front lines', but didn't explain what or where the front lines were. For all we knew we were going to the moon.

Around us, the other inhabitants emerged from the huts they had built of thatch and reeds and pieces of plastic, and started down the paths. It was a cold morning. The 'new' people wrapped their *kramas* around their shoulders to stay warm. Those who didn't have *kramas* or extra shirts shivered and rubbed themselves with their hands. We walked down the paths towards the railroad tracks, but not everybody in Phum Chleav was lucky enough to leave. Through the open door of a hut, we saw an old lady lying unconscious against a wall. Unable to walk and too heavy to carry, she had been left behind.

As we climbed onto the railroad track, which was elevated a few feet above the nearby ground and was the only dry place in the landscape, we looked around at the pitiful spectacle. And then I understood why the rice fields had been so empty of workers. It was as if all the patients I had visited in their huts had been multiplied many times over and put in a parade before our eyes. People with shrunken faces and haunted, vacant eyes, with legs and arms as thin as sticks or else puffy and bloated with edema. Leaning on canes or on relatives' shoulders, or alone, they walked with that terrible economy of movement that signals the approach of starvation.

As Huoy and I watched, a thin, scrawny, middle-aged woman put down the end of the hammock she had been carrying, slung under a bamboo pole. The man inside the hammock called out weakly,

'Sweet, sweet, bring me with you. Don't leave me behind.'

'Sweet, sweet, bring me with you. Don't leave me behind.' But the woman shook her head and trudged off down the railroad track. After a moment of indecision the man carrying the other end of the hammock abandoned it and hobbled off after her. No one went to the hammock to help the man. I didn't. Even if I could have helped him, there was no way that Huoy and I could have carried him. If we tried to carry him, we probably wouldn't make it ourselves.

What made it worse, what made it more appalling was that somehow it was ordinary. You put one foot in front of the other and you kept on walking. You heard the cries of the weak but you didn't pay much attention, because you were concentrating on yourself and your own survival. We had all seen death before. In the exodus from Phum Chleav, the atrocious had become normal.

How fast man changes! How fast he sheds his outer humanity and becomes the animal inside! In the old days – only six months before – nobody abandoned the dead. Now everything had changed – not just our burial customs but also all our beliefs and behavior. We had no more monks and no religious services. We had no more family obligations. Children left their parents to die, wives abandoned their husbands and the strongest kept on moving. The Khmer Rouge had taken away everything that held our culture together, and this was the result: a parade of the selfish and the dying. Society was falling apart. ■

B   Multiple-choice questions.

1   On being told they were going to the 'front lines', the writer felt
    A   apprehensive about being close to the fighting.
    B   resigned at having to embark on another journey.
    C   relieved that they were leaving Phum Chleav.
    D   worried about not knowing the way.

2   The writer describes the people as 'new'
    A   because they had only just woken up.
    B   because they had only recently arrived in the camp.
    C   as an ironical reference to their political re-education.
    D   because they were all going to the 'front lines'.

3   There had been so few workers in the fields because
    A   most of the ground had been flooded.
    B   the weather had been too cold.
    C   there had been a lack of medical supplies.
    D   they had not had enough food.

4   When the man in the hammock was left behind,
    A   his companions did not hesitate before abandoning him.
    B   the writer felt angry with the man's relatives.
    C   the writer knew that the man would die.
    D   the writer tried to persuade Huoy to carry him.

5   What shocked the writer about the exodus from Phum Chleav was
    A   the brutality of the Khmer Rouge soldiers.
    B   the fact that he had got used to seeing such suffering.
    C   the number of people who died.
    D   the poor state of health of the people.

6   The writer suggests that people quickly abandon all values except for
    A   religious beliefs.
    B   old customs and traditions.
    C   the bond between parents and children.
    D   the sense of self-preservation.

C   Style. The reading passage comes from a book by Haing S. Ngor, describing his life in Cambodia after the Khmer Rouge revolution. Read the passage again and answer these questions.

1   Can you find examples of expressions that are informal or colloquial?
2   Apart from the foreign words, is the vocabulary relatively simple or complex?
3   Comment on the length of sentences in the first six lines. In what way do they mirror the feelings experienced by the writer?
4   Would you classify paragraph **3** as mainly narrative or descriptive? What differences are there in sentence length and the use of adjectives compared with the rest of the passage?
5   Would you describe the passage overall as being formal or almost conversational?
6   Why do you think the writer has chosen to adopt this particular style?
7   How do you react to the passage?

language focus

A   *the use, to use, used to do* and *used to doing*. The word *use* can have a variety of different forms and meanings.

1   It can be used as a noun.

    EXAMPLES   *The use of the army to enforce the law was very effective.*
                   It's no use trying to escape.

2   It can be used as a main verb.

    EXAMPLES   *During the war, they used the palace as a prison.*
                   They used sticks and knives to dig the fields.

3   It can be followed by *to* and a gerund or noun to mean 'to be or get accustomed to'.

    EXAMPLES   *The people were used to obeying the soldiers' orders.*
                   I never got used to getting up so early.

4   It can be followed by *to* and an infinitive to talk about past states or habits.

    EXAMPLES   *Cambodia used to be a beautiful country.*
                   I used to walk past the monastery on my way to school.

5   Which examples of *use* have an /s/ sound, and which have a /z/ sound?

B **Comment on the difference in meaning of *use* in the following sentences.**
In which one:

c **1** is the word *use* a noun?   **a** I never got used to the terrible conditions.
d **2** is the word *use* a full verb?   **b** Things used to be much better before the revolution.
a **3** does *used to* mean 'accustomed to'?   **c** The government didn't have any use for intellectuals.
b **4** does *used to* refer to the past?   **d** Spies were used to keep an eye on dissidents.

C **Complete the following sentences with the correct form of the word *use*.** Add any words that are necessary.

1 Before the revolution, Haing S. Ngor ....used to.... work as a doctor.

2 The regime ...used.... terror as a means of controlling the population.

3 It was no ...use... complaining to the authorities.

4 Many of the peasants, who ...were used to.. living in the countryside, coped better than the townspeople.

5 The government ...used.... almost the entire population as unpaid agricultural workers.

6 There was widespread ...use... of torture in the prison camps.

7 Most people abandoned the values and principles that they ...used to... have.

8 Haing Ngor was shocked that he could ..get used to.. seeing so much suffering and remain indifferent to it.

9 The government made ...use..... of informers to identify dissidents.

exam tip
If you have not already done so, plan your revision schedule for the exam; give yourself enough time to look through your vocabulary and grammar notes and at your compositions. Try to ensure that the evening before the exam you have some free time during which you should relax and do no work at all.

Structure

The Scales of Justice

talking points
Use a dictionary if necessary and find out the meanings of the following crimes.

- *attempted murder*
- *arson*
- *reckless driving*
- *fraud*
- *joyriding*

- *blackmail*
- *rape*
- *assault*
- *forgery*
- *possessing a gun unlawfully*

- *libel*
- *shoplifting*
- *armed robbery*
- *tax evasion*
- *drunk driving*

1 Discuss what kinds of punishments would be suitable for these crimes.
2 Are there any crimes in your country that are currently receiving a great deal of attention from the media?
3 Can you think of any crimes that are seen as less serious than they were in the past?
Why do people's perceptions of the seriousness of certain crimes change over time?

cloze development
Read the passage opposite. Insert a verb from the list in each blank using the correct form of the gerund or infinitive. You may need more than one word for some spaces. (Remember, however, that in the examination you are only allowed to choose one word for each space in the cloze test.) The first two have been done for you.

knock	sway	come	concentrate	fire	drive	disregard	hear
report	murder	shoot	serve	get over	ensure	leave	

1 One of the quirks of the English legal system is that it can on occasions give a jury the opportunity (1) ....*to disregard*.... the technicalities of the law and bring in a verdict that conforms more closely to an instinctive feeling of what is just.

2 One of the most famous of these was the case of Stephen Owen, whose 12-year-old son Darren had been killed after (2) .....*being knocked*.... off his bicycle and crushed by a lorry. Mr Taylor, the lorry driver, left the scene without (3) ....*reporting*...... the accident, and it transpired that he had never had a driving licence and was blind in one eye. Mr Taylor showed no remorse for what he had done and, at his trial, he behaved in a very carefree and arrogant manner, which greatly distressed the family. He was sentenced to 18 months in prison for reckless driving, but in the event was (4) ....*to serve*...... only twelve months.

3 Stephen Owen could not (5) ....*get over*.... the death of his son. He was shaken by Taylor's callous behaviour and by how quickly he had been released from prison. The shock of finding that his son's grave had been vandalized was deeply traumatic, and when he discovered that Taylor had not stopped (6) ....*driving*...... after his release, he wrote a letter to the Queen (7) ....*demanding*..... that the ban was enforced. Owen had become totally locked into a repetitive thought pattern that was preventing him from leading a normal life. He traced Taylor to his home in Kent, and confronted him in the street. With a sawn-off shotgun he fired twice at Taylor at point blank range, hitting him in the back and his common-law-wife, Alison Barratt, in the arm.

4 They survived, but Owen was charged with possessing a shotgun and unlawful wounding; the most serious charge was that he had attempted (8) ....*to murder*..... Taylor. At his trial, the prosecution said that his (9) ......*shooting*...... had been pre-meditated. Owen claimed (10) ....*to have fired*... in a moment of near insanity and went on to say that he never intended to kill Taylor. At the end of the trial, the judge told the jury: 'Any parent must feel sympathy, understanding and compassion for a father or mother who receives a phone call only (11) ....*to hear*.......... of the death of a child.' But he warned the jury not (12) ....*to be swayed*...... by understandable sympathy for Owen, and advised them (13) ......*to concentrate*..... on what Owen's intentions were at the time of the shooting, regardless of what had happened beforehand.

5 The jury retired, and (14) ....*coming*......... to a decision was not difficult. The jury returned with a verdict of 'Not guilty' on all charges. Owen was relieved (15) ....*to leave*...... the court a free man. ■

---

gerunds and infinitives

A Read through your answers and find examples of the gerund:

1 in the passive, as in *She hates being told what to do* (paragraph **2**).
2 after a preposition, as in *They left the hotel without paying the bill* (paragraph **2**).
3 after a verb, as in *He enjoys skiing* (paragraph **3**).
4 after a possessive pronoun, as in *Do you mind my smoking?* (paragraph **4**).
5 as the subject of a sentence, as in *Sailing can be an expensive pastime* (paragraph **5**).

exam tip

Gerunds and infinitives are often tested in the blank-filling and rewriting exercises in Paper 3. Bear this in mind when you look through the questions.

B Read through your answers and find examples of:

1 the infinitive after a noun, as in *He has a great determination to succeed* (paragraph **1**).
2 *be* and the infinitive to express the future or future in the past, as in *He is to give a talk next week* (paragraph **2**).
3 the infinitive without *to*, as in *He made her leave the following morning* (paragraph **3**).
4 the infinitive expressing purpose, as in *I called by to see you last week* (paragraph **3**).
5 a verb that is always followed by an infinitive, as in *She decided to turn over a new leaf* (paragraph **4**).
6 the perfect infinitive, as in *He was thought to have bought the gun in London* (paragraph **4**).
7 the infinitive expressing consequence, as in *He arrived home to find his house in flames* (paragraph **4**).
8 the passive infinitive, as in *Justice must be seen to be done* (paragraph **4**).
9 the infinitive after a verb + object, as in *He persuaded them to return* (paragraph **4**).
10 the infinitive after an adjective, as in *She said she was willing to help me* (paragraph **5**).

C Transformations. Rewrite each of the following sentences.

1 It's pointless to appeal against your sentence.

There's no....*in appealing*..

2 He is determined to continue fighting to clear his name.

He has no ...*intention of giving up*...

3 It is thought that he was staying in London at the time of the assault.

He is ...*thought to have been stay*...................................

4 Elizabeth was shocked when she heard the news of her brother's arrest.

It came ...*as a shock to her when she heard*........................

5 The jury couldn't reach a verdict because of the complexity of the case.

The complexity of the case prevented ...*the jury*......................

6 All the other witnesses were called before Mr Jenkins.

Mr Jenkins was the last ...*witness to be called*.......................

7 I would prefer you not to discuss details of this case in public.

I'd rather ....*not discuss c*..................................

8 If you are called to do jury service, you'll have to take time off work.

If you are called to do jury service, it'll mean your ...*having to take*........

9 Leaving fingerprints behind was very foolish.

You were a...*a fool to leave*..................................

10 Craig claimed that he had not fired the gun.

Craig denied ....*having fired*.................................

changes in meaning

A Discuss the differences in meaning in the following pairs of sentences.

1 a I <u>regret</u> to say that we have decided not to offer you the job. *bad news*
  b I <u>regret</u> saying that I don't like your new boyfriend. *did it past*
2 a I've <u>tried</u> to open the bonnet, but it seems to be stuck. *attempt*
  b Have you <u>tried</u> cleaning the spark plugs? *experiment*
3 a He <u>remembered</u> seeing Jane on the way back from work. *saw/remembered fact*
  b She <u>remembered</u> to send her mother a birthday card. *did not forget*
4 a The professor mentioned Botticelli, and <u>went on</u> to talk about the Renaissance. *subseq*
  b He <u>went on</u> talking about himself for hours and hours. *would not stop*
5 a I'll never <u>forget</u> seeing the Taj Mahal for the first time.
  b She was angry with him for <u>forgetting</u> to lock the back door.
6 a I think we ought to <u>stop</u> to have something to eat soon.
  b They <u>stopped</u> going out in the evening when they had their first child.
7 a I <u>dread</u> to think what he's going to say when he sees what you've done to the car.
  b She <u>dreaded</u> having to see her ex-husband again in court.
8 a Your business is a complete shambles – the whole thing <u>needs</u> reorganizing.
  b I <u>need</u> to have a word in your ear. It's about your trip to Italy next week.
9 a I <u>meant</u> to write him a letter of condolence, but I never got round to it.
  b If you do join the Navy, it'll <u>mean</u> being away from home for months on end.
10 a Everyone <u>helped</u> to make the village look its best for the Prime Minister's visit.
  b I can't <u>help</u> feeling that you are making a terrible mistake.

B Complete these sentences by putting the verbs into either the infinitive or the gerund.

1 I've always regretted not ...*learning*...... (learn) to play the piano at school.

2 He became an MP in 1983 and went on ...*to become*.....(become) Prime Minister.

3 I dread .... (think) what he's going to say when he finds out I've crashed the car.

4 It's a very beautiful cottage, but it needs .... (modernize).

5 The house is a wreck; if you buy it, it'll mean ...*living*...... (live) in chaos for months.

6 I'm sure a good holiday would help ...*make*..... (make) you feel more relaxed.

Who Dunnit?

Match the names to these characters and explain why they are / were famous.

Hercule Poirot   James Bond   Batman   Supergirl

Think of a good detective story / thriller you have read or film you have seen and describe why it was entertaining.

extracting information

You are now going to use your skills in extracting information to try and solve a crime. Read the following extract from a story by G. K. Chesterton called *The Oracle of the Dog.*

THE ORACLE OF THE DOG

'Many mystery stories, about men murdered behind locked doors and windows, and murderers escaping without means of entrance and exit, have come true in the course of the extraordinary events at Cranston on the coast of Yorkshire, where Colonel Druce was found stabbed from behind by a dagger that had entirely disappeared from the scene, and apparently even from the neighbourhood.————— • —————

'The summer-house in which he died was indeed accessible at one entrance, the ordinary doorway which looked down the central walk of the garden towards the house. But by a combination of events almost to be called a coincidence, it appears that both the path and the entrance were watched during the crucial time, and there is a chain of witnesses who confirm each other. The summer-house stands at the extreme end of the garden, where there is no exit or entrance of any kind. The central garden path is a lane between two ranks of tall delphiniums, planted so close that any stray step off the path would leave its traces; and both path and plants run right up to the very mouth of the summer-house, so that no straying from that straight path could fail to be observed, and no other mode of entrance can be imagined.————— • —————

'Patrick Floyd, secretary of the murdered man, testified that he had been in a position to overlook the whole garden from the time when Colonel Druce last appeared alive in the doorway to the time when he was found dead; as he, Floyd, had been on the top of a step-ladder clipping the garden hedge. Janet Druce, the dead man's daughter, confirmed this, saying that she had sat on the terrace of the house throughout that time and had seen Floyd at his work. Touching some part of the time, this is again supported by Donald Druce, her brother, who overlooked the garden standing at his bedroom window in his dressing-gown, for he had risen late. Lastly the account is consistent with that given by Dr Valentine, a neighbour, who called for a time to talk with Miss Druce on the terrace, and the Colonel's solicitor, Mr Aubrey Traill, who was apparently the last to see the murdered man alive – presumably with the exception of the murderer.—— • ——

'All are agreed that the course of events was as follows: about half-past three in the afternoon, Miss Druce went down the path to ask her father when he would like tea; but he said he did not want any and was waiting to see Traill, his lawyer, who was to be sent to him in the summer-house. The girl then came away and met Traill coming down the path; she directed him to her father and he went in as directed. About half an hour afterwards he came out again, the Colonel coming with him to the door and showing himself to all appearance in health and even high spirits. He had been somewhat annoyed earlier in the day by his son's irregular hours, but seemed to recover his temper in a perfectly normal fashion, and had been rather markedly genial in receiving other visitors, including two of his nephews who came over for the day. But as these were out walking during the whole period of the tragedy, they had no evidence to give. It is said, indeed, that the Colonel was not on very good terms with Dr Valentine, but that gentleman only had a brief interview with the daughter of the house, to whom he is supposed to be paying serious attentions.————— • —————

'Traill, the solicitor, says he left the Colonel entirely alone in the summer-house, and this is confirmed by Floyd's bird's-eye view of the garden, which showed nobody else passing the only entrance. Ten minutes later Miss Druce again went down the garden and had not reached the end of the path when she saw her father, who was conspicuous by his white linen coat, lying in a heap on the floor. She uttered a scream which brought others to the spot, and on entering the place they found the Colonel lying dead beside his basket-chair, which was also upset. Dr Valentine, who was still in the immediate neighbourhood, testified that the wound was made by some sort of stiletto, entering under the shoulder-blade and piercing the heart. The police have searched the neighbourhood for such a weapon, but no trace of it can be found.'————— • —————

vocabulary

Complete the following information by supplying the correct words from the passage.

The (**1**) .... man was found lying in the summer-house. He had been

(**2**) .... through the heart. Patrick Floyd (**3**) .... and other

(**4**) .... (**5**) .... that no one had entered or come out of the

summer-house during the supposed time of the murder. The police (**6**) .... the

area but the murder weapon seemed to have disappeared without (**7**) .... from

the (**8**) .... of the crime.

comprehension

A   Answer the following questions.

1   Explain the so-called coincidence (paragraph **2**).
2   What was the significance of the two ranks of delphiniums?
3   Find an explanation in the text for Donald's rising late.
4   What kind of welcome had Colonel Druce given to his two nephews?
5   Explain in your own words *to be paying serious attentions* (line 89).
6   Where was Dr Valentine at the time of the supposed murder?

B   Crime-solving. To find out who the murderer is, follow these steps:

1   Make a list of the witnesses / possible suspects in the area at the time of the crime.
2   Make a sketch of the location of the crime and the whereabouts (if known) of the people you have listed.
3   Draw up a timetable of events leading up to the murder.
4   Suggest possible motives for the crime (either implicit or explicit in the text).

summary

The following is an account of the afternoon's events leading up to the murder, according to Patrick Floyd's evidence. Unfortunately three or four important details have been omitted.
Can you insert them in the appropriate places?

Compare your version with another student's.

That afternoon Floyd had been clipping the hedge during the time the murder must have been committed. Consequently he had witnessed Janet offering her father tea. During this time he saw no one else in the vicinity of the summer-house entrance. He was still engaged in his task when Miss Druce reappeared. _____ • _____

problem-solving

In groups of 3 or 4 decide who you think is the most likely suspect. Bear in mind that all the information given in the text is accurate and no one is lying.
CLUE   The solution has something to do with the layout of the summer-house and its position in the garden.

Mr Aubrey Traill   Donald Druce   Nephew   Janet Druce   Nephew   Dr Valentine   Mr Patrick Floyd

Crimes and Punishments

speaking 1

A Picture discussion. Look at the picture and answer the questions.

1 Describe the details of this statue, which stands above a famous court in London.
2 Discuss the symbolic significance of the sword and the scales.
3 Give a brief description of the system of justice that operates in your country.
4 How confident are you that you would be acquitted if you were charged with a crime that you had not committed?

B Weighing the evidence. Imagine you were called to do jury service. Read through the following types of evidence you might be presented with, and rank them in order of reliability.

- statements by independent eye-witnesses
- statements by friends of the defendant
- a signed confession by the defendant (now disputed)
- statements by enemies of the defendant
- your intuition
- circumstantial evidence
- forensic evidence
- police statements

listening

A Listen to the interview. Say whether the following statements are true or false according to Dr Lafford.

1 Sherlock Holmes provides a good example of the right mentality for forensic work.   T/F
2 The aim of the Forensic Science department is to help the police secure convictions.   T/F
3 The most convincing forensic evidence shows traces of mutual contact.   T/F
4 Investigations can now be carried out much faster thanks to sophisticated equipment.   T/F
5 It is principally because of human error that forensic science is not foolproof.   T/F
6 It is possible to determine whether a strand of hair came from a man or woman.   T/F
7 Only genetic fingerprinting can identify a suspect with 100% certainty.   T/F
8 It is important for the findings of forensic investigations to be interpreted properly.   T/F

B White fingerprints. Select and number in the correct order the five steps mentioned in the process of revealing a white fingerprint.

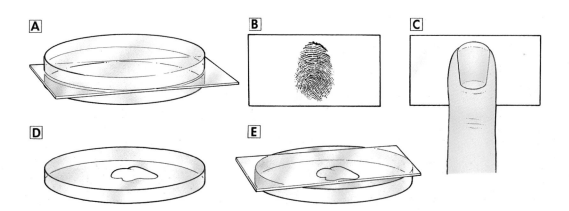

C Expressions. Complete the sentences using the expressions below, making any necessary changes.

- *to be a law unto oneself*
- *to be above the law*
- *the letter of the law*
- *the law of the jungle*
- *to lay down the law*
- *to take the law into one's own hands*

1 The jury freed him because although he was guilty according to . . . ., they all felt that he had done nothing morally wrong.

2 When she came home after midnight for the third time, her mother decided to . . . . and said she could not go out without her permission.

3 Just because he is rich and has powerful and influential friends, he thinks he is . . . . and can do whatever he likes.

4 You can't trust anyone in this prison – the only law here is . . . ., and only the strongest survive.

5 When the police refused to help, he decided to . . . . and to track down and punish the people who had attacked his daughter.

6 Our finance director is brilliant, but he's . . . . and won't have anything to do with normal office routines.

speaking 2

A Commenting on a passage. Read the following passage and answer the questions.

You stand convicted on each of twenty-one counts, on the clearest and most overwhelming evidence I have ever heard, of the crime of murder.

The sentence for that crime is not determined by me. It is determined by the law of England. Accordingly, in respect of each count, each one of you is now sentenced to imprisonment for life. Let them be taken down.

1 Is the passage spoken or written?

2 Who is the passage addressed to?

3 Where might the passage come from?

4 Who do you think might be saying or writing it?

5 What issues does the passage raise?

B Pair work. Choose one of the following two passages, and prepare a set of interview questions. Then ask your partner to answer the questions on the passage you have chosen.

Passage 1 Now, if you see a car with the engine running while stationary, with the bonnet open and a man examining the engine, take a good look. It may turn out to be a getaway vehicle, or they may be looking over a house before doing a job. Note the car number – even in ballpoint on the back of your hand.

Passage 2 My client has admitted that she has done wrong, but consider for a moment her abject poverty, and the cruel blows that life has dealt her. She acted in desperation, not out of greed but solely out of a desire to save her child's life. Could any of you, with your hand on your heart, say that you would have acted any differently?

C Communication activity. Read through the different ways of completing the sentence below. In small groups, discuss each of the statements and say whether you agree with them.

Rioting is …

- usually caused by unemployment.
- often a result of racial tension.
- probably quite good fun.
- often made worse by heavy-handed police tactics.
- inexcusable.

Complete each of the following sentences, then compare your ideas in groups.

1 The death penalty …
2 Going to court …
3 Owning a gun …

4 Prisons …
5 When it comes to justice, the rich …

True Stories

The previous narratives you have studied have been literary in style. In order to write a true story about a personal experience – or one that claims to be true – a different style and tone may be more appropriate. Discuss which of the alternatives, in each of the following, would be more suitable for a true story.

1 first person or third person
2 conversational or literary style
3 formal or informal vocabulary

A Skim read the following true story to get an idea of what it is about. Then complete the exercise that follows.

The Man who Came to Stay

1 The man who came to stay was brought to our house **(1)** . . . . He was hitch-hiking through the country and had been given a lift by some friends of ours. As he too was British and needed a place for the night, we had seemed to be the obvious choice.

2 **(2)** . . . . He was a man of about forty-five, fairly well-built, and full of over-friendly enthusiasm. **(3)** . . . . but Gordon, over a few drinks that evening, did his best to pre-empt any suspicions we might have had. He was a Colonel in the SAS, and, looking around the dimly lit bar, **(4)** . . . . He was in the village to collect money that was being wired to one of the banks, **(5)** . . . .

3 The evening wore on, and Gordon's confidence to tell improbable tales grew. When we mentioned that one of our friends had become a Muslim in order to marry a local girl, he expanded on his life story. By strange coincidence, **(6)** . . . . , he had become a

Muslim, and, as was the custom, had adopted a new Muslim name. While our friend had chosen the name Khaled, Gordon had opted for Ghadaffi. Remembering his rank in the army, we were amused to be having a drink with Colonel Ghadaffi himself.

4 In retrospect, **(7)** . . . . when we went to work and left this homeless, penniless stranger called Colonel Ghadaffi unsupervised at home. When we returned, he had, predictably enough, fled the scene, taking with him my passport, credit cards, cash, and everything he could lay his hands on.

5 He escaped across the border to Thailand and was never found. I presume that the passport was sold, and sometimes I find myself wondering whether **(8)** . . . . But at least if I wake up one morning to find myself surrounded by hordes of armed police with loud-hailers and helicopters, I shall know what has been going on.

B Sentence selection. For each of the numbered blanks, choose one sentence or phrase from the following list. Discuss which sentences or phrases are the most appropriate and why. The sentences are in the right order and are all grammatically acceptable.

1 **a** … while Peter, Chris and I were living and teaching in Alor Janggus, a remote village in Northern Malaysia, just across the border from Thailand.
   b … a few years ago when I lived abroad.

2 **a** Enter Gordon Stirling, or so he claimed.

   b He said he was Gordon Stirling.

3 **a** I wondered why he was travelling around the Far East, …

   b I did wonder quite what a man of his age was doing wandering alone around the Far East, …

4 **a** … he said: 'Don't tell anyone, but I'm a spy.'

   b … he explained to us in hushed tones how he had been engaged in under-cover operations around the world.

5 **a** … so would we mind paying for the drinks and he would pay us back?

   b … and he requested that we should purchase the beverages on his behalf and we would be subsequently reimbursed.

6 **a** … the very same thing had happened to him too

   b … his religious development had progressed along similar lines

7 **a** … perhaps warning bells should have rung the next morning

   b … an error of judgement was made

8 **a** … some drug baron or international terrorist is roaming the world pretending to be me.

   b … a criminal bought it.

focus on style

Irony. When you write a story, the reader normally expects the narrator, ie the person telling the story, to be in control. The narrator presents the information and comments on it where appropriate. However, if you wanted to create a sense of irony, you could present the information in such a way that it failed to match this expectation. The narrator can be 'infected' with the thoughts, feelings, or words of the characters and so give opinions without having to make a direct comment.

Look at paragraphs **3** and **4**, and find examples of where Gordon's words are reported without using direct speech or a reporting verb.

writing task

Write a composition of about 350 words based on the following title.

Write a composition that ends with the words 'I promised myself that I would never do anything like that again.'

Stage 1 General approach. This title allows for a very wide range of interpretations. Try, however, to write the composition as if it were a true story, even if it isn't, and think of two or three possible interpretations. For example, you could write about a mistake you once made that led to having something stolen; or you could write about doing something risky and foolhardy or something wrong from the point of view of personal relations or the law. Spend a few minutes thinking through two or three interpretations and choose the most promising.

Stage 2 Brainstorming. Decide what details will help you tell the story. If your composition is to be based on a real experience, some details will probably need to be filtered out because of length; if you are inventing the story, think of a few small details that will give your story credibility.

Stage 3 Organization. Select your ideas and arrange them into paragraphs. Make sure that your opening paragraph succinctly sets the scene with the place, the people involved and the time. Try and ensure that your story has a clear beginning, middle and end.

Stage 4 Writing. Pay particular attention to the tone of your story – it needs to be more conversational than literary if it is to sound convincing. Include a few short idiomatic phrases (not proverbs). Vary your sentence length, using a very short sentence once or twice for dramatic effect if appropriate.

Stage 5 Check your work, paying particular attention to vocabulary and tone. Try to ensure that you haven't used any words that are too formal, poetic or literary. Look for words that have been repeated and choose alternatives where necessary.

Overview 12

Choose the word which best completes each sentence.

1 When the bombing started, plans were made for an immediate .... of the city.
   A evacuation   **B** exodus   **C** departure   **D** vacation

2 He wrapped all his possessions up in a sheet and carried the .... on his back.
   A case   **B** rucksack   **C** bundle   **D** bag

3 I'm sure your bank manager will lend you a .... ear when you explain the situation to him.
   A merciful   **B** compassionate   **C** pitiful   **D** sympathetic

4 People who are squeamish are afraid of the .... of blood.
   A spectacle   **B** view   **C** sight   **D** look

5 She was furious after the argument she had had, and .... out of the house, slamming the door behind her.
   A stormed   **B** staggered   **C** trudged   **D** hopped

6 The witness's account was not .... with the facts.
   A matched   **B** reliable   **C** consistent   **D** confirmed

7 He is very ill, and the doctors are not sure whether he will .... it through the night.
   A last   **B** survive   **C** endure   **D** make

8 If you go on a diet, you'll find that giving up butter will help you .... a few pounds.
   A shed   **B** drop   **C** leave   **D** fall

9 He was forced to get out of the city and had to .... his family behind.
   A desert   **B** abandon   **C** let   **D** leave

10 A large number of tourists were waiting in front of the .... ground to see the soldiers.
   A parade   **B** procession   **C** demonstration   **D** rally

Fill each of the blanks in the following sentences with a suitable word or phrase.

1 After sharing a flat with friends for several years, it took him ages to ... get used to .... alone.

2 I was nervous about renting out my house, but it turned .... out to be .... a good decision.

3 We had the most terrible maths teacher at school – he was incapable ..... of explin .... anything clearly.

4 Be careful what you say – she isn't used .... being .... criticized.

5 There's .... no use in .... phoning the bank – everyone will have gone home by now.

6 She's very independent and hates ... anyone telling her .... how to run her life.

7 My sister prefers to cut her hair herself .... rather than having /to have .... it cut at the hairdresser.

8 The burglar wiped everything he had touched with a cloth ..... so as not ...... to leave any fingerprints.

9 I couldn't ...... get used to .... using the new computer, so I returned it and went back to my old one.

10 I regret ..... to tell you .... that the part you requested is not in stock.

For each of the sentences below, write a new sentence as similar as possible in meaning to the original sentence, but using the word given in capital letters. These words must not be altered in any way.

1 He didn't lock the front door when he left the house.

   WITHOUT...

2 It's a waste of time to try and get your money back.

WORTH ..... *trying* ....

3 They sent him to prison for three years.

SENTENCED ....

4 This mix-up is not my fault.

BLAME .... *not to blame* ....

5 The new equipment means that the work can be done more safely.

THANKS ....

6 In what way was his evidence important?

SIGNIFICANCE ....

7 If you send her away to boarding school, you won't see her for months on end.

MEAN .... *Sending* ...... *will* ....

8 Turning down that job was very foolish of you.

FOOL ....

9 We were not very surprised to hear that he had been stealing money from the company.

CAME ....

10 Peter was our first visitor in our new home.

VISIT ....

transformations Finish each of the following sentences so that it means the same as the sentence printed before it.

1 Everyone noticed that Jane was absent.

Jane was conspicuous..

2 I took little notice of the man standing at the gate.

I didn't pay ....

3 Soldiers obey orders as a matter of course.

Soldiers are..

4 He didn't say goodbye when he left.

He left without ....

5 Is it all right with you if I smoke?

Do you ....

6 I used to see a lot of her until she went to London.

I stopped ....

7 The colonel and the doctor did not get on well.

The colonel was not on ....

8 The three men were each sentenced to prison for life.

The three men each received...

9 Try to stay inconspicuous when you get there.

Try to keep ....

10 I'm afraid that I think he shouldn't marry her.

I can't ....

THAT'S ENTERTAINMENT

Getting your Act Together

Read the following extracts and discuss:
a what they are about.
b who might be speaking or writing them.
c where you might find them.

When you are doing the passages for comment section, try to approach it with a mental checklist of questions, asking who, what, when, where, what about, etc. for each passage.

1

grew up on Mozart and Schubert, so jazz was certainly a shock. At first I couldn't see how they could improvise for hours, it went so against my background. Even when they write things down in jazz, if you interpret it according to a classical training it comes out wrong, and there's no way to write down swing. I couldn't change myself into a jazz musician, of course, there's a fundamental difference of attitude and feeling.

2

An unusual double bill is playing for three days. *Dead Again* is Kenneth Branagh's stab at directing and starring in a murder / mystery alongside his wife Emma Thompson. The recently-released *Ruby* explores the theory of a Mafia / CIA conspiracy in the assassination of John F Kennedy. While *Ruby* is more compelling than *Dead Again*, the line-up is certainly value for money. ▷ ▷ ▷ ▶ ▶ ▶

3

I think it was bad luck rather than bad judgement. I had nursed *Reflected Glory* for weeks and weeks, but it just didn't find an audience. *Body And Soul* was only contracted to play for four weeks.

If it had done well, of course, it could have transferred, but the Albery Theatre wasn't very good for it and it never really made it.

4

With such colourless music and absurdly self-regarding but naive text, the sheer energy and commitment of the performers is remarkable – and very welcome. Timothy Lole conducting keeps a straight face and plays a brisk baton. At least one can believe dramatically and musically in the luxuriance of the singing and unaffected passion of the acting.

5

The two most enjoyable records of the New Year for me have both been groovacious compilation albums. **'Talkin' Loud 2'** functions as a credible shop window for new attractions such as **Bryan Powell, Urban Species and Perception**. It's a groove of one sort or another from start to finish, and it's a lot cheaper to buy than 15 CD singles. Also, look out for **'R U Conscious'**, an 11-track compilation of (very) basic underground British soul on the new Conscious label. Two ways to explore the margins and stay in the pocket. ◆

- -

Walk the Plank

Annie Wilson on how Walk the Plank got their financial act together and took to the sea

The Fitzcarraldo is an iron-clad Norwegian island ferry formerly named the Bjarkov. It bears little resemblance to the 350-ton steamship Werner Herzog hauled through the jungle in his film about building an opera house in Amazonia, from which the old ferry gets its new name, except in the proportions of its voyage and the dreams which made it possible.

The ship sailed into the grey waters of Glasson Dock early in the New Year. The storms had been tremendous, the wait in the Caledonian Canal long and expensive, but at last she arrived to dwarf every other vessel in the marina and capture the imagination of the small fishing village. The adventure had begun.

The Fitzcarraldo is the achievement of a dream for John Wassell and Liz Pugh and their company Walk the Plank, the "world's first marine theatre contractors". Their vision: to tour a theatre ship around the beaches and docks of Britain during the summer. There are two shows: one an extravagant fairy tale with a "green" environmental theme, written for them by Adrian Mitchell, the poet and playwright; the other a pyrotechnic spectacular for up to 2,000 people, combining music, magic, drama and dance with fireworks. The project has attracted arts departments around the coast, and the ship is booked from May to September.

"I think people like the spirit of adventure, the romance of it appeals," says Liz. "And conventional arts departments know that people who wouldn't necessarily buy tickets for the theatre or go to an art gallery might come and see our show."

Bringing the dream to life has been hard work. Their success in selling the tour, raising a £40,000 grant and an £82,000 bank loan – no mean achievement – has been dulled somewhat by the extra costs of the delays en route from Norway and of converting the ship to UK marine specifications.

But enthusiasm has not dimmed. The bank manager was persuaded (with difficulty) to extend the loan, the decks and sides of the ship were transformed with riotous paintwork, the rear deck has been converted into a seating area for an audience of 150 and the company of performers and musicians is ready for anything the seas can throw at it.

"The project has a momentum that can't be stopped," said Liz Pugh.

Her experience of boats was limited to the Norfolk Broads until three years ago, when she and John Wassell bought a wooden launch which proved the starting point for the Fitzcarraldo project. They spent the summers of 1989 and 1990 touring the Scottish islands with the Boat Band, literally singing for their supper. "That was the springboard for this idea, to expand it into a show on a ship, although it was a leap of the imagination from a 50ft boat to a 120ft ship with a 28ft beam."

For John, a former builder of wooden narrow boats, it was a lesser leap. Having organised large, site-specific events for an arts company and experienced the immense cost of touring, he realised that keeping everything on board ship would cut costs.

Glasson Dock is a small village but it has taken Liz and John to its heart. Over the last three years the couple have made a name for themselves by turning the traditional Bonfire Night of November 5 into a community event for 1,500 people, with a children's lantern procession and a 30-strong organising committee. Word about the Fitzcarraldo project spread like wildfire.

"They all knew the ship was coming because we sold them sea miles to raise funds and make ends meet," Liz said, "and then it took so long, two months instead of three weeks, that when it arrived it was very exciting. We were inundated with offers of anything from carpets to welding equipment, and all offers of help (there was a constant stream of willing helpers) were accepted."

Money may be tight indeed, but when the ship sailed at the beginning of May there was a distinct feeling that, if nothing else, the goodwill of the community alone would keep it afloat.■

Annie Wilson, *The Financial Times Weekend*

B Multiple-choice questions. Choose the best answer.

1 The ship bought by the theatre company was originally
   A used in the film *Amazonia*.
   B built in the Caledonian Canal.
   C used for touring the Scottish Islands.
   D employed as a passenger ferry.

2 The productions presented by *Walk the Plank* include
   A an appealing romantic drama.
   B a tale of adventure set in the countryside.
   C an art exhibition on board.
   D a legendary tale to encourage conservation.

3 Despite their initial success with the project the company owners
   A failed to raise the necessary finance.
   B failed to persuade enough people to book their shows.
   C had to cope with later unexpected expenditure.
   D were unable to comply with UK marine specifications.

4 Since John and Liz went to live in Glasson Dock
   A they have found accommodation in the centre of the village.
   B they have transformed a local celebration into a spectacular event.
   C they have had to sell most of their possessions to make ends meet.
   D they have run out of funds for their project.

C Comprehension. Explain the meaning of the following as they are used in the passage.

1 iron-clad (line 1)
2 to dwarf every other vessel (line 16)
3 a pyrotechnic spectacular (line 31)
4 has been dulled somewhat (line 49)
5 riotous paintwork (line 58)
6 the springboard (line 73)
7 a leap of the imagination (line 75)
8 spread like wildfire (line 95)
9 we sold them sea miles (line 97)
10 keep it afloat (line 111)

vocabulary

Expressions with *make*. The expressions *made a name for themselves* and *make ends meet* appear in the text. What do they mean? Here are some explanations of other idiomatic uses of the verb *make*. Try and fill in the missing words.

1	to establish your reputation	to make a … for yourself
2	to do what you can given the circumstances	to make the … of a bad job
3	to try and compensate for	to make …
4	to take some action	to make a …
5	to acquire more (money) by working or investing	to make a …
6	to do something laboriously or with much fuss	to make a … of something
7	to pretend	to make …
8	to exaggerate the importance of something	to make a mountain out of a …
9	to spoil or unsuccessfully try to do something	to make a … of

discussion

You are preparing a short item for a radio programme about *Walk the Plank*. Prepare your talk, a short text to be read aloud, by answering the following questions:

1 What is the Fitzcarraldo and how did it get its name?
2 What kind of shows does it put on?
3 How did John and Liz manage to finance the project?
4 How did they get the idea for the project?
5 What impact have they made on the village of Glasson Dock?
6 What are their plans for the future?

Formal Constraints

talking points

> *David Blackwood*
> requests the pleasure of your company for
> ## Dinner
> on Thursday, 6th June, 1994
> at the Randolph Hotel
>
> R.S.V.P. Law Society
> 8.00 for 8.30pm   White tie

Look at this formal invitation.

Discuss how you would reply to an invitation like this:
a if you were able to attend;
b if you were unable to attend; and what you would be expected to wear.

would like to thank but regrets

cloze development

Read the passage about preparing to go to a Law Society dinner. Fill each of the numbered blanks with one suitable word.

Any day now I am (**1**) .....about/going..... to reach my fiftieth birthday, and I had hoped to arrive at that safe (**2**) .point/landmark/have. without ever having to go skiing, enjoy opera, become a poker player or wear a white tie. I was (**3**) ...mistaken/wrong. about one of them. Last week I was (**4**) ...invited....... to a grand dinner for the legal profession and accepted because the guest list also (**5**) ....included.... my boss, a man whom I never get to meet (**6**) .normally/chat..us. I did not realize (**7**) ...until......... it was too late that it was white tie. So I rang a friend at *The Times* newspaper for his (**8**) ....advice..... . He does not run an advice column but until four years ago he was my next door (**9**) ...neighbour.. in London and I know that he knows about dressing grandly for strange (**10**) .occasions/events. 'When I go to hire this (**11**) .suit/coat/out.., Philip, what do I ask for exactly?' 'Dear boy, you don't hire it. Not only (**12**) .will/do/can.

you spend £35 hiring it but you will also go looking like a man who has just spent £35 hiring it. Now, I have at home a whole selection of stuff (**13**) ...inherited...... from uncles and fathers and if you go to my place and let my wife (**14**) ....kit........ you out, you will go to the dinner looking like a man whose white tie has been in the family for three (**15**) ..generations..... .' And so it was. The best fitting jacket was somewhat frayed, but cosily (**16**) .....so......... . It was also (**17**) ...missing..... a button, but Myrtle Howard flourished a spare one and sewed it on.

I entered my white tie and evening dress like a man becoming his own wax (**18**) .in.model.off. at Madame Tussauds. Like a waiter going to a restaurant, Myrtle thought. Or a conductor going to a (**19**) ...concert........... . 'A conductor wouldn't go on a bike,' I said. 'You're going on a bike?' she said. 'This I (**20**) ....must...... see.' ∎

vocabulary

A **The words below appeared in the passage.** Look at the context of these words, then find words or phrases which mean the opposite.

EXAMPLE   *hoped to arrive*   *dreaded arriving*

1 safe (line 2) – dang/pred treach
2 grand (line 6) simple
3 accepted (line 7) decline/turn down
4 boss (line 8) sub/infer

5 strange (line 15) ordinary/mundane/commurne
6 frayed (line 26) pristine/second
7 cosily (line 26) uncomfor
8 entered (line 30) took off

B **Now use one of the words or phrases you have found to complete these six sentences.**

1 It was a(n) .....ord........ day, just like any other. Nothing was going to happen and we knew it.

2 As he ....took off..... the uncomfortable uniform, he sighed with relief.

3 As we shall be away for the whole of August, I had to ...decline...... the invitation.

4 There are some ....dang/prec.. bends on these mountain roads.

5 Unfortunately, as well as being cheaper in price, the goods are also ....inferior....... in quality.

6 They lived a .....simple..... life with no extras, no luxuries.

discussion

Answer the following questions, then discuss your answers with a partner.

1 What do you think the writer would have done if he had noticed initially that the invitation called for formal dress?
2 How did the writer's friend feel about hiring evening dress?
3 How did the writer feel having *entered* his white tie and evening dress?
4 How did Myrtle react to the writer's announcement that he was going to the dinner on a bike?

inversions

A **In the passage above we had the sentence** *Not only would you spend £35 hiring it but you will also go …* . **Why does the writer use an inversion in this sentence? When do we normally use an inversion in English? Which verb in a complex sentence is inverted?**

neg adv/ words considered

B **Answer the following questions about inversions.**

1 If there is no ready-made auxiliary like *have* or *be* to form the inversion, what do you need to use? Fill in the missing words in these sentences.

 a Not only .do.... they hate going abroad but they also hate going on holiday.

 b Never .... he arrive on time. He is always at least half an hour late.

 c Not a sound .... they make, they were so frightened of being discovered.

2 We use an inversion when words like these appear at the beginning of a sentence, *rarely*, *little*, *only then*. Why? *neg / restricted meaning*

3 What differences in construction must you make when using *hardly*, *scarcely* and *no sooner*? Fill in the missing words.

 a Hardly / Scarcely had they closed the door ...than... the alarm went off.

 b No sooner had they closed the door ..than.. the alarm went off.

4 Often the inversion of the verb in the main clause appears later in the sentence.

 EXAMPLE *He managed to unlock the door by trying again and again.*
 Only by trying again and again **did he manage** *to unlock the door.*

 Transform this sentence.

 She realized that something was wrong when she set foot in the house.

 Only.. when she.. had set foot ....

C **Finish each of the following sentences in such a way that it means exactly the same as the sentence printed before it.**

1 He was working all day and all night as well.

 Not only...

2 He hadn't ever stayed in such a dreadful hotel before.

 Never had...

3 She dances beautifully and sings sweetly too.

 Not only...does...

4 I have never met such an infuriating person before.

 Never ..have..

5 She didn't spill a drop.

 Not a...drop...did...

6 They don't spend much money on entertainment.

 Rarely..

7   She doesn't understand how much suffering she has caused.

Little . . . .

8   We had only just finished putting up the tent when it started to rain.

No sooner . . . .

9   They discovered a cure for the disease by trial and error.

Only. . . . .

10   They didn't understand what the fuss was about until they saw the evidence for themselves.

Only when . . . .

Summary Skills	# The Perks of the Job

talking points

A   Describe the pictures and the activities. How might the people in the pictures be feeling?

B   Expressing opinions. Some companies offer employees and clients outings and entertainment as an incentive to motivation or winning contracts, or as a perk / benefit. Which of the following would appeal most / least to your friends and colleagues where you work / study?

- a night at the ballet
- a meal in an expensive restaurant
- free tickets to a pop concert
- a day's sailing on a yacht
- a day's training to be a racing driver
- a free weekend in a capital city of your choice

What about you?

comprehension

A Often a paragraph can convey far more information than its length might suggest.
Look at the following paragraph and answer the questions below. Your answers will give you clues about the underlying meaning of the paragraph.

> THE idea, the slim and smartly suited PR lady told me, was to gather together a group of key journos and take them fishing. Key journos, eh? The expression was undeniably
> 5 revolting. But to be thought of as one was – dare I say it? – soothing to the ego.

1 PR means Public Relations. What information does this convey about the lady?
2 *to gather together a group of key journos* (line 2)
  What does *key journos* mean and what does this tell you about the event?
3 *undeniably revolting* (line 4)
  What does this tell you about the writer's reaction to the expression used?
4 *soothing to the ego* (line 6)
  What does this tell you about the writer's reaction to being included in the event?

B Now write your own clues, like the ones above, to focus on the information highlighted below.

In the past I've tended to take **a dusty view** of outings arranged by public relations people for journalists – the **so-called freebie**. I now realise,
10 though, that **I had confused high moral principle with envy.** What was wrong with freebies was not that they were immoral, but that I was not on them.

This **philosophical sea-change began to dawn on**
15 **me** as the aeroplane **skimmed through the skies** towards Scotland.
The sea **sparkled** on my right, while on the other side, the snows of the Cairngorms **glittered** in the sunshine. I counted a score and more of rivers and
20 streams, **threading their way down** Scotland's heather-brown valleys.

C Read the rest of the article then answer the questions below.

By the time I was sitting in a spacious chalet by the river, spooning date pudding and fudge sauce down my throat and sipping my wine, I was
25 thoroughly converted to the new thinking. How else, I reflected – as I held up my plate for more of the heavenly suet – would I ever get to fish on Scotland's most famous salmon river?
I know next to nothing about fly fishing for
30 salmon and the conditions – brilliant sunshine and a stiff easterly wind – were not helpful. I did, however, learn something.

Among the genuinely key journos in the party was the renowned angling expert, Crawford Little. And
35 he, most kindly, gave me a casting lesson. I cannot boast that I was one of Mr Little's aptest pupils. But I think I was beginning to get the hang of it, when I was told it was time for me to go to the Lodge for the malt whisky tasting. I realised at
40 this point that whoever had devised the jaunt was showing an acute appreciation of the angler / journalist's requirements.

Tom Fort, *The Financial Times Weekend*

1 Explain why and to what the writer had been converted.
2 What is the heavenly suet and what has the writer just been treated to?
3 What exactly had the *freebie* outing offered?
4 Explain the meaning of *next to nothing* (line 29).
5 Who or what is Crawford Little?
6 What does the writer mean by *get the hang of it* (line 37)?
7 Rephrase the last sentence in your own words.

summary

Write a summary of 60 to 80 words outlining the writer's reasons for accepting the freebie and what seems to be the company's reason for organizing it.

speaking

A **Picture discussion: electronic wallpaper.** These pictures were taken by cameras inside television sets. They show what is happening in the room and, inset, the TV programme that was on at the time.

1 Describe what is happening in the photographs.
2 What do the photographs indicate about the attentiveness of the television audience?
3 Do you think the photographs give an accurate impression of how most people watch television?
4 How might broadcasters and advertisers react to the impression that these photographs give?
5 How many hours, on average, do you watch television every week? Do you watch to relax, for entertainment, for education, or as a result of addiction?
6 Do you think television has any effect on you or your family?
7 Did you have any controls imposed upon you by your parents as to what you watched and how often you watched TV? What controls would you impose if you had children?
8 To what extent do you think the government should control what is broadcast?

exam tip

Try and relate the content of the passages for comment to the overall theme of the interview. Be prepared to comment on the new issues raised.

B **Passages for comment.** In pairs, select one of the passages and prepare a set of interview questions about it. Write some specific questions and some general questions. When you are ready, ask another pair to read the passage before answering your questions.

O PENNESS is important to the cause of justice, but only sufficient openness as is necessary for that justice. Second-hand reporting meets that requirement. Direct reporting, live from the courthouse, intrudes too far. Justice might think it can use television for its own purposes, but more likely television will use justice for its.

A

B

C

NEIGHBOURS, *BBC1.*
With the possible exception of Skippy, the bush kangaroo, it's hard to imagine that anyone could play Joe Mangel any worse than Mark Little. Even for an Australian, he looks dim. But mercifully, the long and ludicrous cliffhanger, involving Joe's secret love for moronic Melanie, is over. What should have been a heart warming scene turned into a joke. Because Mark doesn't so much act as shout in the right direction and attempt to avoid the furniture. A more suitable end to this cliffhanger would have been for them both to jump off a cliff.

'Till at last the child's mind *is* these suggestions, and the sum of these suggestions is the child's mind. And not the child's mind only. The adult's mind too – all his life long. The mind that judges and desires and decides – made up of these suggestions. But all these suggestions are *our* suggestions!' The Director almost shouted in his triumph.

C **Discussion activity: moral issues and the media.** Read through each of the following situations, and discuss your reactions in small groups.

SITUATION 1 A TV company making a documentary about the secret services has discovered the identity of an army major who has been on a number of undercover anti-terrorist operations. The man's exploits are well-known to the public but his real name has never been divulged. Should they broadcast the information?

SITUATION 2 A frantic woman telephoned the police for help as a man was breaking into her house. The man then cut off the call and attacked her. The tape recording of this real phone call was used in a TV advertisement for a burglar alarm company. Should this have been allowed?

SITUATION 3 An American TV show features home movies of actual accidents, shootings and incidents such as people jumping to their deaths from burning buildings. How would you react to having such a programme on your national network?

SITUATION 4 While investigating a miscarriage of justice, a TV documentary crew have discovered that a man found guilty of a terrorist offence was innocent; they have interviewed another man who confessed confidentially to committing the crime. Should they be obliged to tell the police their source of information?

SITUATION 5 A TV news crew filming in a remote African village find a number of children in need of urgent medical attention. Their only hope of survival is to be taken to the hospital in the crew's Landrover, which will entail a considerable delay to the filming. What should the news crew do?

listening

exam tip

Remember to read through the task carefully and try and anticipate what you will hear on the tape!

A **Camcorder man.** Listen to the interview and choose the best answer.

1 The interviewer implies that camcorders
A are an expensive fad.
B are beginning to decline in popularity.
C represent excellent value for money.
D have improved technically.

2 One of the reasons why June wants a camcorder is that
A she has been offered a £300 discount.
B so many other people have one.
C she felt she would be better at making films than her neighbours.
D she wants to take it on her next skiing holiday.

3 The interviewer's comments on June's proposed films are
A sympathetic.
B enthusiastic.
C respectful.
D sarcastic.

4 The home movies shown on the TV programme
A are largely uneventful.
B are selected from thousands of entries.
C depict ordinary domestic scenes.
D are usually bizarre.

5 John Munroe suggests that a *camcorder anorak* is someone who
A has little sense of humour.
B sometimes takes a camcorder to work.
C is a genuine enthusiast.
D uses their camcorder excessively.

B **Communication activity: radio broadcast.** Work in small groups to prepare a two-minute feature for a radio programme.

Format
Follow the same pattern as the radio interview you have just heard. You will need a presenter / interviewer to read the majority of the report, into which there should be inserted a number of very short extracts (typically four or five lines long) from different interviews to illustrate the main points. Your overall result might have the following pattern:
Presenter / Interview 1 / Presenter / Interview 2 / Presenter / Interview 3 / Summary from presenter.

If you are in doubt about this, listen to the model passage again.

introduction

A **A common type of composition requires you to blend together two separate descriptions into a cohesive passage.** Here is an example of this kind of question:

In what ways is your national character reflected by the sports and pastimes that are popular in your country?

B **Outline planning.** Read through the three possible approaches to the composition. Discuss the merits and drawbacks of each one and say which one would be the most suitable.

1 Introduction
2 Description of national character
3 Description of popular sports
4 Conclusion

1 Introduction
2 First set of traits reflected in sports and pastimes
3 Second set of traits reflected in sports and pastimes
4 Third set of traits reflected in sports and pastimes
5 Conclusion

1 Introduction
2 Dismiss the idea that there is such a thing as a national character
3 Discuss the sports that prove that there is no such thing
4 Discuss the variety of pastimes that prove there is no such thing
5 Conclusion

sample composition

A **Read the following composition and say which of the three outlines above it follows.**

This statement certainly holds true for the English. One only has to consider a few of the most obvious features of our national character to realize that it is continually reflected in the sports and pastimes
5 we enjoy.

One thing that distinguishes the English from the other nations of Europe is the influence of the class system, and we choose sports according to our position in society. The prime example of this
10 is the way the upper classes choose sports like polo and croquet. The urban middle classes, on the other hand, play golf with their bank managers on Saturday afternoons, while the working classes have turned football into a religion.

15 There are some games we do not play because of our distrust of foreigners and sense of separateness. One such is 'boules', which is the ideal sport in many ways. It can be played by almost any number of people, of any ability, of any
20 age, in any weather, anywhere, but it is almost unknown in this country. The reason is not hard to find – it is French. Instead we select stranger pastimes. Take cricket, the national sport. It is so complicated and dull that it is shunned by almost

25 the entire world, but we carry on playing it because it makes us feel separate and different. Yet cricket, it must be said, exemplifies some of the better sides of the English character – for example it is calm and is played in a spirit of fairness and
30 politeness; and apart from occasional moments of excitement, when, for instance, it is time for tea, the five days that it takes to complete a game are entirely unemotional.

It is said that an Englishman's home is his
35 castle, and this is amply demonstrated by the most popular pastime of all – gardening. It reflects our general unfriendliness because gardens mark out territory, and flowerbeds and hedges warn strangers to keep out. This obsession also reveals
40 an aggressiveness that has been part of the national character throughout history; we are no longer trying to build an empire, but the same war-like spirit lives on in events such as trying to grow the biggest marrow for the village show.

45 So there can be no question that our national character is reflected in our sports and pastimes, but they also reveal more fundamental and perhaps less pleasant truths.

B **Language study: illustrations and examples.** Look through the text and underline where the following words or phrases are used in the process of giving examples and illustrations.

the prime example   like   one such   take   exemplifies   for example
for instance   is amply demonstrated by   such as

Now complete the sentences below using one of these words or phrases.

1 There are a number of sports .... tennis that have become popular all over the world.

2 Our poor performance in the Olympic Games .... what poor sportsmen we have become.

3 Certain games will never catch on in England. American football, ..., is never likely to be played over here.

4 Games fall in and out of favour; .... of this is ice skating, which shot to prominence after Britain won an Olympic medal, and then was dropped.

5 Some sports will remain amateur pursuits in England – .... skiing, for example, which is something that we will probably never be good at.

6 Different regions often have their own sports. .... game is Aunt Sally, which is popular in Oxfordshire pubs, but which is found nowhere else.

writing task   **Write a composition of about 350 words on the following subject.**

What do the forms of entertainment you enjoy most reveal about your character?

Stage 1 General approach. There are two possible basic approaches. Either base your central paragraphs on three or four forms of entertainment you enjoy, such as the cinema, music, theatre, TV, etc. Alternatively, you could take three or four related character traits and match these to the things you enjoy doing.

Stage 2 Brainstorming. Jot down features of your character and the kinds of entertainment you like, and see which features match up. Think also of examples of behaviour patterns that will illustrate these characteristics. For example, you might come up with sentences like: *I am a fairly self-contained rather than a solitary person – I would not choose particularly to spend a weekend alone, but would on the other hand be quite happy and content if I had to.*

Stage 3 Organization. Decide on the order of your paragraphs, and exactly which forms of entertainment, characteristics and illustrations you will discuss in each paragraph.

Stage 4 Writing. Make a note of exactly how long it takes you to write your passage. Remember that, in the exam, you will only have an hour for each composition, but that time must be divided between planning, writing and checking. Try and include some of the appropriate structures and idioms you have learned and use these where appropriate.

Stage 5 Checking. Proficiency candidates are not expected to make elementary grammatical mistakes. You will be penalized severely if your work is very inaccurate, however interesting it may be. If you suspect a sentence may be wrong, rewrite it, because getting even complicated structures wrong will do you no good.

Overview 13

vocabulary

Choose the word which best completes each sentence.

1 The opera singer was .... by the reception she received from the audience.
   A deluged   **B** inundated   **C** overwhelmed   **D** flooded

2 Hourly news bulletins keep the public .... of current affairs.
   A afloat   **B** abreast   **C** afresh   **D** afield

3 The theatre lights were slowly .... as the curtain rose on the first act.
   A dulled   **B** dampened   **C** deadened   **D** dimmed

4 News of the celebrity's arrival .... through the small town like wildfire.
   A flared   **B** moved   **C** grew   **D** spread

5 Not only .... visit Japan but they plan to stop off in the USA as well.
   A they plan to   **B** they must   **C** will they   **D** are they paying

6 Champagne is a .... wine, which originally came from the north-east of France.
   A glittering   **B** sparkling   **C** glistening   **D** gleaming

7 Although the producer is .... to the reactions of his audience, he feels he must portray a 'real' situation.
   A enthusiastic   **B** respectful   **C** sarcastic   **D** sympathetic

8 Films sometimes overdo their portrayal of reality – .... example is the 'horror' movie.
   A like   **B** such as   **C** take   **D** one such

9 .... had the curtain been raised than the lights went out.
   A Scarcely   **B** Hardly   **C** Only when   **D** No sooner

10 They've sold out of tickets for the football match tonight, so we'll just have to make .... of it and go to the cinema instead!
   A a mess   **B** a meal   **C** the best   **D** a mountain

transformations

Finish each of the following sentences so that it means the same as the sentence printed before it.

1 We rarely see such a high standard of performance in an amateur production.
   Rarely ...do we see..

2 I've never come across such a horrifying film.
   Never ...have I ...... come across..

3 They little suspected that the musical was going to be a runaway success.
   Little ...did they ...... suspect......................................

4 We'd only just started the performance when there was a loud explosion.
   No sooner ...had we ...... started......................................

5 You can enter the competition to meet the cast only if you purchase a ticket for the show.
   Only ...when ...... you ...... enter ...the ...... comp................

6 I had just begun my solo when there was a noise of breaking glass off-stage.
   Scarcely ...had I ...... begun..

7 You will enhance your posture and improve your acting ability on this course.
   Not only ...will ...... you..

8 As soon as we had finished dinner, the thunderstorm broke.
   Hardly ...had we finished..

9 He booked tickets for the afternoon performance and the evening performance as well.
   Not only ...did he book..

10 She didn't shed a tear when the story ended in tragedy.

Not... *a tear did she shed*

blank-filling

Fill each of the blanks in the following sentences with a suitable word or phrase.

1 Not only ..... *did her* ...., but he forgot his money as well!

2 Only when she got to the theatre ... *did she realise* .... she had forgotten the tickets.

3 No sooner ... *had* .... the doorbell rang.

4 We ...... *made* .... pact never to tell anyone our secrets.

5 The refugees' only hope of ...... *survival* .... is to be taken to hospital for medical treatment immediately.

6 The company offers a competitive salary with ... *the added perh/benefit* ... of monthly theatre tickets for employees and their families.

7 He liked ... *to be thought* .... of as the best Shakespearian actor of the century.

8 What's ..... *wrong/matter with* ..... the seats? I can see perfectly well and they're comfortable!

9 I know next ...... *to nothing* .... about opera but I'd love to go and see *Turandot*.

10 To the north lay the mountains, while ... *to the south* .... the golden stretches of sandy beaches and blue seas.

rewriting

For each of the sentences below, write a new sentence as similar as possible in meaning to the original sentence, but using the words given in capital letters. These words must not be altered in any way.

1 We wouldn't want to restrict the freedom of the students in any way.

IMPOSE ... *impose* ....

2 I suddenly realized the meaning of a 'freebie'.

DAWNED ....

3 I wanted to learn Russian before I visited Moscow.

WITHOUT...

4 When I noticed it was formal dress, it was too late.

UNTIL... *it was too late* ....

5 Don't panic about something so trivial.

MOUNTAIN ....

6 What you have done is inexcusable.

AMENDS ... *impossible* ....

7 The fact that they are always in trouble doesn't surprise me.

WONDER ....

8 The pressures of being in the public eye have proved too much for him.

COPE ....

9 Raising the necessary finance for the venture proved impossible for them.

FAILED...

10 No sooner had he bought the car than it broke down.

SCARCELY...

THE WORLD IN OUR HANDS

Day and Night

Janet Blair, *The Observer Magazine*

talking points

Eco quiz. Discuss in pairs whether you think the following statements are true or false. When you have finished, check your answers with the key on page 215.

1 There has been more economic growth since 1950 than in all the time from the beginning of civilization up to 1950.
2 Brazil contains half of the world's tropical rainforest.
3 At current rates of deforestation, the tropical rainforests will have disappeared by 2050.
4 On average, every car produces double its own weight in CO_2 every year.
5 One day's breathing in Bombay is equivalent to smoking 10 cigarettes.
6 The greatest increase in population in the next 25 years will be in the industrialized West.
7 Oxygen is intensely poisonous.
8 On average, no more than one species becomes extinct every day.

reading

A Read the following passage and decide on a suitable title for it. Compare your answer with the original title on page 215.

Has the whole country gone mad? I am referring to the current practice of illuminating every street, corner, nook and cranny with bright penetrating light, every night, all night. Take our road – a quiet residential thoroughfare in semi-detached suburbia. Once it was a peaceful haven, where the streetlights popped on discreetly at dusk, and popped off quietly as soon as it had gone midnight. There isn't much nightlife here, apart from the stirring of cocoa spoons at 10.30pm. After that no one goes walkabout except the feline population.

Yes, I know that 'streetlights prevent crime', but *do* they? A recent consumer report found that 'sensor' lights, which go on only when a car or person approaches, are the only deterrent to would-be intruders. So why do councils insist on flooding the country with harsh, blazing light? I remember mellower times when our Victorian streetlamp beamed benignly down on the footpath, casting a safe but civilized pool of light. If it ever went out, a local phone call brought someone from the council straight round to replace the bulb.

Times have changed. Now our street lighting is masterminded from County Hall. An agency operates under instructions from afar. No longer do we feel cared for or in control. Big Brother

No longer the star-studded Plough but a uniform orange glow arches over Britain, blotting out the once well-known constellations

is watching us. The mellow yellow light was replaced with a harsh white glare which bounced light back to the houses, penetrating the curtains and turning life into a magnesium-lit stage set. Worse followed. Streetlights stayed on until nine in the morning, in a useless waste of money and energy.

It is all a disgraceful waste of resources, burning up electricity, using fossil fuels and causing vast amounts of carbon dioxide to be pumped into the atmosphere, penetrating the ozone layer and accelerating the greenhouse effect. Light pollution is a growing menace to our once black velvet skies. Formerly the scourge of London, the dreaded orange light is creeping northwards. No longer the star-studded Plough but a uniform orange glow arches over Britain, blotting out the once well-known constellations.

Indignant astronomers are threatening to set up protest groups.

Apparently the Observatory at Greenwich can hardly function thanks to light pollution – they have had to move to darker southern climes, with a naturally dark night sky.

So, councils and Government, please note. There is a growing band of people who do *not* want their darkness lightened. If the current trend continues, the birds will go mad too, and we shall hear a dusk chorus instead of a dawn chorus! ■

B Comprehension. Explain the meaning of the following words and expressions as they are used in the passage.

1 nook and cranny (line 4)
2 semi-detached suburbia (line 7)
3 haven (line 9)
4 would-be (line 22)
5 masterminded (line 33)
6 Big Brother (line 36)
7 the scourge of London (line 53)
8 star-studded (line 55)
9 uniform orange glow (line 56)
10 dawn chorus (line 70)

C   Multiple-choice questions. Choose the words that best complete the following sentences.

1 Most of the people who live in the writer's neighbourhood
  A prefer old-fashioned streetlights.
  B go to the pubs or restaurants in the city.
  C go to bed early.
  D are afraid to walk around at night.

2 The writer preferred Victorian streetlamps because
  A they were a greater deterrent to burglars.
  B they were more economical to run.
  C their light was less harsh.
  D they were less expensive to repair.

3 According to the writer, one effect of the new lighting policy is that
  A it has made her almost feel as if she is living in a totalitarian state.
  B it is becoming difficult to tell day from night.
  C the lights go on and off at unusual times.
  D centralized control has brought greater efficiency.

4 The orange glow caused by night lighting
  A is damaging the atmosphere.
  B now affects the whole of the country.
  C has led to a strike at the Greenwich Observatory.
  D has affected the visibility of the stars.

vocabulary

A   Adjectives. The writer uses a number of expressions to contrast the old lights with their modern replacements. Read through the passage and find as many adjectives as you can that refer to light, and classify them according to whether their use is positive or negative.

EXAMPLE   *mellow yellow* (positive)

B   Read through the following list of adjectives connected with sound, smell and taste. Classify them according to what they describe (sound, smell or taste), and whether they are positive or negative.

- *musty*
- *insipid*
- *shrill*
- *acrid*
- *catchy*
- *tasty*

- *tasteless*
- *fragrant*
- *bland*
- *fetid*
- *scented*
- *strident*

- *cacophonous*
- *harmonious*
- *mellifluous*
- *palatable*
- *delicious*
- *aromatic*

C   Expressions. Match the following expressions about light and dark with their meanings.

1 *light at the end of the tunnel*
2 *the bright lights*
3 *to come to light*
4 *to make light of something*
5 *to see the light*
6 *to go out like a light*
7 *a shot in the dark*
8 *to keep someone in the dark*
9 *a dark horse*

a to withhold information from someone
b a risk with unknown consequences
c not to take something seriously
d a mysterious person
e to be revealed
f the excitement and entertainment of a big city
g to understand
h to fall asleep immediately
i a sign that a difficult period will finish

Now complete the following sentences using the idioms, making any necessary changes.

1 Gail is a bit of .... – she never talks about her family and no one knows much about her past.

2 The police appealed to the public for witnesses, and as a result a number of interesting new pieces of information ....

3 He is always immensely sympathetic to others, but he always .... his own troubles.

4 She was absolutely exhausted; when she finally got to bed, she ....

5 No one had considered offering mail order before, so setting it up was a bit of ....

6 He never communicates with his parents – he even . . . . them
. . . . about his own wedding until afterwards.

7 After months of unemployment, the actor had been offered a small part in a TV film, and felt
he could at last see . . . .

8 Despite everyone's warnings, I trusted them completely, and it was only when they failed to
pay me that I began . . . .

9 My sister would never be happy in the country – she loves . . . .
and all her friends are in London too.

Choose three of the idioms and write your own sentences that illustrate the meaning.

Structure   Tomorrow's World

cloze development   **Read the following passage and fill in the blanks.**

Although the rise in the global temperature by 4 per cent predicted by many scientists may not sound like much, it is the difference between now and the last Ice Age, when huge glaciers covered Europe and most of Britain. Nobody knows
5 **(1)** . . . *quite precise* . . . what would happen in a warmer world, but we **(2)** . . . . *do* . . . . know some things. Heat a kettle and the **(3)** . . . . *water* . . . . . inside it expands. The **(4)** . . . . *temp* . . . . . . of the world has climbed more than half a degree this century, and the oceans have
10 **(5)** . . . . . *risen* . . . . . by at least 10 cm.

But **(6)** . . . *just* . . . . as it takes several minutes for a kettle to begin warming, **(7)** . . . . *so* . . . . . . it may have taken the oceans thirty years to swell. This **(8)** . . . *means* . . . . that the global warming we are now experiencing is a result only of
15 the carbon dioxide we have dumped into the atmosphere **(9)** . . . . . . *up* . . . . to the 1960s. Since then, the **(10)** . . . . . . *use* . . . . . . of fossil fuels has increased rapidly.

Scientists **(11)** . . *working* . . . . for the United Nations and European governments have been warning that
20 **(12)** . . . . *what* . . . . . . the Dutch and the people of East Anglia will need to do will **(13)** . . . . . *be* . . . . to build more extensive sea defences. Many of the world's great cities are **(14)** . . . *at* . . . . risk, because they are **(15)** . . *located* . . . . . . at sea level. Miami,
25 **(16)** . . . *almost* . . . . . entirely built on a sandbank, could be **(17)** . . *swept* . . . . away. But the effects of rising sea levels will be much **(18)** . . . . *worse* . . . . for the developing countries. With a metre rise in sea levels, 200 million could become homeless.
30 There are other fears too, **(19)** . . *according* . . . . . . to a recent United Nations report. The plight of the hungry in northern Africa could **(20)** . . . . *worsen* . . . . . . , as rainfall in the Sahara and beyond is reduced by 20 per cent. ■

exam tip   *Some sentences may seem to be complete and contain blanks that appear to be unnecessary. If you come across blanks like this, you will probably need a word to change the emphasis of the sentence.*

tenses in future time clauses

A **In future time clauses, a present or present perfect tense (either simple or progressive) is used after the time word, as the 'will' future is not acceptable.**

EXAMPLE *When I see him next week, I'll tell him what you said.* (not 'will see')
After I see him next week, I'll tell you what he said.

The use of the present perfect in the time clause after *when* emphasizes that one action must be completed before the other starts, and this may or may not be significant. Which of the pairs of sentences on the next page show a significant difference in meaning?

1   **a**   I'll give you a ring when I arrive.
      b   I'll give you a ring when I've arrived.

2   **a**   You must come and see me when you visit London.
      b   You must come and see me when you have visited London.

B   **Put the verb in brackets into an appropriate tense.**

1   I'll put some sun-tan oil on when I . . . . (be) on the beach.

2   I'll let you know when he . . . . (leave) so you can come and give him your present.

3   You'll feel more confident when you . . . . (swim) for a few weeks.

4   From now on, I'm going to tear my newspapers up and use them to light the fire when I
. . . . (read) them.

5   I'll give you a lift when you . . . . (want) to go home.

6   We'll be able to get to the duty-free when we . . . . (wait) for the plane to leave.

the future

A   **There are many different ways of referring to the future (or future in the past).** Study the following sentences and say which way is the most appropriate and why.

1   Could you ring the cinema and find out what time the film <u>begins / shall begin</u>?
2   Nuclear waste <u>will continue / is continuing</u> to damage the environment for years to come.
3   We'd better book the hall for the party. They say it <u>rains / is going to rain</u> tomorrow.
4   I'm afraid I'm tied up this afternoon – I <u>will play / am playing</u> tennis with Graham.
5   I've bought some cement because I <u>am going to mend / will mend</u> the wall.
6   I really can't decide which coat I like best. I know what – I'll <u>take / am taking</u> them both.
7   It's not surprising your car <u>won't start / isn't going to start</u>. There isn't any petrol.
8   I <u>was writing / was going to write</u> to you but I couldn't find your address.
9   That case looks heavy. Hold on and I'll <u>give / am giving</u> you a hand if you like.
10   There's someone at the door. That <u>is going to be / 'll be</u> John. He said he might drop in.

11   Now remember you <u>are not firing / are not to fire</u> until you receive the order.
12   Just think. This time next week we'll <u>be sitting / will sit</u> on the plane on our way home.
13   I <u>am seeing / was seeing</u> Sally tomorrow but she has had to go to New York.
14   The Palace have announced that the Prince and the Princess <u>shall separate / are to separate</u>.
15   You can come and collect it on the 17th – I <u>will have finished / finish</u> by then.
16   Oh, it's no trouble to post the letter. I'll <u>be going / am to go</u> past the Post Office anyway on my way to work.
17   We're having a small celebration for Mr Merry; on Friday he <u>will have been working / will be working</u> for us for 25 years.

B   **Complete these grammar notes with examples from the first ten sentences above.**
The first one has been done for you.

1   **The present simple can be used for**

a definite future action based on a timetable / an itinerary / a programme.

EXAMPLE *Could you ring the cinema and find out what time the film begins?*

This cannot be used for things outside human control, for example, you can't say 'It rains tomorrow.'

2   **The present progressive can be used for**

arrangements. . . . .

This cannot be used for things outside human control, for example, you can't say 'It's snowing tomorrow.'

3 *Going to* **can be used for**

 a decisions and intentions. ....

 b definite predictions based on firm evidence. ....

 c the 'future in the past'. ....

4 *Will* **can be used as a temporal auxiliary**

to make predictions or state facts about the future. ....

5 *Will* **can be used as a modal auxiliary to express**

 a spontaneous decisions. ....

 b offers and requests. ....

 c a deduction or probability. ....

 d willingness or lack of willingness. ....

C **Complete the remaining grammar notes with examples from sentences 11 to 17.**

6 **The future progressive can be used for**

 a an unfinished activity or action in progress at a point in time in the future. ....

 b something that will happen as a matter of course. ....

7 **The infinitive future can be used for**

 a formal orders. ....

 b plans and intentions (particularly found in newspapers). ....

8 **The future perfect can be used for**

an action that will have been completed by a stated future time. ....

9 **The future perfect progressive can be used for**

the past duration of an activity up to a point in time in the future. ....

10 **The past progressive can be used for**

changed arrangements. ....

context and
future tenses

At sentence level, it may at times seem that all these future forms are possible and grammatically correct. It is, for example, impossible to say which form of the future would be most appropriate to complete the following sentence.

He .... (visit) New York.

There are a wide range of options, but these are limited by the overall context.

Read the paragraph below. Which ways of referring to the future would be acceptable here?

Peter's driving me mad at the moment, and he's being very difficult about our holiday. We're going to America, as you know, and we've got one of those multiple air tickets that means you can go pretty well anywhere you want within two weeks or whatever. And that's the problem – he wants to spend the time in LA and San Francisco. Now I want to see the Statue of Liberty and see Times Square and Manhattan, but he .... (not visit) New York, and he's quite adamant about it. He says it's full of gangsters and muggers and just refuses to discuss it.

PAIRWORK Write one short paragraph incorporating the sentence *He .... (visit) New York* in one of the future forms above. When you have finished, discuss which alternative ways of referring to the future would be possible in your paragraphs.

Where do we go from Here?

Describe the picture below. Suggest reasons for the monument's unusual appearance. How important is the preservation of our ancient monuments?

Read the article quickly. Then, in small groups, choose what you consider to be the best title for it from the list below.

1 Pyramids at risk
2 The perils of pollution
3 Death on the Nile
4 Surrounded by scaffolding
5 Endangered species

NOTHING PREPARES YOU FOR THE SHEER INHUMANITY OF THE TITANIC ABSTRACT SHAPES

NOTHING prepares you for their impact. You might think you must know their every detail beforehand; they have, after all, been described, endlessly, by travel writers for over 2,000 years. Their images have appeared again and again in publications ranging from solemn academic treatises to advertisements in fashionable magazines, so that as a result their shapes have become as familiar as that of your local place of worship. But no: nothing prepares you for the sheer inhumanity of the titanic abstract shapes.

For all the Middle East and the Western world the Pyramids and their guardian Sphinx have become symbols of eternity.

But now no one is quite sure how long the pyramids – and Egypt's other antiquities – can last. Recently a leading member of the Egyptian Antiquities Organisation was quoted as saying: 'All of the monuments are endangered. If we don't do something soon, in 100 years the paintings will be gone, and in 200 years the architecture will be gone.'

All Egyptologists agree that the problems are getting worse – an analysis which has precipitated an involved, confused and at times bitter debate about the nature of conservation. The causes of the accelerated deterioration of structures that have so far managed to survive 4,500 years of sun, sand, wind and war are depressingly familiar: pressure of population, pollution and – perhaps most dangerous of all – the devastating effects of mass tourism.

The benefits of the building of the Aswan High Dam are undeniable: it controlled the flooding of the Nile, releasing more land for agriculture and providing more water for irrigation. Yet the changes of water patterns have contributed greatly to the problems of conservation. The imbalance in the stone of the monuments, which is now very salty, means that the stone is trying to "drink" water from below, like a wick or a sponge. But the water that it is drinking up is salt-saturated, so the level of salt in the stone itself is increased. In the heat the water evaporates, leaving damaging deposits of salt on the outside of the structures.

The problems of underground water have been exacerbated by the presence of sewage leaking into the ground from Cairo's inadequate drainage system. In 1900 Cairo had a population of around one million; today it is nearer 14 million, and there has been no appreciable expansion of the sewage system.

The effects of airborne pollution are less severe, but are certainly contributing to the eating away of the outside of the great pyramids. Fifty years ago, Cairo was six miles distant, but today the Giza suburb extends to the foot of the plateau itself. Traffic fumes combine with emissions from the cement, steel and chemical industries a few miles away at Helwan, an area which has become known to some environmentalists as the Death Triangle.

The continuing fascination held by Egypt – the only country to have a complete science named after it – does nothing to improve the situation. Archaeologists still arrive in droves, lured by what remains hidden. But the archaeologists are vastly outnumbered by the hordes of tourists who come to Giza – nearly two million last year alone. Every ancient country has its tourist horror stories to tell, but Egypt has suffered more than most.

If international rescue efforts are successful, the preservation of the Nile Valley monuments can act as a model for the rest of the world's ancient structures. If it is not, then the world must resign itself to the fact that the great structures which bejewel the planet will survive or not survive on an arbitrary basis, in a cultural free-for-all conducted in an increasingly hostile physical environment. ▲▲

vocabulary

Many of the words and phrases used in the passage have unfavourable connotations.

EXAMPLE *problems* *getting worse* *dangerous* *fumes* *emissions*

Match the words on the left with the meanings on the right.

1	*endangered*	a	dilapidation
2	*confused*	b	destructive
3	*bitter*	c	disorganized
4	*deterioration*	d	multitudes
5	*depressingly*	e	contamination
6	*pollution*	f	harmful
7	*devastating*	g	at risk
8	*imbalance*	h	disproportion
9	*damaging*	i	discouragingly
10	*hordes*	j	acrimonious
11	*suffered*	k	inhospitable
12	*hostile*	l	been badly affected

comprehension

Explain in your own words what is meant by these words and expressions as they are used in the article.

1 solemn academic treatises (line 9)
2 the sheer inhumanity of the titanic abstract shapes (line 14)
3 precipitated (line 32)
4 pressure of population (line 39)
5 no appreciable expansion (line 67)
6 Death Triangle (line 81)
7 arrive in droves, lured by (line 86)
8 tourist horror stories (line 92)
9 on an arbitrary basis (line 101)
10 a cultural free-for-all (line 102)

summary

Summarize the problem and its causes which have been outlined in the article above in 100 to 120 words. When you have finished your summary, give it an attention-seeking headline which will make people aware of the seriousness of the problem.

Listening and Speaking

A Tangled Web

listening 1

The park.

Indicate whether the following statements are true or false according to the speaker.

1 The speaker's organization accepts responsibility for creating a park. T/F
2 In the previous press conference there had been better news. T/F
3 The speaker is worried that the authorities will not fulfil their promises. T/F
4 The gold miners have little contact with the local population. T/F
5 A major problem caused by the miners is the destruction of forests for airfields. T/F
6 The governor of Roraima state will take over the running of the park. T/F
7 Some pressure groups suspect concerned foreigners of having ulterior motives. T/F
8 The highway will not be needed if the Indian population continues to fall. T/F

speaking

A Picture discussion.

1 Describe what is happening in the two photographs on page 193.
2 What are the environmental effects of the activities in the photographs? Which activity do you consider to be more damaging?

B Read the following passage and answer the questions below.

'You in the North got rich by doing what we now aspire to do: using your land, raw materials and energy sources to fuel a process of economic growth and industrial expansion. In the process
5 you have caused untold ecological damage in your own countries and in ours. You now expect us to hold back from a pattern of development that has served you so well because you fear that in the process we will exacerbate the pollution you
10 have already caused and accelerate the process of ecological collapse you first set in train. And you apparently expect us to do this out of the goodness of our hearts when millions of our people are dying of malnutrition or preventable
15 diseases, or living in grinding poverty. Well, you can get stuffed – unless you are prepared to pay up.'

1 What job might the speaker have?
2 Which country might the speaker come from?
3 Which countries is the speaker referring to by the term 'the North'.
4 What is the tone of the passage?
5 What, according to the speaker, are the main priorities of the North?
6 What are the speaker's main priorities?
7 What do you think of the points the speaker makes?

C Write a short speech (that relates to one or both of the photographs) given by one of the people below. When you have finished, read out your speech. Ask the other students to guess which character you chose, and discuss the issues the speech raises.

- a botanist searching for new medicines
- a Yanomami (local Indian) chief
- a western banker
- a landless peasant
- a poor urban worker
- a politician

D Discussion. Look at the following factors which threaten our future well-being. Choose three that are, in your opinion, the *most* significant and three that are the *least* significant. Discuss the reasons for your choice with a partner and try to come to an agreement.

- air pollution
- deforestation
- mineral extraction
- global warming
- toxic wastes
- international debt
- desertification and soil erosion
- water shortages
- population increases
- energy consumption
- arms spending
- ozone depletion

listening 2

A lot of hot air. Listen to the tape and choose the best answer.

1 The guest speaker became interested in the theory of global warming because it
   had been accepted so uncritically.   T/F
2 According to the speaker, the figures from thermometer readings are more accurate
   than satellite data.   T/F
3 The speaker says that rises in sea levels are likely to cause dramatic changes. T/F
4 The speaker says carbon dioxide emissions may have a beneficial effect
   on agriculture.   T/F
5 The speaker is saddened by the attitude of scientists.   T/F

Writing

Putting your Case

introduction

The argument composition. There are different ways of approaching the argument composition, and the method you choose will depend partly on the question you are asked and the strength of your views. A common question type gives you a proposition and then says 'Discuss'. This can be approached using the balanced discussion (see Unit 1). A different approach is to write an 'unbalanced discussion'. For this, you take the various elements of the opposing view, expose their weaknesses, and then destroy them.

Think of the three or four main points you want to make. Then work backwards, thinking of what someone with the opposite view would say. Then think of reasons why this opposing view is wrong. Your aim is to end up with a series of paragraphs that each has the following structure.

a opposing view
b comments on this view and why it is wrong
c the correct view (ie your own)

language focus

To avoid repetition, you will require a variety of words and phrases that make the stages of your argument clear. Below are examples of useful language for each section.

Read through the sample composition on the next page. Indicate with a tick which of the following words and phrases are used in the composition.

A Introducing a false argument
   It could be argued that …
   Some people would argue that …
   There is also an idea implicit in the statement that …
   It is often suggested that …

B Demolishing a false argument
   This is partly true, but …
   To a certain limited extent, there is some truth in this …
   However, the implication that … is an over-simplification.
   This argument has a certain superficial logic, but …

C Proposing a correct argument
   It is clear that …
   The real situation …
   Obviously …
   It is therefore quite wrong to suggest that …; on the contrary, …

sample composition

The West should put more pressure on developing countries to stop damaging the global environment. Discuss.

There can be very few people who have not read about the destruction of the rainforests, and fewer still would say that nothing should be done. However, the idea that this could be achieved by
5 pressurizing developing countries is a highly dubious proposition.

It is often suggested by the media that the industrialized countries of the world have worked hard to limit pollution. To a certain limited extent,
10 there is some truth in this, and measures have been taken to stop the increase in CFCs and other ozone-destroying gases; some cars are fitted with catalytic converters, recycling is commonplace and lead-free petrol is widely
15 available. However, the implication that we in the West are doing something to combat pollution whereas the developing world is not is an over-simplification. We are continuing to pour billions of tons of pollutants into the atmosphere every
20 year. It is clear that compared with the damage that we are doing to the environment, the contribution of the developing countries is almost negligible.

There is also an idea implicit in the statement
25 that the West is not responsible for the environmental damage that is taking place in the developing world. Some people would argue that if the rainforests are being destroyed in Brazil, then the Brazilians ought to be doing something about
30 it. This argument has a certain superficial logic, but, on closer examination, it turns out to be untenable. The real situation is more complex. Many of the developing countries owe money to the western banks, and they now need economic
35 growth, whatever its environmental consequences, to pay back the interest on these loans. It is therefore quite wrong to suggest that the West is not responsible for environmental damage; on the contrary, the West is the cause
40 of it.

To sum up, we are in no position to lecture the developing countries on ways of reducing pollution and environmental damage. Ultimately, it is in everyone's interest that the environment should
45 be protected; however, rather than putting more pressure on the developing world, we need to set an example and to show substantially less self-interest than we have done to date.

writing task

Write a composition of about 350 words on the following subject.

The increased use of nuclear power would be the best way to provide energy whilst protecting the environment. Discuss.

Stage 1 General approach. Use the basic outline of the sample composition.

Stage 2 Brainstorming. You may like to consider the following points.

- Some people suggest that nuclear power is environmentally friendly because it does not produce greenhouse gases (but what about the radioactive waste?).
- The statement assumes that nuclear power is very safe (mainly true, but accidents do happen, and then massive damage occurs).
- Some people consider nuclear power to be environmentally friendly because it does not use up fossil fuels (but what about other forms of energy – wind, solar, wave, etc?).

Stage 3 Organization. Start with your most important point first, and then move on to the others.

Stage 4 Writing. You may find it useful to refer to the title of the composition as 'the statement' or 'the proposition'. Use some of the phrases given on page 194 to help you introduce false arguments, dismiss them and propose your own.

Stage 5 Checking. Pay special attention to your use of link words.

exam tip

When writing a discursive composition, try to refer to real examples – the passage mentioned the rainforests in Brazil. You do not need to know all the details of a specific case to use it. However, do not invent examples that are obviously not true. If you say 'The world's worst nuclear accident, which destroyed half of Athens in 1992 …', the examiner will not be impressed.

vocabulary

Choose the word which best completes each sentence.

1 I'm not all that interested in politics and .... affairs.
   A actual   B recent   C modern   **D** current

2 After the revolution, the ex-president eventually found a safe .... in the Far East.
   A refuge   B sanctuary   **C** haven   D asylum

3 Because of the dominance of retail chain-stores, most shopping centres show the same bland .... and no imagination.
   A similarity   B likeness   C equality   **D** uniformity

4 Kylie's new song ought to do well in the charts – it's got good lyrics and a nice .... tune.
   A catchy   B harmonious   C melodious   D strident

5 Some intriguing new facts .... to light during the course of the investigation.
   A came   B brought   C turned   D made

6 Conservationists are worried that many potentially valuable .... of plants and animals are threatened with extinction.
   A examples   B variations   **C** species   D brands

7 My dog's being very difficult at the moment; I don't know what the trouble is but he just .... not eat.
   A shall   **B** will   C may   D has

8 The evidence that carbon dioxide levels are rising is ....
   A inevitable   B unavoidable   C indelible   **D** undeniable

9 The pollution problems in the town have been .... by mass tourism in the summer months.
   A exacerbated   B developed   C augmented   D contributed

10 During the height of the season, tourists arrive in .... to see Shakespeare's birthplace.
   A loads   B flocks   C shoals   **D** droves

11 You really shouldn't buy that car. I know the engine is fine, but most of the bodywork has been .... away by rust.
   A eaten   B dissolved   C erased   D crumbled

12 The Pyramids are perhaps the most famous of the seven .... of the ancient world.
   A structures   B spectacles   **C** wonders   D constructions

13 I've given up trying to make my sister see sense, and now I'm .... to the fact that she is going to marry Jason.
   A adapted   **B** resigned   C adjusted   D accepted

14 They split up on very bad terms and went through a bitter and .... divorce.
   A acrid   B aggravated   C aggrieved   **D** acrimonious

15 I am rather suspicious of your brother's sudden concern for your welfare and fear that he may have .... motives.
   A underlying   B concealed   C secondary   **D** ulterior

blank-filling

Fill each of the blanks in the following sentences with a suitable word or phrase.

1 Do you realize that by this time tomorrow we .... living here for exactly a year?

2 I expect .... be from Mary – she said she had written to us.

3 The blackmailer's voice became colder. 'Get me the money by noon tomorrow

. . . . send those photographs to the newspapers.'

4 I'll let you have the book back as soon . . . . it.

5 Now listen carefully – you . . . . to open fire unless the order is given by your officer.

6 As you've been divorced twice, you're in . . . . to lecture me about marriage.

7 It's a . . . . talking to him – he won't listen.

8 I'm going past the station – I . . . . lift if you like.

9 She didn't want any payment, she helped them out of the . . . .

10 As the most senior boy in the school, you are expected to set . . . . the others.

rewriting

107

For each of the sentences below, write two new sentences as similar as possible in meaning to the original sentence, but using the words given in capital letters. These words must not be altered in any way.

1 Mass tourism has been one of the causes of the problem.

CONTRIBUTED . . . .

BLAME . . . .

2 He was not given details of the company's new plans.

DARK . . . .

WITHHELD. . . . .

3 Changes in the water table have adversely affected the monuments.

GOOD . . . .

DAMAGE . . . .

4 A rise in temperature in the next century seems likely.

PROBABILITY . . . .

CHANCE . . . .

5 The 'environmentally friendly' label on this product is misleading.

CONTRARY . . . .

DESPITE . . . .

6 You must accept the fact that she has left you.

RESIGN. . . . .

TERMS . . . .

7 The report says that the pyramids will deteriorate.

ACCORDING . . . .

DETERIORATION . . . .

THE MEDIA AND THE MESSAGE

Windows on the World

talking points

Look at these two English newspapers.

A

B

1 How do the papers differ in terms of size, headlines, photographs, and use of colour? What sort of reader is each paper appealing to?

2 Which of the following would you be more likely to find in Paper A, Paper B or both?

- horoscopes
- a gossip column
- sports pages
- stock market prices
- page 3 girls

- an analysis of foreign news
- arts reviews
- law reports
- a problem page
- crosswords

3 In your country, are there similar differences between serious broadsheets, middle market papers and popular tabloids?

register in the news

Read through the extracts taken from the two papers above and answer the following questions.

1 Which paper does each extract come from? Mark them **A** or **B**.
2 In what ways does the content of the two sets of extracts vary?
3 What do you notice about the way individuals are described in the popular paper (Paper B)?
4 What other differences in language are there between the two sets of extracts?

A **financial**

Weak Italian governments have habitually met budget deficits by borrowing and permitting inflation. That option is no longer open because of the size of the deficit, the high cost of borrowing and, until recently, the belief that the Maastricht treaty would demand monetary discipline. ●

B

Bar owner Wayne Lineker – 29-year-old brother of soccer ace Gary – cuddled his 15-year-old girlfriend last night and vowed: "I'm no Bill Wyman."

Wayne is furious after being spotted kissing beautiful schoolgirl Zoe Davey at an Essex nightclub. He said: "I'm absolutely crazy about Zoe and think she is the most beautiful sexy girl I have ever met."

Linda's s...

 D

● BUDDY racket! Linda McCartney grabbed hubby Paul and burst into song after a slap-up lunch to commemorate Buddy Holly. Linda, 49, and ex-Beatle Paul joined showbiz pals at a Mexican restaurant in West London. Paul, 50, who owns rights to many of the 50s rocker's hits, was toasting Buddy's birthday in a tribute week to the star.

ro... McC rtne bol tit ho lo r a sl h

C **M**r Ryder said young criminals often committed crimes because of pressure to conform to the norms of their group or gang. That subculture, he argued, was fostered by society's reliance upon machismo, a culture which was also fostered in prisons. _____

DEVIANTS RAKI

reading

A Read the following extract from a book. According to the writer, what do popular and serious newspapers have in common?

LANGUAGE IN THE NEWS

As readers of newspapers, and viewers of television, we readily assume that the *Nine O'Clock News*, or the front page of the *Daily Express* or the *Guardian*, consists of faithful reports of events that happened 'out there', in the world beyond our immediate experience. At a certain level, that is of course a realistic assumption: real events do occur and are reported – a coach crashes on the autobahn, a postman wins the pools, a cabinet minister resigns. But real events are subject to conventional processes of selection: they are not intrinsically newsworthy, but only become 'news' when selected for inclusion in news reports. The vast majority of events are not mentioned, and so selection immediately gives us a partial view of the world. We know also that different newspapers report differently, in both content and presentation.

The pools win is more likely to be reported in the *Mirror* than in *The Times*, whereas a crop failure in Meghalaya may be reported in *The Times* but almost certainly not in the *Mirror*. Selection is accompanied by transformation, differential treatment in presentation according to numerous political, social and economic factors.

As far as differences in presentation are concerned, most people would admit the possibility of 'bias': the *Sun* is known to be consistently hostile in its treatment of trades unions, and of what it calls 'the loony Left'; the *Guardian* is generous in its reporting of the affairs of the Campaign for Nuclear Disarmament. Such disaffections and affiliations are obvious when you start reading carefully, and discussing the news media with other people. The world of the Press is not the real world, but a world skewed and judged.

Now what attitude might one take towards the 'bias'? There is an argument to the effect that biases do exist, but not everywhere. The *Daily Express* is biased, the *Socialist Worker* is not (or the other way round). In a good world, all newspapers and television channels would report the unmediated truth. This view seems to me to be drastically and dangerously false. It allows a person to believe, and to assert, complacently, that *their* newspaper is unbiased, whereas all the others are in the pockets of the Tories or the Trotskyites; or that newspapers are biased, while TV news is not (because 'the camera cannot lie').

The danger with this position is that it assumes the possibility of genuine neutrality, of *some* news medium being a clear undistorting window. And that can never be.

Language in the News by R. Fowler

B Match the following words with their meanings as used in the extract.

1 *readily* (line 2)
2 *faithful* (line 5)
3 *immediate* (line 8)
4 *certain* (line 8)
5 *intrinsically* (line 15)
6 *generous* (line 39)
7 *unmediated* (line 55)

a favourable
b particular
c inherently
d willingly
e unaltered
f accurate
g personal

C Comprehension. Explain the meaning of the following words and phrases.

1 admit the possibility (line 35)
2 the loony Left (line 38)
3 disaffections and affiliations (line 41)
4 in the pockets of the Tories (line 60)
5 the camera cannot lie (line 63)

D Multiple-choice questions. Choose the best answer.

1 We have a distorted picture of the world beyond our immediate experience because
   A real events are deliberately distorted by the media.
   B we are selective in what we read.
   C a limited number of events are reported.
   D the stories that are presented are not fully researched.

2 The writer implies that *The Times*
   A never deals with any human interest stories at all.
   B has large numbers of overseas readers.
   C carries reports that would not interest *Mirror* readers.
   D has the same political slant as the *Mirror*.

3 According to the writer, newspapers
   A shape the political views of their readers.
   B vary greatly in their degree of objectivity.
   C are widely perceived to be politically biased.
   D are funded by political pressure groups.

4 When the author says 'the *Daily Express* is biased',
   A he in fact means the opposite.
   B he is citing an opinion he may not hold personally.
   C he wishes to imply that the *Daily Express* is a special case.
   D he wants to defend the *Socialist Worker*.

5 The writer's attitude towards distortion of news is that
   A it happens more in the press than on TV.
   B its incidence varies between different newspapers.
   C it is far too prevalent.
   D it is inevitable.

vocabulary

In the passage there was the expression 'the loony Left'. Below are a number of other common expressions. Match the expressions with their meanings and complete the sentences that follow.

1	*an entirely different kettle of fish*	**a**	an environment cut off from the harsh realities of life
2	*a far cry from*	**b**	reservations
3	*the gutter press*	**c**	a completely different (and unacceptable) matter
4	*a few home truths*	**d**	tabloids carrying sensational stories and scandals
5	*an ivory tower*	**e**	be motivated by hopes of personal gain
6	*a raw deal*	**f**	unfair treatment
7	*second thoughts*	**g**	unpalatable but correct criticism
8	*have a vested interest*	**h**	not at all the same as

1 As Kim's manager, I obviously .... in seeing that her new record gets a lot of good publicity.

2 I am tired of reading about sex scandals involving ministers that constantly seem to appear in

....

3 I had tentatively agreed to sharing my office with Jonathan, but I'm having ....

.... about it now, and would like to keep it for myself.

4 I had to point out .... to Sophie; she was upset by what I said but, as a friend, I could not let her behave so selfishly without saying anything.

5 There was a lot of sympathy for the manager after he was sacked so unfairly: most people thought that he had got ....

6 It's no use asking university professors to solve the problem of football violence – they all live in their .... and don't know what is happening in the real world.

7 I agreed that your mother could stay for a couple of weeks, but I'm afraid that having her here on a permanent basis is ....

8 The village now has a golf course, there's a car park and it's full of tourist shops; all in all, it's

.... the sleepy little hamlet that I knew thirty years ago.

Making Headlines

Headline news. Look through the following newspaper headlines where inadvertent puns have created second meanings. Can you explain what the news stories are probably about and what the other interpretations might be?

MILK DRINKERS ARE TURNING TO POWDER

L

THUGS EAT THEN ROB PROPRIETOR

GRANDMOTHER OF EIGHT MAKES HOLE IN ONE

MAN HELD OVER GIANT L.A. BRUSH FIRE

POLICE DISCOVER CRACK IN AUSTRALIA

IRAQI HEAD SEEKS ARMS

DRUNK GETS NINE MONTHS IN VIOLIN CASE

STOLEN PAINTING FOUND BY TREE

CARIBBEAN ISLANDS DRIFT TO LEFT

TRAFFIC DEAD RISE SLOWLY

---

cloze development   **Fill in each of the blanks in the following passage with one suitable word.**

There are few industries that have embraced new technology with as much enthusiasm as the press. (**1**) ...*gone*... are the days when typesetters would laboriously set out each word letter by letter. Nowadays computers with sophisticated graphics and word-processing (**2**) ...*prog*... have almost made misprints and spelling errors a thing of the (**3**) ...*past*... .

While it may be true that papers have – at (**4**) ...*least*... in linguistic terms – become more accurate, it does not necessarily (**5**) ...*mean*... that the same can be (**6**) ...*said*... for their content. Few papers (**7**) ...*have*... printed stories that they knew to be entirely false, but new technological developments (**8**) ...*such*... as the advent of colour printing have meant that the visual appeal of a paper has taken (**9**) ...*on*... a new importance in the circulation war. This pressure (**10**) ...*to*... pander to the

tastes (**11**) ...*of*... the television generation, to opt (**12**) ...*for*... the visually exciting or sensational (**13**) ...*rather*... than the analytical, has already transformed the popular press and is making inroads (**14**) ...*into*... the more serious papers. Where it all will lead is still (**15**) ...*open*... to question, but already there are some pointers. There is a popular paper (**16**) ...*where*... headlines like 'ELVIS PRESLEY FOUND ALIVE AND WELL ON MOON' are regularly splashed across the front (**17**) ...*page*... ; fact is blended with fiction, and the accuracy of a story is immaterial as (**18**) ...*headlong*... as it entertains. Harmless fun, you may say, and you may be right. But as the trend continues and papers bear less and less (**19**) ...*relation*... to the real world, the dangers of the press falling into the wrong (**20**) ...*hands*... become ever greater.

review of expressions

A Tabloid talk. Read the following editorial in a popular newspaper criticizing a rival paper. Replace the underlined words with the most appropriate expression from the list below.

EDITORIAL

ROYAL SCANDAL FATIGUE

SUPER SNOOPER Cyril, who taped Princess Di's private phone conversations, is (**1**) too inquisitive. Listening in on other people's phone calls is absolutely illegal. The police ought to (**2**) prosecute him.

And what's all the fuss about anyway? Absolutely nothing. *The Daily Sun* is (**3**) exaggerating the importance of the story. In a few months it will all look like (**4**) a short-lived furore. We're fed up with hearing the same stories in the paper day after day. I think it's time *The Daily Sun* (**5**) changed its behaviour. ●

1 **A** a dark horse
   B a nosy parker
   C an armchair critic
   D a wet blanket

2 **A** throw the book at
   B get wind of
   C speak volumes about
   D short-change

3 **A** making a mountain out of a molehill
   B doing the donkey work
   C taking it as read
   D seeing the light

4 **A** a drowned rat
   B a storm in a teacup
   C a stuffed shirt
   D a big fish in a small pond

5 **A** looked a gift horse in the mouth
   B went out like a light
   C picked up the pieces
   D turned over a new leaf

B Write five sentences of your own to practise the other idioms above. Leave a blank where the idiom should be. See if your partner can guess the correct answers.

C Rewrite each of the following sentences using an idiomatic expression that contains the word given.

1 He was so overcome with emotion that he didn't know what to say.

WORDS .... *lost for* ....

2 The police caught the burglar in the process of committing the crime.

RED ....

3 I always try to be optimistic about things.

BRIGHT ....

4 After my divorce, she helped me to recover.

PIECES ..... *pick up* ....

5 My brother's not feeling terribly well these days.

WEATHER ....

6 They managed to get to the airport with only seconds to spare.

NICK ....

7 I resent the way that she clearly feels herself to be superior to me.

NOSE .... *looks down her nose* ....

8 The staff were upset not to have been informed about the company's plans.

DARK .... *kept in dark* ....

grammar review

A April fool. It is a common practice amongst newspapers to play jokes on their readers on April Fool's Day (April 1st), and to print stories that are not true. As you read through the following April Fool story, look for ten grammatical mistakes.

CHANNEL TUNNEL WILL NOT MEET

Red-faced executives at Eurotunnel were trying making light of a report that the two sides of the channel tunnel, which has been under construction for the last five years, are not meeting in the middle. Not until the latest surveyor's report was published they realized the terrible truth: the two ends will be approximately 300 metres apart when the digging is completed at the end of the year, that will cost an additional £20 million to put right. The error thinks to have stemmed from the fact that while English engineers have been doing calculations in feet and yards, the French have been used to centimetres and metres. A Eurotunnel spokesman denied this a serious matter and said: 'We never actually expected the two ends would meet up exactly. It can have been a lot worse, and we are absolutely pleased to have got so close. All we need to do is putting in a few sharp corners and everything will be all right.' ■

B Read through the second story and fill in the missing words.

THAT CERTAIN SMILE

Picture restorers working (**1**) .... Leonardo's masterpiece, the Mona Lisa, famous (**2**) .... her enigmatic smile, have been ordered to bring their work (**3**) .... a halt amid fears that restoration might rob the world's most famous painting (**4**) .... its mysterious expression. (**5**) .... the centuries, a layer of dust and dirt has gradually built (**6**) .... forming a film over the paint, slightly distorting the colour and bringing (**7**) .... other subtle changes. X-ray photography has revealed that (**8**) .... the original painting, contrary (**9**) .... popular belief, the Mona Lisa's expression was closer (**10**) .... a snarl than a smile. Now an acrimonious argument has blown (**11**) .... between academic art historians who are interested (**12**) .... seeing the painting as Leonardo intended, and the curators of the Louvre, who are anxious (**13**) .... preserve their most famous crowd-puller as it is.

....

C Transformations. Finish each of the following sentences in such a way that it means exactly the same as the sentence printed before it.

1 I was very annoyed by his refusal to listen to reason.

What *annoyed me* ....

2 The company have been reviewing their recruitment policy for the last three months.

The company's recruitment policy has ....

3 The comedian soon made everyone in the audience laugh.

The comedian soon had ....

4 I am absolutely sure he took the money on purpose.

He couldn't possibly ....

5 Starting smoking was a big mistake.

I wish ....

6 Winning the crossword competition made him extremely happy.

He was absolutely ....

7   It is thought that the Prime Minister is considering raising taxes.

The Prime Minister . . . .

8   He did not pass his driving test until he was nearly 30.

It . . . .

9   It was the weakness of the foundations that led to the collapse of the building.

If . . . .

10   Next Saturday is our tenth wedding anniversary.

We will . . . .

11   'I think you ought to see a doctor,' he said.

He suggested . . . .

12   I do not intend to discuss this matter any further.

I have . . . .

13   It started to pour with rain moments after we had started our walk.

Hardly . . . .

14   Could you tell me the time of the last train to London?

Could you tell me when . . . .

newspaper activity   **Work in groups of three and look through a selection of newspapers.** Each group should summarize two unusual news items and write one fictitious April Fool story. Read out your stories to the rest of the class, and see if the other students can guess which of the three stories is untrue.

Summary Skills

Getting your Message Across

talking points   **Role-play.**

STUDENT A
A friend of yours is very much against 'new-fangled' gadgets and inventions. Persuade your friend to purchase **one** of the gadgets below. Remember that you have to **convince** them of the indisputable advantages of possessing one of these objects.

STUDENT B
You are against possessing objects which you consider to be unnecessary. Explain to your friend why you have no intention of purchasing what he or she recommends and why you would derive no benefit from doing so.

  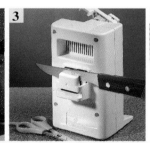 

Now reverse roles and choose a different object.

summary 1   **A**   **Read the first paragraph of the article on the next page, which contains conflicting opinions about the old and the new.** This is a different kind of passage to summarize. It is an amusing, metaphorical piece of writing whose subject matter is not immediately obvious.

SLAVES OF THE SCREEN

Monica and I, we go way back. It hasn't always been easy, there have been a few screaming arguments – I'm ashamed to admit that once or twice I've knocked her about a bit. It's the way her K jumps and one of her fractions sticks that drives me wild. I've never seen eye to eye with her about her blasted ribbon. But we're staying together, Monica and I: after all, we've been through a lot – two books, reams of journalism, hundreds of 'Dear Sir' letters, another book on the way. We're partners, I suppose, and basically we understand each other. In my line of business, that means a lot.

B Which of the following statements best sums up what the passage is about?

1 Despite their differences of opinion, the writer and his secretary are still together.
2 In spite of the problems, the writer is still with an old and trusted friend.
3 Although there have been difficult times, the writer would not consider employing anyone else.
4 Notwithstanding the problems, the writer nostalgically remembers a relationship he once had.

comprehension 1

A Possible answers. Now choose the best answers to the following comprehension questions.

1 What does *we go way back* mean (line 1)?
   A We have travelled extensively together.
   B We have always gone on holiday together.
   C We have known each other for quite some time.
   D We have decided to return to where we came from.

2 Explain *knocked her about* (line 4).
   A was unkind to her
   B treated her roughly
   C travelled everywhere with her
   D dropped her on several occasions

B Now write your own definitions of

1 *never seen eye to eye with her* (line 6).
2 *reams of journalism* (line 8).

Could you now hazard a guess as to the identity or profession of Monica?

comprehension 2

Read the rest of the article and answer the questions on the next page.

exam tip

Do not jump to conclusions about the subject matter of a passage. Read the whole passage before you decide on its overall tone / mood and content.

Monica's other name is Olympia. She is a rather battered manual typewriter, of a no-nonsense, no-extras variety. Over the years of my bullying, she has weathered into a unique identity, her most intimate nooks and crannies clogged with dust and splattered with Tippex. In the inevitably lonely business of writing, she is, for better or for worse, my one and only companion.

But my friends and colleagues regard me as either completely insane or a pitiable dinosaur. They insist, in patronising tones, on telling me about their word processors. 'Oh, but you should get one. They are so much quicker. You can do amazing things on them. I've just bought a Pamplemousse XJ6, with an inscape print-out facility and double declutch tab which you can transfer on to a ...' I nod politely, but I don't listen any more, as they bore on for England, like people who tell you to take the second right for the B3456 signposted Cullompton after a pub called The Pig and Whistle.

Now I'm going to defend my position. I dare say that word processors are very useful for accounts and telling you the time in Tokyo. But writing is a long, slow 40 grind; sentences are born out of my blood, sweat and tears, with every syllable a sort of torturing responsibility. By giving you the illusion of speeding-up, word processors only encourage slapdash prolixity. Fast 45 writing is almost invariably bad writing. Good writing is head – not finger – work. And anyway, process them into what? Words are not cheese slices. Second, I don't think I want anyone or anything to take 50 responsibility for my poor little words. I am fanatically possessive of every single one. I want to maintain maximum control over them, and pen, paper and Monica are quite problems enough, thank you, without 55 another machine butting in.

With that poisoned offer to assume responsibility goes an incredible capacity to muck things up. Even more tiresome than babble acrobatic declutch tabs are the tales 60 of catastrophe, of 500-page tomes lost to humanity because someone pressed the wrong button. Monica, let me tell you, has never lost anything, though I have. Then we are told that word processors are 65 subject to viruses and that they can give you RSI. Well, what do you expect? They're electric, for heaven's sake. Electricity kills. Let's get back to candle power. ■

1 Explain in your own words
  a *weathered into a unique identity* (line 16).
  b *her most intimate nooks and crannies* (line 16).
  c *pitiable dinosaur* (line 23).

2 What effect is the writer creating by including descriptions of people talking about the Pamplemousse XJ6 and people giving road directions?

3 Explain in your own words
  a *writing is a long, slow grind* (line 39).
  b *slapdash prolixity* (line 44).
  c *butting in* (line 55).

4 What point is the writer making when he says *Words are not cheese slices* (line 48)?

5 Explain the terms *viruses* and *RSI* (line 65).

summary 2

A **Note on style.** The skill of a passage like this lies in the writer's ability to put forward his own point of view in an amusing and unusual way, eg the personification of Monica. A summary of writing of this kind should capture the essence of the writer's train of thought and not merely sequence events or gather factual information.

B **Now write a complete summary.** Summarize the attitude of the writer's friends and colleagues towards him, his feelings towards them, and his attitude towards an old friend, and to new technology. Write between 120 and 140 words.

Listening and Speaking

Lack of Communication?

talking points

Choose two of the following items. Tell your partner what they are and what might go wrong with them. Consider the consequences if they go wrong.

- a stop watch
- a tannoy system
- a microchip
- a black box
- a remote control device
- a nuclear power station
- an automatic sprinkler system

listening 1

A **The trouble with technical equipment is that things do go wrong and need to be serviced or repaired.** Listen to the conversation on tape and complete the following information.

1 speakers ....

2 place ....

3 the problem ....

4 cause of problem ....

5 solution to the problem ....

6 misunderstanding about solution...

Discuss your answers in small groups.

B **Sounds similar.** The words on the left all appeared on the tape. Read the pairs of words aloud showing the differences in pronunciation, then explain the differences in meaning.

1	fix	flicks	**7**	dirt	dearth
2	fax	facts	**8**	word	ward
3	tiny	tinny	**9**	illegible	ineligible
4	spots	sports	**10**	screwed	skewed
5	havoc	haddock	**11**	fence	fends
6	shedding	shredding	**12**	cages	gauges

listening 2

A **Listen to three people complaining on the phone and the manner in which these complaints are dealt with.** As you listen, decide which of the people dealing with the complaints is:
a assertive.
b aggressive.
c passive.

Which do you think would be the correct attitude to have when dealing with customers' complaints?

B **Listen again and put A, B or C in the correct column on the skills feedback form for conversations 1 to 3** (**C** = ineffective, **B** = could be better, **A** = effective).

Areas for comment	1	2	3
Introducing themselves / department			
Obtaining information / clarifying what the customer wanted			
Calming the customer down			
Repeating and recording information			
Stating what will be done			
Giving information to the customer			
How do you rate the customer care?			

simulation

You are a member of a small team responsible for staff training in customer relations in a large department store. With your colleagues, draw up a list of points which you could focus on in a training session to encourage your staff to deal effectively with customers' complaints. You can base your points on the charts in the listening above and include some of your own. After drawing up your list, compare and discuss your advice with another group.

Task-based Composition

Types of task. The task-based composition sometimes requires you to give instructions, describe a process, or give formal or informal explanations of how something works. In this kind of exercise it is important to choose a suitable style for the specified task.

Read the following passages and complete the exercises that follow.

1 MITAC is creating a name for itself by building reliable, price performance computers with advanced modular design for future expansions. Take Mitac MD4033, for example. The lightning speed Mitac MD4033 should be the first computer of your choice. It has an Intel® 33MHz 486DX microprocessor inside to give you the fast performance you want. But wait, there's more to MD4033 than just a superior microprocessor and ample system and cache memory. It also has non-interlace VGA® graphics, whose extended features offer 1024x768, 16 colours, making it a machine perfect for professional desktop publishing or any other office or business application.

2 Incidentally, you can check the arrival times on the TV in case the plane is late. I'll tell you what to do. Well, first of all, you just turn on the TV and get ITV. Then you get the bleeper and press 'Text', OK, and you get Ceefax or Oracle on the screen, I'm not sure which, but actually it doesn't really matter either way. Anyway, you get kind of a series of headings – you know, the news, financial reports, TV times, and so on. Now, you want travel, so you take the number printed next to it, say 300, and you sort of dial it up on the bleeper, you see, and the number comes up in the top left hand corner of the screen. You might have to wait a second for the right page to come up. And then you basically get another menu which says something like Heathrow arrivals, and you dial that number as well, and all the arrival times come up. And then to get back to the TV, just press the TV button on the bleeper and it takes you back to the normal TV.

3 Tobacco is made from the leaves of various narcotic plants of the *Nicotiana* family, which contain a volatile oil and an alkaloid called nicotine. Tobacco undergoes various processes of preparation. The leaves are first dried, then cut into small pieces, moistened and compressed, and in this form it is known as cut or "shag" tobacco; when moistened with syrup or treacle and pressed into cakes, it is Cavendish; when twisted into string form it is "twist" or "pig-tail". For cigars the midribs of the dry leaves are removed, and what is left is moistened and rolled into a cylindrical shape. For snuff, the tobacco leaves are moistened and allowed to ferment, then dried, powdered and scented. *See* Section P (Respiratory Diseases) for the connection between tobacco smoking and lung cancer.

1 Where would you find or hear these passages, and what are they about?
2 Who are the passages aimed at?
3 Grade the three passages in terms of their degree of formality.
4 Which passage uses the most descriptive adjectives and why?
5 How would you describe the key vocabulary in each passage?
6 Comment on the way each passage uses or does not use contractions.
7 Comment on the use of the second person singular.
8 Which passage makes the most extensive use of the passive and why?
9 Find ten examples of verbal padding in passage 2, which could be removed without changing the meaning of the text.

Read this extract from a letter. It was written by a mother to her son who is away from home for the first time and is unable to cook. Change the vocabulary and structures to rewrite the passage in a form that is more appropriate for this task.

The cooking of an omelette is not a time-consuming project, nor does it necessitate a particularly high degree of culinary skills. The prerequisites in terms of provisions are two eggs, water and butter, and the essential equipment comprises a frying pan and heat source. The procedure is as follows. Initially, the two eggs are broken, and the contents, both egg yolk and white are placed in a bowl, where they are beaten. A small quantity of water or milk is then added and the mixture stirred again. The butter is placed in the frying pan, heated to melting point, and the egg mixture is subsequently added to the pan. The process of cooking is complete in approximately one minute, after which time the omelette is folded in half and served.

writing task

Read the advertisement below and write two of the following passages.

1 *An advertisement for the product. (150 words)*
2 *A technical description of the way in which a telephone or fax or photocopier works (you may consult an outside source for this). (150 words)*
3 *An extract from a letter to your non-technically-minded grandmother, who has won this machine in a lottery, explaining briefly what the machine can do and how she might use it. (150 words)*

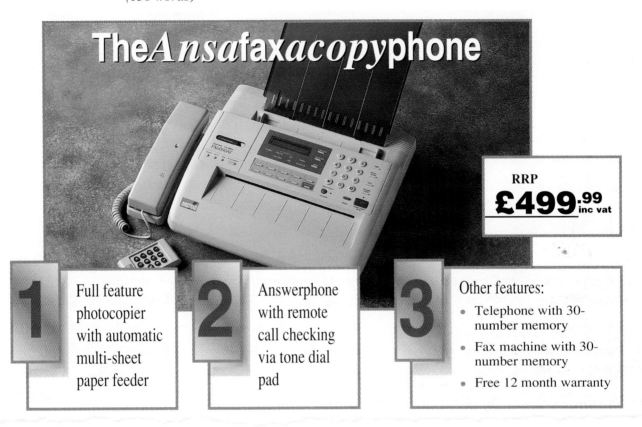

The*A***nsa**fax**a***copy***phone**

RRP
£499.99
inc vat

1 Full feature photocopier with automatic multi-sheet paper feeder

2 Answerphone with remote call checking via tone dial pad

3 Other features:
• Telephone with 30-number memory
• Fax machine with 30-number memory
• Free 12 month warranty

exam tip

Here is one way of organizing your time in the compositions. For each composition allow yourself about 10 minutes for planning, 40 minutes for writing and 10 minutes for checking.

Composition 1

Good advertisements answer the basic question 'What can it do for me?'. Write your text so as to answer this question directly. You can use the word 'you', as was shown in the model, and keep to a relatively informal tone. Make sure sentences are relatively short. Think of a good range of adjectives for the product so that you do not have to repeat key words, but avoid pretentious adjectives like 'expeditious'. You could organize your advertisement into three parts: firstly, outline some of those moments when a machine like this would be essential; secondly, give a brief but glowing description of the things this machine can do; thirdly, encourage the reader to phone for more information or a demonstration.

Composition 2

The tone for this passage needs to be neutral or formal, as you are describing the technical side rather than explaining to someone what to do. The passive is likely to be used fairly extensively in your answer. The structure of the composition is very simple, starting with what happens to a sound once it is picked up by the microphone in the handset, following the process through to the reproduction of the sound through the speaker at the other end.

Composition 3

Before writing, ask yourself what your grandmother's reaction is likely to be to this machine; begin with some reassuring words. Then take each of the separate elements of the machine, starting with the features she is most likely to use. Give illustrative examples of when she might use the various features, and explain why the machine would be useful. Conclude with some practical tips. Remember also that you are asked only for an extract rather than a complete letter.

Overview 15

vocabulary

Choose the word which best completes each sentence.

1 The Red Cross is .... an international aid organization.
    A intriguingly   **B** intrusively   **C** intrinsically   **D** intrepidly

2 The quality papers are a different .... of fish from the gutter press.
    A pan   **B** basket   **C** box   **D** kettle

3 Politicians interviewed on TV seldom see eye .... eye with their interviewers.
    A for   **B** to   **C** at   **D** by

4 The invasion of the small country was an .... act which violated the peace treaty.
    A assertive   **B** aggressive   **C** affirmative   **D** abrasive

5 A new .... of programmes on wildlife will be shown on Channel 4 in the autumn.
    A episode   **B** series   **C** serial   **D** sequel

6 The in-depth news bulletins are aimed .... a middle-aged, professional audience.
    A for   **B** to   **C** in   **D** at

7 I have no idea whether the restaurant will be open – we'll just have to take pot ....
    A choice   **B** chance   **C** luck   **D** fortune

8 As I boarded the train, I was suddenly .... by the arm and ushered towards a first-class carriage.
    A clutched   **B** grabbed   **C** caught   **D** plucked

9 As a result of ...., the price of new cars has risen dramatically over the last few months.
    A inflation   **B** escalation   **C** distension   **D** extension

10 Although she has three children of her own, this 32-year-old mum has .... four others for the local authority.
    A upheld   **B** supported   **C** fostered   **D** sustained

transformations

Finish each of the following sentences in such a way that it means exactly the same as the sentence printed before it.

1 Jane was coming this evening but she has apparently changed her mind.

Jane seems ..... to have chan ....

2 The phone stopped ringing the moment I got downstairs.

No sooner ... had ....

3 He is determined to carry on working when he is 65.

He has no .... intention ....

4 He was very sorry that he didn't see Audrey on her trip to London.

He greatly ... regretted not seeing ....

5 His disabilities did not prevent him from sailing around the world.

Despite the fact ....

6 She agreed to go out to dinner with him because she assumed he was not married.

Had she ... known ....

7 The police let him leave after they had questioned him.

He was ... allowed to leave ....

8 The music teacher managed to make the whole class sing in tune after a few weeks.

The music teacher had .. the whole class ....

9 Everyone was surprised that the singer had very little money when he died.

The singer had ... little ....

10 They only found out who Peter really was when they read about him in the paper.

It was ....

blank-filling   *Fill each of the blanks in the following sentences with a suitable word or phrase.*

1 I couldn't even hazard a .... *a guess* .... as to the number of people in need of accommodation in the city.

2 Living a sheltered life in the countryside is .... *far cry* .... cry from confronting the perils of city life.

3 .... *Con/vrane* .... to public belief, he had never been involved in any financial scandals.

4 It's an old house with some marvellous .... *nooks* .... and crannies for the children to hide in.

5 What impressed me ..... *more* .... else were his amazing feats of memory.

6 I wish ...... *I didn't have I* .... to live in this noisy street!

7 Hardly .... *had* .... it began to rain and we had to run for shelter.

8 If you .... *could* ...., what would you have done?

9 It's not my decision; as .... *far as I'm* .... concerned you can please yourself.

10 Ring the airport and check the departure times just in case .... *plane* .... delayed.

rewriting   *For each of the sentences below, write a new sentence as similar as possible in meaning to the original sentence, but using the words given in capital letters. These words must not be altered.*

1 I just didn't know what to say.

LOST .... *lo* ....

2 The press seem to have found out about the MP's indiscretions.

WIND ....

3 They arrived at the station with only a minute to spare.

NICK ....

4 He was beginning to change his mind about moving house.

SECOND ....

5 All this violence on TV makes me sick and tired.

FED ....

6 We should be going home now.

WENT ....

7 I enjoy being the boss of a small company.

FISH ....

8 I think you should try and be as optimistic as you can.

SIDE ....

9 The sound is detected by the microphone hand set.

UP ....

10 This is the procedure.

FOLLOWS ....

1

2

3

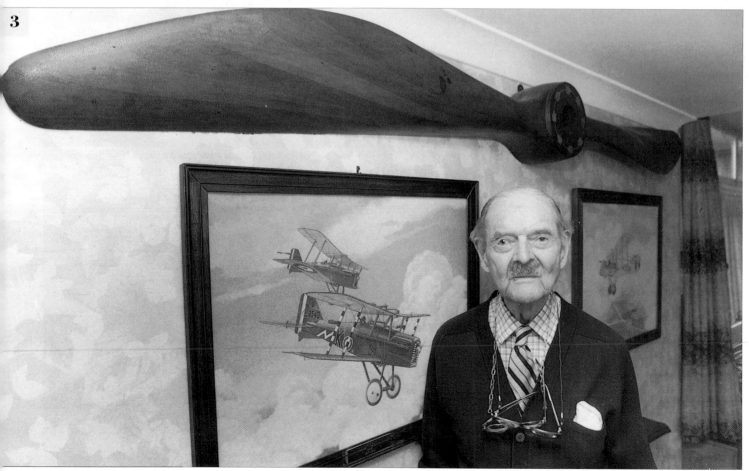

Student's Book Answers

Unit 3, p35 *talking points*

Official statistical ranking	Days of life expectancy lost
being male rather than female	2, 700
remaining unmarried	1, 800
working as a coal miner	1, 500
riding in cars (10, 000 miles per year)	200
choking on food	12
being struck by lightning	6
being bitten by an animal or insect	0.3
exposure to radiation	0.05

Unit 5, p59 *reading*

A The title of the passage is *Mindless in Gaza*, which is a reference to the belief that Samson, a strong man in the Bible, was blinded in Gaza, and so he became 'Eyeless in Gaza'. The modern tourist is now 'Mindless in Gaza'.

Unit 6, p72 *talking points*

A Portrait of Dr Gachet by Vincent Van Gogh. This was sold for a record amount at £ 49, 100, 000.

Patterned vase – £10. Although this might look like ancient Chinese pottery, it is a modern mass-produced item that is not worth a great deal.

Persian carpet – £25. The carpet is imitation and can be bought fairly cheaply.

Teddy bear – £6, 000. Some of these have become exceptionally valuable, and this particular example dates from the 1890s.

Unit 7, p95 *comprehension*

1 Repeats one of the words used and does not explain the meaning.
ANSWER An important point to consider when drawing conclusions.

2 Similar to 1, although slightly better as it explains *head*.
ANSWER What each individual is earning on average.

3 A line reference is not sufficient, an explanation is needed.
ANSWER The rise in population is 2.7 per cent a year in South Africa.

4 The answer is too narrow and needs clarification.
ANSWER Ensuring that the income per head is equal to the rise in the population so that it can be supported by the work force.

5 Copies almost verbatim what is written in the text.
ANSWER Because there are fewer people to support, growth in the economy has resulted in the income per head rising, but not in equal proportions.

6 Doesn't explain *economically active*.
ANSWER Generating money by being a member of the workforce.

7 Only half of the explanation.
ANSWER The mutual relation between those relying on others to support them and those who are capable of earning their own living.

8 Merely changes the order of the words.
ANSWER Because the more dependants there are in the population (students, retired people), the harder it is for the state system to provide enough money to make sure they can be looked after by the state.

9 Too abrupt, no explanation.
ANSWER The longer people live, the more money taxpayers will be required to pay in order to provide money for pensioners.

10 Too narrow, only half of the story.
ANSWER Because not every member of society who could be employed actually has full- or part-time work.

11 Too abrupt, no proper explanation given.
ANSWER Although attitudes have changed, the fact remains that far fewer women are employed in the workforce than men, and those women with small children and full-time employment are exceedingly rare.

Unit 14, p186 *talking points*

Eco quiz

1 True. In fact, every decade since 1950 has seen an amount of growth equivalent to the economic output added from the beginning of civilization until 1950.
2 False. The figure is nearer a third.
3 True. At current rates, it is estimated that the rain forests will have disappeared within about 50 years.
4 True.
5 True. Bombay is only an example and many other badly-polluted cities can have similar harmful health effects.
6 False. It is estimated that the world's population will increase by 3.2 billion by the year 2025. Three billion out of the 3.2 billion will live in the Third World.
7 True. Oxygen is detoxified by the bio-chemistry of our body cells. However this is only partially successful, as the metabolization of oxygen releases very small amounts of substances which can cause cancer.
8 False. According to recent estimates, the figure is far higher than this. Some studies have estimated that the figure (including plants and insects) may be as high as 100 species per day.

reading

A The title of the passage is *Let there be Darkness*, an ironic reference to God's words on the first day of creation, 'Let there be Light'.

Grammar and Vocabulary Index

Oxford University Press Walton Street, Oxford OX2 6DP

Oxford New York
Athens Auckland Bangkok Bogota Bombay Buenos Aires Calcutta Cape Town
Dar es Salaam Delhi Florence Hong Kong Istanbul Karachi Kuala Lumpur Madras
Madrid Melbourne Mexico City Nairobi Paris Singapore Taipei Tokyo Toronto

and associated companies in Berlin Ibadan

OXFORD and OXFORD ENGLISH
are trade marks of Oxford University Press

ISBN 0 19 432823 6

Acknowledgements

The authors and publisher would like to thank the following for permission to use extracts
and adaptations of copyright material in this book:

Actionaid: leaflet about sponsoring a child; **Amstrad plc:** press advertisement; **Mark
Archer:** extract from book review in the *Financial Times*; **Armand Colin Éditeur:** extract
from Fernand Braudel: *Les structures du quotidien (Structures of Everyday Life)*; **BBC
Enterprises Limited:** extract from Jonathan Porritt: *Where On Earth Are We Going?* (BBC
Books, 1990), and map of Brazil, Ann Linge/*BBC Wildlife Magazine* (December 1991);
Curtis Brown London Ltd: extract from Josephine Bell: *Easy Prey*, Copyright ©1959
Josephine Bell; **James N. Devin:** cartoon, 'Cowboy after O.S.H.A.'; **Express Newspapers
plc:** article from the *Daily Star*; **The Financial Times Ltd:** extract from book review and
article by Annie Wilson in the *Financial Times*; **Tom Fort:** article from the *Financial Times*;
The Guardian: extracts from Russell Thomas: 'Music and muscle', ©The Guardian, from
Trader Horn: 'The rain man cometh', ©The Guardian, from David Brindle and Ben
Laurence: 'Population time bomb', ©The Guardian, from Michael Robinson: 'The comfort of
the cage', ©The Guardian, and from Richard Whitehouse: 'Not so green and pleasant land',
©The Guardian, articles by Jack Shamash: 'Mindless in Gaza', ©The Guardian, Michael
Marland: 'Fact and reading fiction', ©The Guardian, and Jim Shelly: 'Please don't call me
and I won't call you', adaptations of articles by Richard Newton and David Worley: 'Turtles
in danger', ©The Guardian, T.M. Radford: 'The greatest threat to the world', ©The
Guardian and Judy Williams: 'Hidden Clues to Crime', ©The Guardian; **Vernon L. Grose:**
excerpt from his book *Managing Risk: Systematic Loss Prevention for Executives* (Prentice
Hall); **Hampstead Theatre:** from Michael Slater: 'Dickens and his public', in the Hampstead
Theatre programme for *Dickens' Women* by Miriam Margolyes and Sonia Frazer, and '10
point plan' in the Hampstead Theatre programme for *Back Up the Hearse and Let Them Sniff
the Flowers* by William Gaminara; **HarperCollins Publishers Ltd:** extract from Fernand
Braudel: *Structures of Everyday Life*, (Collins, 1986), and jacket illustration for Josephine
Bell: *Easy Prey* (Pandora Press, 1988); **The Independent/Newspaper Publishing plc:**
extracts from Patrick Brogan: 'Whatever happened to Baby Doe?', *Independent Magazine*,
and David Bowen: 'Blowing bubbles may damage your wealth', *Independent on Sunday*;
International Creative Management, Inc: extract from Allan Gurganus: 'Blessed
Assurance', Copyright 1990 by Allan Gurganus; **James Joll:** extract from book review in the
Financial Times; **The Robert Lanz-Joy Harris Literary Agency:** on behalf of the author,
Haing Ngor: *Surviving the Killing Fields* (Chatto & Windus); **Lemon Unna & Durbridge:**
extract from William Boyd: 'Transfigured Night'; **Bernard Levin:** adapted article from The
Times; **Mitac Europe Ltd:** publicity brochure; **The Observer Ltd:** from *The Observer
Magazine*, 'Spleen' articles by Dina La Vardera: 'Muscle binds', The Observer ©, and
Rupert Christiansen: 'Slaves of the screen', The Observer ©, Ena Kendall: 'A room of my
own – Mara Amats', The Observer ©, Willy Newlands: 'Safari holidays', The Observer ©,
and Janet Baird: 'Let there be darkness', The Observer ©; **The Oxford Story/Heritage
Projects:** commentaries, ©The Oxford Story exhibition; **Pan Books Ltd:** extracts from
Douglas Adams: *The Hitch Hiker's Guide to the Galaxy* (1979); **The Peters Frazer &
Dunlop Group Ltd:** extracts from John Collee: 'A slippery slope' and 'Suspension of
belief', in *The Observer Magazine*; **Sir John Plumb:** extract from book review in the
Financial Times, ©J.H. Plumb, 1992; **Prometheus Books:** extract from Terence Hines:
Pseudoscience and the Paranormal (1988); **Reed Consumer Books:** cover of Douglas
Adams: *The Hitch Hiker's Guide Omnibus* (Heinemann, 1986); **Relate:** statistics and general
information; **Routledge:** extract from Roger Fowler: *Language in the News* (1991); **Serious
Productions Ltd** and **Dove Audio:** for audio rights to Douglas Adams: *The Hitch Hiker's
Guide to the Galaxy* (produced and distributed by Dove Audio); **The Spectator:** article by
Simon Courtauld from *The Spectator*; **Abner Stein:** extract from Haing Ngor: *Surviving the
Killing Fields* (Chatto & Windus/Pan); **Patrick Stephens Ltd:** extract from George Behe:
Titanic: Psychic Forewarnings of a Tragedy (Patrick Stephens Ltd, Sparkford, Nr Yeovil,
Somerset, BA22 7JJ); **The Sun/Rex Features:** extracts from *The Sun*; **The Telegraph plc:**
article from the *Daily Telegraph*, ©The Telegraph plc/Russell Chamberlain, 1989; **Time Inc:**
extract from Nancy Gibbs: 'At the end of their tether', in *Time* magazine, Copyright 1991
Time Inc; and **Times Newspapers Ltd:** adapted extracts from Brian Appleyard: 'Master of

the Universe', in the *Sunday Times Magazine*, ©Times Newspapers Ltd. 1988, and 'The
Theory of Inequality', in *The Times Saturday Review*, ©Times Newspapers Ltd. 1991, and
extract from editorial, *The Times*, ©Times Newspapers Ltd. 1991.
Despite every effort to trace and contact copyright holders before publication, we have been
unsuccessful in a few cases. We apologize for any apparent infringement of copyright and if
notified, the publishers will be pleased to rectify any errors or omissions at the earliest
opportunity.

The publishers would like to thank the following for their permission to reproduce
photographs:

Amstrad Plc: page 209; **Archive Photos:** page 148; **Banx:** page 151, cartoon from *FT
Weekend*; **BBC Photo Library:** page 110; **Bettman Archive/Hulton Deutsch Collection:**
pages 43, *(Houdini escaping)*, 86, *(Baby Doe, Baby Doe's cabin, Horace Tabor)*; **Bridgeman
Art Library:** pages 50, 145; **Gyles Brandreth:** page 111, cartoons reproduced from *The
Wordbook* (Robson books); **Brotherton collection, Leeds University:** page 52; **Camera
Press:** page 16, (Homer Sykes – *Stephen Hawking*); **Christie's Images:** page 72, *(portrait of
Dr Gachet by Van Gogh)*; **John Cleare Mountain Camera:** Progress Test 1 *(John Cleare in
action)*; **Dr Peter Collett:** page 180; **James Davis Travel Photography:** page 147, *(street
trader)*; **Philip Dunn:** page 24; **E.T. Archive:** page 73, (George French Angas); **Mary Evans
Picture Library:** pages 21, *(Ada Bryon)*, 60, 146 *(Amsterdam)*; **Financial Times:** page 174,
(Ashley Ashwood); **Format:** page 93, (Sheila Gray – *father and son*); **Fortean Picture
Library:** pages 49, (Hannah McRoberts – *UFO*, Frederick C. Taylor – *crop circles)*; **Brian
Froud:** page 52, rephotographed from *Fairies* by Alan Lee and Brian Froud (Pan); **GMW
Partnership/Richard Turpin:** page 214 *(Office building)*; **Ronald Grant Archive:** page
165, *(Supergirl, Murder on the Orient Express, Batman, Dr No)*; **Sally and Richard
Greenhill:** page 7; **V.L. Grose:** page 31, reproduction of cartoon from *Managing Risk*
(Prentice Hall); **The Guardian:** Progress Test 1 (Tom Jenkins – *camera man*), Progress Test
3 (Edward Hamilton), pages 118, (artwork from *Turtles* by R. Newton and D. Worley), 167,
illustration to show taking fingerprints, from the *Education Guardian*; **Sonia Halliday:** page
116, (James Welland); **Robert Harding Picture Library:** pages 147 (Duncan Maxwell – *car
boot sale*), Progress Test 2 *(Henry Moore bronzes)*; **Heritage Projects Management Ltd/
The Oxford Story:** page 67; **HMSO:** page 28, permission to reproduce the Gulf War medal,
Crown copyright; **David Hughes:** page 44; **Images Colour Library:** pages 16 (*Cambridge*),
49 *(ghosts)*, 53, 178 *(gold eater)*; **Jarrold Publishing:** page 122 *(safari park)*; **Hugh
Johnson:** page 191; **Tony McSweeney/Observer Magazine:** page 124; **Magnum:** pages 14,
(Ian Berry – *Stephen Hawking*), 28 (Susan Meiselas – *Women's artillery Battalion*), 139
(Martin Parr – *bored couple*), 155 (J. Griffiths – *poster in India*, Alex Webb – *poster in
Egypt*), 160 (B. Barry – *paddy fields*), 161 (Steve McCurry – *two people*), 178 (Ferdinando
Scianna – *art gallery*), 198 (Sebastian Salgado – *gold mine*), Progress Test 1, (A. Abbaas –
soldiers), 142 (Susan Meiselas – *Crack on New York streets*); **H.F. Marks:** page 199,
Progress Test 2, *(person in library)*; **Mansell collection:** pages 20, 21 *(air pump)*, 104, 140,
187; **The National Trust Photo Library:** page 65; **NSP Catalogue Holdings Plc:** page 204
(humidifier, portable seat, knife sharpener); **Performing Arts Library:** page 178, (Clive
Barda – *theatre*); **Photo Press Defence:** page 28 *(Royal Marine recruits)*; **Photographers
Aspen:** 87, (David Hiser); **Louis Psihoyos/Matrix/Colorific!:** Progress Test 3 *(dinosaur on
lorry)*; **RAF Lyneham:** page 96; **Graham Rawle:** page 125 (rephotographed from *Lost
Consonants*, the *Guardian*); **Retrograph Archive:** page 43, (Martin Breeze – *Houdini
poster*); **Scientific American:** page 103, illustration by Thomas C. Moore from 'The Early
History of Indo-European Languages'. ©March 1990 by *Scientific American*. All rights
reserved; **Sotheby's:** page 72 *(teddy bear)*; **Frank Spooner Pictures/Gamma:** page 131;
Sporting Pictures: page 178 *(Brazil fans)*; **Still Pictures:** page 193 (Mark Edwards –
burning forest); **Tate Gallery, London 1993:** pages 74 (Kandinsky – *Cossacks*), 80 (Burne
Jones – *King Cophetua*, Orchardson – *The First Cloud*), 81 (Holman Hunt – *The Awakening
Conscience*, Rothko – *Black on Maroon*); **Telegraph Colour Library:** page 14 *(business
woman)*, 204 *(portable television)*; **Titanic Historic Society:** page 46; **Topham Picture
Source/ Observer Colour Library:** pages 9, 77; **Zefa:** pages 14 *(Chinese man, child)*, 40,
61, 93 *(male nurse, teacher)*, 122 *(wolves, elephants)*, 167.

We have been unable to trace or contact the copyright holder of the following items. If
notified, the publisher will be pleased to rectify any omissions at the earliest opportunity:

Alan Lee: page 56, reproduction of artwork from *Fairies*; **the Guardian:** page 89, artwork of
table.

Illustrations by:

Ken Binder/Satchel Illustrators: page 59
Jenny Brackley: pages 66, 98/99, 166
Nicki Elson: pages 25, 32, 38
Diana Gold: page 189
Robina Green: page 183
Sophie Grillet: page 137
Sue Hillwood-Harris: pages 4, 206

Margaret Morgan: page 102
Jacqueline Pestell: page 79
Carol Roberts: page 67
Stuart Robertson: page 1
Alex Tiani: pages 1, 6, 18, 63, 107,
133, 135, 164, 194, 200, 203
Harry Venning: pages 3, 34, 91, 119, 120, 128, 181

Studio photography by:

Mark Mason: pages 22, 28 *(military realia)*, 198   **Martyn Chillmaid:** pages 72 *(vase)*, 169

Location photography by:

Rob Judges: page 147 *(pawn broker, charity shop)*
Emily Andersen: page 37

We would also like to thank the following for their time and assistance:
Oriental Crafts, Oxford; The RAF, Brize Norton

The authors and publisher are grateful to all the teachers who have contributed
to the development of this course and would like to give special thanks to:
George Antoniadis, Paul Carne, William Hawkridge,
Sue Inkster, Mary Geaney, Pamela Murphy, Goodith White, Lynne Zafiropoulos.